# Art and Celebrity

**Frontispiece: Vladimir Dubosarsky & Alexander Vinogradov,**
*En Plein Air* **(detail), (1995).**
Painting, oil on canvas, 240 x 240 cm,
reproduced courtesy of the artists and Vilma Gold Gallery, London.

# Art and Celebrity

John A. Walker

Pluto Press
LONDON • STERLING, VIRGINIA

First published 2003 by Pluto Press
345 Archway Road, London N6 5AA
and 22883 Quicksilver Drive,
Sterling, VA 20166–2012, USA

www.plutobooks.com

British Library Cataloguing in Publication Data
A catalogue record for this book is available from the British Library

ISBN 0 7453 1850 9 hardback
ISBN 0 7453 1849 5 paperback

Library of Congress Cataloging in Publication Data
Applied for

10  9  8  7  6  5  4  3  2  1

Designed and produced for Pluto Press by
Chase Publishing Services, Fortescue, Sidmouth EX10 9QG
Typeset from disk by Stanford DTP Services, Towcester
Printed in the European Union by
TJ International Ltd, Padstow, Cornwall, England

# Contents

# Acknowledgements

My thanks to Derek Manley and Rob Orman for assistance in obtaining research materials and to Mike Hazzledine for references supplied and comments on early drafts of the book. I am also grateful for information and comments to Gen Doy, Katy Deepwell, Rita Hatton, Dr Jan-Christopher Horak (curator of the Hollywood Entertainment Museum), Professor Brandon Taylor, Sharon Hayes of Bedford Borough Council, Helen Wylie of Tate Liverpool, Sue Watling, Renee Coppola of the Broad Art Foundation (Santa Monica), Michael Marek (public relations officer of the Crazy Horse organisation), Danielle Rice of the Philadelphia Museum of Art.

Thanks are also due to all the artists, galleries and photographers who have supplied me with information and images, and given permission for the latter to be reproduced: the Andy Warhol Museum in Pittsburgh, Anthony Reynolds Gallery, Clive Barker, Mary Barone, Gerard Basquiat/Estate of Jean-Michel Basquiat, Stephen Bates of the Catto Gallery (London), Sandow Birk, David Bowie, Michael J. Browne, Roderick Coyne, Eugene Doyen, André Durand and the Camera Press Agency, Matt Faber of Associated Press, the Fogg Art Museum, Chris Glass, Timothy Greenfield-Sanders, Greenwich Public Libraries, Alexander Guy, Maggi Hambling, Susan Hiller, Peter Howson, Wendy Hurlock of the Archives of American Art, Alison Jackson, John Keane, Karen Kilimnik, Scott King, Jeff Koons, Richard Krause, Sebastian Krüger and Edition Crocodile, Johnnie Shand Kydd, Hugh MacLeod, Andrew Macpherson, David McCall of PA Photos, Sir Paul McCartney, Kerry Millett of Mother, Yasumasa Morimura and Natsuko Odate of Yoshiko Isshiki Office (Tokyo), Gerald Ogilvie-Laing, Julian Opie, Elizabeth Peyton, Grant Rusk of the Los Angeles County Museum of Art, the Sadie Coles HQ, Sebastião Salgado, A. Thomas and Cynthia Schomberg, Martin Sharp, Joanne Stephens, Celia Sterne of the Photographic Library of English Heritage, Gavin Turk and the Jay Jopling/White Cube Gallery, Winnie Tyrrell of Glasgow Museums Photolibrary, Gerrie van Noord of the Artangel Trust, Jessica Voorsanger, Ian Walters and Tim Wilcox of Manchester Art Gallery.

While every effort has been made to trace the copyright holders of art works and photographs, the publishers would be glad to hear from anyone who should have been credited so that corrections can be made in any future editions.

# Introduction

Celebrity is the main currency of our economy, the prime value in our news and the main impetus in our charitable works. It is the predominant means of giving and receiving ideas, information and entertainment. Nothing moves in our universe without the imprint of celebrity.[1]

In the past 30 years, the interpenetration of the domains of art and celebrityhood has had a significant impact on the image-making strategies of the media industry. The mutual influences have been so great that sometimes it is hard to distinguish art from advertisement.[2]

... the incremental celebritization of the contemporary artist has been fuelled by big sales and a buoyant market, which helps, but it is not the whole picture ... New Fame ... is achieved via headlining, instantly recognizable work, sexy galleries, high profile events, media ease and an extraordinary cross-fertilization into other arenas. Top of the Pops. Advertising. Food. Fashion. Film. Brands. Not since David Hockney painted the fashion guru Ossie Clark have artists fused their traditional world of private creativity with such a popular market of commerce and publicity.[3]

While Ziauddin Sardar's claims – see quotation one above – about celebrity, which are shared by a number of commentators, are somewhat exaggerated, there is no denying its considerable importance in contemporary developed societies. This book will argue that artists are imbricated in the culture of celebrity because they contribute images, statues, monuments and simulated relics to it, because some artists impersonate celebrities, and because others participate in its social rituals and enjoy the status of celebrities (they will be called 'art stars'). The kind of art the latter produce is often influenced by their desire for fame and fortune. At the same time, other artists seek to criticise or deconstruct or play with celebrity or to find alternatives to the depiction of celebrities. In addition, some celebrities outside the world of art collect art while others are spare-time artists (they will be called 'celebrity-artists').

Furthermore, the sociologist Chris Rojek has argued that, since the eighteenth century, the growth of celebrity culture has been closely bound up with the aestheticisation of everyday life, that taste 'is pivotal in celebrity culture' and that 'groupings of fans can be regarded as taste cultures'.[4]

The history of fame has been described in detail by Leo Braudy in his book *The Frenzy of Renown* (1986), and the main characteristics of celebrity and how is it constructed or manufactured have been analysed by sociologists, journalists and historians of the mass media and entertainment industries (see Bibliography). Theorists have also discussed the various social functions – such as social integration – celebrity culture is thought to perform and its paradoxical relation-ship to democracy.[5] While it will not be possible to repeat all their findings, a summary of the celebrity system that emerged during the twentieth century is in order:

1)  Psychological desires, social needs and economic demands for celebrities.
2)  A pool of celebrities, exhibitionists and wannabes eager to fulfil those demands no matter what the personal cost.
3)  Support agencies and marketing companies ready to promote aspirants and to organise events for their public appearance so that they attain 'high visibility'.
4)  A range of cultural industries, such as film and sport, which employs celebrities.
5)  A spectrum of mass media willing to discuss, glorify or denigrate them.
6)  Mass audiences, celebrity-watchers and groups of fans fascinated by celebrities.
7)  Celebrities, designers and manufacturers happy to generate mer-chandise for fans to buy; plus dealers and auction houses willing to sell memorabilia to collectors.
8)  Organisations and businesses willing to pay celebrities to promote and endorse their products and services; charities and political parties that rely on celebrities to support their causes.

Evidently, celebrities and the images and products based on them are all commodities (objects with both use and exchange values) within capitalism. Celebrities sign legal contracts so that managers, businesses and corporations can exploit them for profit. The fact that many celebrities are highly paid and can accumulate fortunes does not alter their status as commodities except that, once they realise their economic power, many celebrities try to take more control over their careers.

It has been estimated that human beings each know personally about 250 people. However, via hearsay and the media they know about a much larger number of people even if it is just their names and professions. Most humans are curious about their fellow creatures and enjoy gossiping about them. We also seem to need people to admire and detest; hence, role models, heroes, hate figures and scapegoats. Doubtless, such needs have their origin in children's dependent and subservient relationships with their parents, authority figures that are both admired and feared. However, children soon discover that society beyond the family is governed by other powerful figures such as teachers, the police, employers and political, religious, military and business leaders. Many teenagers reject parental control and experience strong sexual desires, which prompt them to seek alternative, younger role models in their peer group and in film, fashion, pop music and sport.[6] Teenagers are also the group most troubled by identity issues and most concerned about their appearance; consequently they try out various identities and looks. The popular American illustrator Norman Rockwell represented such a moment in his 1954 painting *Girl at Mirror*: a girl studies her reflection while holding a movie magazine open at a portrait of the film star Jane Russell. Many teenagers copy the way pop stars dress but eventually find they cannot afford to keep pace with stars like Madonna who regularly change their image.

In the ancient and medieval worlds, the populace may only have known about their rulers via edicts and legends, and visually by such means as public statues or the profiles of heads stamped on coins. (Fame and money were thus early bedfellows. The profiles on coins were not necessarily accurate likenesses because what was important were the leader's virtues; martial prowess, for instance.) Even in the ancient world, certain artists, philosophers and entertainers enjoyed considerable fame. The crowds in the arenas of Roman cities, for instance, followed and acclaimed the strongest gladiators. Coins did enable the image of a Roman emperor to be widely disseminated across the Empire but most scholars argue that in the past fame was much more geographically limited than in the present era of mass media, international travel and globalisation. Today's pop music and movie stars can have fans in virtually every country in the world. Even so, many stars have a local or regional appeal: a leading British cricketer is not likely to be well known in China or the United States. Furthermore, the leaders of certain cults may be known only to devotees and may have no desire to reach a broader audience.

A celebrity is a person of renown, one who is celebrated (the word itself derives from the Latin to celebrate) – but what for? Daniel J. Boorstin, the American author of a critique entitled *The Image or What Happened to the American Dream* (1962), has provided a circular definition: a celebrity is a person 'known for his well knownness'.[7] Neal Gabler, writing in 1998, updated this idea:

> In what was an entirely new concept, celebrities were self-contained entertainment, a form of entertainment that was rapidly exceeding film and television in popularity. Every celebrity was a member of a class of people who functioned to capture and hold the public's attention no matter what they did or even if they did nothing at all. The public didn't really seem to care. The star's presence, the fact that they deigned to grace our world, was sufficient. That is why newspapers could run pages of celebrities at parties, sitting in restaurants, attending benefits or arriving at premieres and why a magazine like *Vanity Fair* could devote long sections to what it called photo portfolios, which were nothing more than pictures of celebrities whom we had already seen dozens of times.[8]

Anyone who doubts that this description applies to the art world should access the Artnet.com website where they will find pages of photographs of artists, dealers, curators, etc., taken at exhibition openings.

The authors of *High Visibility* (1997) cite this definition: 'a celebrity is a name which, once made by news, now makes news by itself' but they also claim that the core essence of celebrity is 'commercial value'; hence their preferred definition: 'a person whose name has attention-getting, interest-riveting, and profit-generating value'.[9]

Fame is common to both celebrities and heroes but what differentiates them? Heroes are generally considered exceptional human beings noted for their courage, abilities, intelligence, strength, daring and powers of leadership. David, the Biblical hero, is still remembered for his bravery and victory over Goliath, and Michelangelo's sculpture of him (*David*, 1501–04, Galleria dell'Accademi, Florence) remains one of the most famous and revered icons of Western art. Heroes have thus been celebrated in art and literature since earliest times and their general function has been to inspire others. The American anthropologist Joseph Campbell (1904–1987) defined the hero as 'someone who has given himself to something bigger than, or other than, himself'. In *The Hero with a Thousand Faces* (1949), a study of hero myths and stories in many cultures and religions, Campbell argued that a single pattern of heroic journey of personal evolution underpinned them and he identified various stages (twelve in all) through which the hero passed from birth to death.[10] Today we are more cynical and sceptical. Whether or not stories about real historical heroes can still inspire modern audiences is unclear, but what is certain is that fictional heroes with mythic overtones can entertain millions: the plots of George Lucas' first three *Star Wars* movies were based on Campbell's analysis.

In Boorstin's view, 'The hero was distinguished by his achievement; the celebrity by his image or trademark. The hero created himself; the celebrity is created by the media. The hero was a big man; the celebrity is a big name.'[11] Boorstin also observed acerbically: 'Two centuries ago when a great man appeared, people looked for God's purpose in him; today we look for his press agent.'[12] The title of Dick Keyes' book about Christ – *True Heroism in a World of Celebrity Counterfeits* (1995) – exemplifies the sharp distinction so many make between the true and the false, the authentic and the inauthentic. However, one wonders if the difference between heroes/people of achievement and celebrities really is so clear-cut. Do they not overlap or shade into one another and share the same media space? Furthermore, how do millions who were not eyewitnesses learn about heroic achievements except via communication and media systems?

Let us consider an example. Nelson Mandela, the first black president of South Africa, is a widely acclaimed figure of recent years comparable to the great political leaders of the past (although his enemies once dubbed him a terrorist). In a 1997 photo shoot, he posed with Prince Charles – a royal famous because he is heir to the British throne – and the Spice Girls, a successful British pop music group. This gathering revealed the eclectic character of today's elite. It demonstrated that celebrities from different realms often attend the same events and seek mutual benefits; that different magnitudes and types of fame coexist and are represented by the mass media. As we shall discover, national portrait galleries and waxwork museums do not bother to distinguish between famous heroes and celebrities. Waxworks are also willing to feature notorious criminals.

At the time of writing, there is a proposal to erect a statue to Mandela in London's Trafalgar Square where Admiral Lord Nelson is already commemorated. (Ian Walters is the sculptor working on the project.) However, one cannot envisage a bronze monument to the Spice Girls being permitted in this public space alongside such important male heroes. Incidentally, a giant bronze bust of Mandela already exists on London's South Bank, outside the Royal Festival Hall. It was sculpted by Walters in 1982 to mark the 70th anniversary of the ANC and unveiled in 1985. Walters had to rely on photographs for his naturalistic likeness because Mandela was still in prison at the time. This sculpture, which was originally made from fibreglass, was the focus for much political activism and was repeatedly vandalised.

Another encounter between a rock music group and a world famous politician occurred in Cuba in 2001 when the Welsh band Manic Street Preachers met Fidel Castro. In this instance, radical, left-wing political convictions were a common denominator. The Manics have attracted intensely loyal supporters, many of whom are fascinated by the fact that one of the band's founders – Richey James (aka Richard James Edwards) – disappeared without trace in 1995. It is presumed he committed suicide.

The practice of politicians appearing with entertainers in order to gain popularity by association with the popular (the opposite was true in the case of Mandela: he has been dubbed 'the celebrities' celebrity') dates back at least to the 1960s when Prime Minister Harold Wilson was photographed with the Beatles. (Such associations can prove counterproductive if the pop star later becomes critical of the politician's policies.)

The life story of Audie Murphy (1924–1971) demonstrates that sometimes the divide between heroism and celebrity can be crossed. Murphy, a small, modest orphan from Texas who happened to be a crack shot, emerged from World War II as America's most decorated combat soldier. In July 1945, he was featured on the cover of *Life* magazine and this led to a career in movies. In 1949, he recorded his wartime experiences in a bestseller entitled *To Hell and Back*, which was made into a film in 1955. Unusually, Murphy played himself. In most of his other films, numerous B-Westerns, he appeared as a gunfighter. Therefore, Murphy was a real war hero who became a

**1. Ian Walters, 'Bust of Nelson Mandela', 1985.**
Public sculpture, bronze, South Bank, London.
Photo © Roderick Coyne.

Hollywood star playing heroic roles even though his acting skills were limited and his boyish features made him an unconvincing tough-guy. (A movie actor who travelled in the opposite direction was Ronald Reagan who became a politician and then President of the USA.) Murphy suffered from symptoms of post-traumatic stress and, at the age of 46, he met a violent death in a plane crash. In 2000, the American artist Richard Krause (b. 1945) produced a set of seven oil paintings, based on photographs, memorialising Murphy as war hero and film star. Krause then donated them to the Audie

Murphy Research Foundation, which keeps his memory alive via a website and newsletter. Murphy also has a fan club and is commemorated in the National Cowboy Hall of Fame, Oklahoma City.

The authors of *High Visibility* maintain that celebrities 'are manufactured, just like cars, clothes and computers'; but surely potential celebrities must have some natural attributes or abilities that enable them to become famous even if it is only physical beauty? In fact, good looks are crucial to most celebrities. Camille Paglia has remarked: 'we should not have to apologise for revelling in beauty. Beauty is an eternal human value. It is not a trick invented by nasty men in a room someplace on Madison Avenue.'[13] However, there are those who argue that the plethora of images of beautiful men and women appearing in magazines and advertisements are repressive because they set impossible standards for the rest of us.

Attractive faces and bodies are an advantage in virtually all professions. Some journalists have claimed that editors working for book publishers are more likely to accept and promote a new book if the author is young and attractive so that they will look good in jacket photographs, magazine spreads and television interviews.[14] Of course, people no longer have to accept their inherited physique. Today's celebrities spend lavishly on hairdressers, dentists, make-up, clothes, dieting and exercise regimes, personal trainers and even cosmetic surgery – via such clinics as the Beverly Hills Institute for Reconstructive Surgery – to 'improve' their appearance. One has only to read a biography of Sylvester Stallone to appreciate the punishing regimes required to put on and take off weight and muscles.

However, while youth and beauty are often prerequisites for celebrity, they are not always essential. There are a number of plain or even ugly film stars, such as Ernest Borgnine and Edward G. Robinson, who managed to become famous for their acting abilities. To overcome the reluctance of potential employers, Robinson used to tell them that what he lacked in 'face-value' he made up for in 'stage-value'. In London, there is even a character agency called the Ugly Model Agency. Such actors are often needed to add flavour to a film and to serve as a foil to the good-looking but bland leading players.

The British professional footballer David Beckham may not impress as an intellectual but he is a handsome, highly skilled athlete. However, the media are as interested in his various hairstyles as in his sporting prowess. It is obvious that he deliberately changes style from time to time to maintain a high media profile. His marriage to another celebrity from a different field – Victoria/Posh

Spice – adds to his newsworthiness. For this reason – synergy – celebrities frequently date and marry one another. At least they both understand the rewards and problems of the celebrity lifestyle. Some observers have suggested that many such affairs and marriages are 'arranged' for career reasons, are in fact PR exercises, rather than being instances of genuine passion. An example of a celebrity marriage involving a fine artist and a porn star, to be discussed later, was that between Jeff Koons and Ilona Staller.

One can distinguish between major and minor celebrities; indeed, journalists use a graded system: A-list, B-list, C-list, etc. Today, ranking celebrities is a small industry. *Forbes*, the American business magazine, for example, issues an annual list of the top 100 celebrities ranked according to such criteria as money earned, numbers of magazine covers, press clippings, radio/television appearances and website hits.[15] A comparable system for contemporary fine art called the *Kunstkompass* was devised in 1969 by Dr Willi Bongard (?–1985) to assist art collectors and investors. Every year it listed the top 100 artists selected and arranged according to a reputation scale based on a points system. The British artist Peter Davies (b. 1970) has also produced a many-hued painting entitled *The Hot One Hundred* (1997, Saatchi Gallery), which ranks 100 artists, mostly twentieth-century, by name and a comment. According to Davies, Bruce Nauman is number one, Andy Warhol is five, Jackson Pollock is 24, Damien Hirst is 28, Julian Schnabel is 30, Joseph Beuys is 41, Jeff Koons is 57, Cindy Sherman is 70 and last of all is Ivon Hitchens.

Fame is a volatile and often transient phenomenon; consequently, one can distinguish between long- and short-term celebrities. Some writers also employ the categories earned/unearned or deserved/undeserved. Among the unearned are those sexually alluring individuals – so-called 'It Girls' – who attract photographers by wearing almost nothing while attending public events such as film premieres. Hundreds of aspiring starlets are also willing to pose nude to increase their appeal. In Britain, for example, the Scottish-born television presenter Gail Porter (b. 1971) posed nude for the cover of *FHM* magazine in June 1999. (Today there are fine artists – both male and female – who are equally willing to flaunt their bodies in public.) To publicise the issue and the magazine's poll to find the 100 Sexiest Women, a 60-feet-high image of Porter was projected at night (10 May) on the side of the Houses of Parliament (a landmark building and voting place). This smart example of 'ambient advertising' or 'guerrilla marketing', devised by the London agency Cunning Stunts, was indebted to the 1980s projected art of Krzysztof Wodiczko.

**2. Mick Hutson (photographer), 'Image of Gail Porter projected on
the side of the Houses of Parliament', 10 May 1999.**
Photo courtesy of Cunning Stunts, © *FHM* magazine, London.

Boorstin dismissed such happenings as 'pseudo-events' but they
could also be called 'publicity events'. (As the annual Turner Prize
ceremonies held in Britain indicate, publicity events are now characteristic of the art world.) Individuals whose only claim to fame is
that they attend publicity events infest the media. However, even
they, if they want to remain in the public eye, must work hard to
retain the interest of photographers and journalists. Sometimes,
being a minor, underserved celebrity results in job offers so that,
eventually, he or she may achieve something more substantial.

Another category of minor/short-term celebrities consists of people who accomplish physically demanding but rather futile tasks such as rowing alone across the Pacific. (One is reminded of the endurance tests of some performance artists.) Their goal and destiny seem to be an entry in the *Guinness Book of Records*.

Fame, Joey Berlin has maintained, is often 'toxic', causing 'immense pressure and alienation'.[16] (John Updike once remarked: 'Celebrity is a mask that eats into the face.') Given the negative aspects of celebrity lifestyles, it is surprising that so many individuals yearn to become one. Humans have conflicting desires: to conform but also to stand out. Wannabes are driven by the desire to be different, to gain admiration and love, immortality, fortune and success. Freud once argued that artists (that is, male ones) were motivated by the desires 'to win honour, power, wealth, fame and the love of women' but since they could not obtain these goals directly, they tried to reach them indirectly via their art. Freud's theory certainly fits Picasso because once he established a reputation in Parisian art circles as a radical modern artist, international fame, wealth and the adoration of a succession of women followed.

We have probably all encountered a few individuals who, because of their exceptional energy or force of personality or striking physique or glowing health, possessed a special presence – an aura or charisma. Paglia has remarked: 'An inborn force of personality, always present in great teachers, speakers, actors, and politicians, automatically marshals people into ordered groups around a focal point of power.'[17] Jesus Christ was clearly such an exceptional person. Even before the age of mass media, visual elements played their part in his appeal to audiences. Students of the psychology of visual perception will know that the auratic effect is often due to simultaneous contrast: if one stares at a figure silhouetted against a light sky then the dark/light contrast will be mutually reinforced so that an aureole of light hovers around the edges of the figure. When a person's head occludes the disc of the sun, rays of light are emitted from behind it as in a lunar eclipse. In Christian mosaics and paintings, the nimbuses around the heads of Jesus, angels and the saints were made concrete and portable via golden halos and discs, while soft focus and back lighting achieved a comparable luminosity for movie stars in studio portraits.[18] During stage performances and in music videos, spotlights function like heavenly beams and clouds of smoke or dry ice enable performers to materialise as if by magic. The word 'star' meaning 'a light-emitting object found in the heavens' applied to a human is, of course, a metaphor. However, just as the light of real stars attracts the gaze, so does the light reflected from the jewellery and glitter-encrusted clothes favoured by female movie stars and male glam rockers. Furthermore, combining 'glitter' and 'literati' yielded the word 'glitterati' (rich, fashionable people or 'the smart set'). In 1980, Warhol produced a series of paintings – *Diamond Dust Shoes* and a portrait of Joseph Beuys – whose surfaces literally sparkled because of the addition of 'diamond dust', a powder derived from the manufacture of industrial diamonds, to his pigments. During the 1960s, Warhol himself acquired an aura and was once approached by a commercial company that wanted to buy it!

In the cases of the amateur painter Hitler and the professional artist Picasso, piercing eyes impressed those who met them. (The photographer David Douglas Duncan once took a close-up of Picasso's face that foregrounded his 'penetrating gaze' or *mirada fuerte*.) In many instances, the acquired or natural attributes of a charismatic individual can be conveyed and enhanced by mechanical means. In Hitler's case, for instance, microphones and the radio amplified his powers as an orator. He also struck theatrical poses for his personal portrait photographer Heinrich Hoffmann and 'starred' in Leni Riefenstahl's disturbingly powerful propaganda films. Hitler, of course, is now remembered for his crimes against humanity. (In 1944, in a painting entitled *Cain or Hitler in Hell*, George Grosz depicted Hitler as a pathetic, seated figure mopping his brow amidst the devastation he had caused.) To distinguish such monsters from heroes such as Florence Nightingale, Tom Paine and Gandhi who benefited society, they are normally referred to as 'infamous', 'notorious' or 'anti-heroes'. However, some degree of transgression of social norms, Rojek has argued, 'is intrinsic to celebrity, since to be a celebrity is to live outside conventional, ordinary life'.[19] This was also a characteristic of bohemian and avant-garde artists of the nineteenth and twentieth centuries.

Major transgressors – violent criminals, outlaws and terrorists such as Al Capone, John Dillinger, Ned Kelly, Jesse James, the Kray brothers, Charles Manson, Mark 'Chopper' Read and Osama bin Laden – fascinate and repel at the same time. They are often admired for their ruthlessness and readiness to break society's laws; their extreme actions attract reporters, biographers and scriptwriters; films about them are popular and even their funerals are well attended. Ned Kelly, the nineteenth-century Irish-Australian bushranger who became a folk hero, was the subject of a series of paintings Sidney Nolan produced in the 1940s and was played by Mick Jagger in a 1970 movie. Warhol represented such dangerous but exciting figures in his 1964 *Thirteen Most Wanted Men* series of paintings based on mug shots of criminals issued by the New York Police. The British artists Pauline Boty and Marcus Harvey have also painted notorious criminals and the German artist Gerhard Richter has depicted the Baader-Meinhof gang of terrorists.

When celebrities themselves commit or are accused of crimes – Jeffrey Archer, Gary Glitter, Hugh Grant, Michael Jackson, Mick Jagger, Jonathan King, O.J. Simpson, Mike Tyson, Sid Vicious, et al. – the two categories overlap. (The FBI opened files on both Picasso and Warhol!) A few artists have also been accused of serious crimes. For example, Walter Sickert has been accused of being Jack the Ripper and during the 1980s, the American minimalist sculptor Carl Andre was tried in a New York court on the charge of murdering his wife and fellow artist Ana Mendieta.[20]

It is not only the attributes and skills of celebrities that account for their fame. Major celebrities seem to embody or exemplify cultural aspirations, social trends or moods; such personalities, one might say, personify something grander than themselves. For example, during the 1960s, the Beatles exemplified everything that was creative, youthful, energetic and swinging about cool Britannia; late in the same decade, Bob Dylan became the spokesman for a new generation of radicals; in the 1980s, the British Prime Minister Margaret Thatcher embodied the right-wing ideology known as Thatcherism; and in the 1990s, Princess Diana exemplified the qualities of compassion and vulnerability. Picasso's biographer Arianna Stassinopoulos Huffington has claimed that his life was 'the twentieth century's own autobiography. And it was by mirroring, reflecting and epitomising our century and all its torments both in his life and art that he became a culture hero and the legendary personification of our tumultuous times.'[21]

What has been well documented is the part played by modern means of representation and communication dating from the nineteenth and twentieth centuries – the press, photography, radio, film, television and the Internet – in creating celebrities. The difference between a master chef appreciated by the clientele of a restaurant where he or she cooks and a 'celebrity chef' is that millions know the latter via television cookery programmes and lucrative tie-in recipe books. Apart from Albert Einstein, male scientists are not noted for their glamour but the British physicist Stephen W. Hawking became famous for his best-selling account of the universe – *A Brief History of Time* (1988) – and so earned the description 'celebrity scientist'. Dinos and Jake Chapman, two British artists, commemorated him in a sculpture, which showed his crippled body – itself a vivid signifier of difference and suffering – confined in a wheelchair, but situated on a mountain peak, so that, in spite of his physical infirmity, he was reaching for the stars.

A precondition for art stars is thus mass media coverage that enables them to become famous far beyond their principal profession. For this reason, my contention is that they are a phenomenon associated with the present and last centuries although, of course, there are historical precursors and cults of certain artists have developed after their deaths. The number of art stars is still quite small but they do hog a high proportion of the media's attention. (Chapter 5 considers 14 examples.) Another characteristic of art stars is that their lives and personalities become as important (or even more important) as their work. The latter is also routinely regarded as a direct expression of their lives and personalities.

Visual representations of celebrities facilitate voyeurism because we can watch to our heart's content without ourselves being observed by the object of our gaze. Zoom camera lenses also enable the private lives of celebrities to be recorded without their knowledge or permission. To curb this intrusive practice, some celebrities are currently invoking privacy and human rights acts.

Many actors and models are described as 'photogenic' or it is said 'the camera loves them'. Photographers also know how to flatter their subjects and to remove any facial blemishes by retouching. Artists who have made works based on publicity shots taken by professional photographers include Warhol and Richard Hamilton. As in the case of close-up camera shots of movie actors' faces projected onto huge cinema screens, the media intensify and magnify visual appearances. (This is one reason why so many celebrities, seen in the flesh, seem diminutive.) In addition, the presence of those images on cinema and television screens around the world ensures that the actors become familiar to millions who have never met them. Nevertheless, viewers feel they know stars; hence, the paradoxical expression 'intimate strangers' employed by Richard Schickel.[22]

Additional information about stars is conveyed by secondary means such as magazine interviews and profiles, appearances on television chat shows, documentary films, confessional autobiographies and debunking biographies. (Biography is currently a popular literary genre and there are television channels screening nothing but biographies and series with titles like *Reputations*, *Legends* and *Hollywood Greats*.) It follows that fans often know more about the lives and personalities of their idols than they do about their aunts and uncles. The visibility and disseminating power of even the smaller screens of television means that such minor figures as programme presenters can become household names rather than the staff hidden from the public gaze, such as commissioning editors and programme producers. Only in the movie industry, it seems, do directors receive as much credit as the principal players.

Furthermore, the existence of so many channels and types of media means that there is a voracious appetite for infotainment and gossip, even when there is little worth reporting; hence, the media's need for a galaxy of established celebrities and a constant flow of new ones. Today, one cannot imagine a television channel closing down early or a newspaper appearing with fewer pages because they had nothing worth showing or reporting. Content expands to fill the spaces available and the spaces themselves continually expand. The result is a huge redundancy of information through repetition plus immense amounts of trivia. To cite just one example of the latter: on 28 August 2001, whole front pages of British tabloids were filled with photographs of Victoria Beckham because she had added a metal ring to her lower lip! It is evident from gossip columns that no detail of a celebrity's existence is too small to be overlooked by the media. (And if there are no news stories to report, unscrupulous publicists and journalists are willing to make some up.) This rule now applies to British art stars such as Damien Hirst and Tracey Emin. In March 2002, after Emin's cat Docket went missing in London, she placed posters in the street but people who thought they might be saleable art works tore them down. The story, which was reported in *The Times*, had a happy ending: Docket was found.

In addition to the mainstream media that include celebrities as part of their coverage, there are magazines that specialise in news and features about celebrities; for example, *Bliss*, *Celebrity Bodies*, *Heat*, *Hello!*, *Interview*, *OK!*, *National Enquirer*, *Now*, *People*, *Star* and *Vanity Fair*. Visual images are crucial to the appeal of *Hello!* (1988–) and *OK!* (1993–), two virtually identical magazines, which mainly consist of colour photographs of attractive, smiling, well-dressed celebrities preening in expensive settings. In contrast to media reporting bad news, the overwhelming impressions conveyed by these magazines are optimism, enjoyment, luxury, and the good life. A vision of utopia, one may conclude, that provides readers with a refuge from harsh realities and the boring routines of everyday life.

In the United States there are also women's magazines published by such celebrities as Oprah Winfrey (*O Magazine*), Martha Stewart (*Martha Stewart Living*) and Rosie O'Donnell (*Rosie Magazine*).[23] On the Internet too, there are dozens of websites devoted to celebrities in general and to particular individuals. Many of the latter have been established by the celebrities themselves or by their fan clubs. Fine artists now promote themselves via websites, witness <www.peterhowson.co.uk>.

Three differences between the present and the past are: the sheer quantity of individuals who now enjoy some degree of fame; the speed with which they can become famous; and the rapid turnover of celebrities. Another difference is the role of the many experts and support organisations that help to fabricate and sustain celebrities: Hollywood studios with their portrait photographers, make-up artists, hairstylists, dress makers, talent scouts, publicity and marketing departments; the managers, drug dealers, press agents, psychotherapists, plastic surgeons and lawyers employed by major celebrities; the image consultants, speech writers and 'spin doctors' employed by politicians; and so on. Assistants are essential to busy celebrities and are now called Celebrity Personal Assistants (CPAs) or Celebrity Assistants (CAs) and in the United States, there are agencies that specialise in supplying them. Successful fine artists such as Jeff Koons, Julian Schnabel and Damien Hirst also employ personal and studio assistants.

Max Clifford is one British public relations consultant who has himself become highly visible in the mass media. Pat Kingsley, of the American public relations firm PMK, is reported to wield enormous power on behalf of her movie star clients.[24] Today, celebrities often tip off journalists and photographers about their whereabouts; their press agents routinely plant rumours and stories and, if necessary, they will use their client's wealth to buy publicity.

In the past, the celebrity fabrication process was mostly concealed but today exposing it increasingly serves to entertain rather than to demystify; witness the television series documenting the step-by-step creation of pop music groups consisting of singers selected from a pool of unknowns, such as Hear'Say. The latter achieved a number one hit in 2001, just a few months after being formed, and a book about the group was immediately published.[25] Watching such series makes viewers feel like experts. Another example is the so-called 'reality' television show that places unknown people in competitive situations under constant camera surveillance. One reason for the increasing popularity of such shows is cheapness: television companies do not have to pay unknowns huge fees. Audiences seem enthusiastic about such shows because they can easily imagine that, given the same opportunity, they too could make the transition from anonymity to celebrity.

Moviemakers, celebrities and fine artists are all capable of reflecting upon the experience of celebrity and fame. In 1998, Woody Allen directed a satirical film entitled *Celebrity* and, as we shall see, David Bowie and Madonna are two singers who made stardom the subject of several songs and Warhol is an artist who published his thoughts on fame.[26]

Besides the media's elevation of a personality, what is also familiar is the reverse process. For various reasons (but mainly the need for a fresh storyline, a juicy scandal), the media regularly turn against celebrities in order to degrade and humiliate them. The media undermine their reputations by criticising their bodies and dress sense, by reporting their drug and alcohol addictions, eating disorders, hell raising antics, adulteries, divorces and failed love affairs, excessive earnings and profligate spending habits. Furthermore, the British tabloid press is willing to deceive and entrap celebrities in order to catch them off guard. Mazher Mahmood, an undercover reporter employed by the *News of the World*, is noted for his sting operations. Several times, he has posed as an Arab Sheik or businessman and lured celebrities to London hotel suites in order to record indiscretions via concealed tape recorders. Paradoxically, while such attacks and exposures ruin some celebrities, they fail to damage or even enhance the reputations of others.

Graphic artists contribute to the public criticism of celebrities by producing caricatures of them that generally involve grotesque distortions of their faces and bodies. Gerald Scarfe (b. 1936) is a long-established British practitioner and Sebastian Krüger (b. 1963) is a brilliant German exponent.[27] Among the celebrities Krüger has depicted are several artists: Joseph Beuys, Jasper Johns, Picasso and Warhol. In Britain during the 1980s, animated puppets made from foam or latex rubber pilloried politicians, royals and celebrities of all kinds. The puppets were designed by Peter Fluck, Roger Law and a team of assistants, and reached a mass audience via the ITV television comedy series *Spitting Image*.[28] Another, more recent ITV

**3. Sebastian Krüger, 'Three caricatures – Jack Nicholson, Robert DeNiro and Madonna – from the book *Stars*', 1997.**
© Sebastian Krüger, courtesy of Edition Crocodile, Switzerland.

television series made by Triffic Films Ltd that began transmission in October 2001 was entitled *2DTV*. The programmes consisted of up-to-the-minute satirical sketches rendered in colourful, computer-assisted animation. Among the famous personalities attacked were Prince William, Tony Blair, and Osama bin Laden and his 'Talibannies'. The laughter prompted by such caricatures served a cathartic function by diffusing the hostility so many people felt towards the politicians and celebrities who held power over them.

Fine artists who provoke the public by means of shock tactics can also expect pictorial assaults by newspaper cartoonists. However, the media's ultimate sanction is to ignore the celebrity who is then consigned to the black hole of oblivion. Of course, comebacks, reha-bilitations and revivals are always possible.

Finally, there are the audiences, celebrity-watchers (who attend to a range of celebrities) and particularly the fans (who follow particular stars) that underpin the whole celebrity system. Their adoration, enthusiasm, collecting zeal and spending power fuels the cult of celebrities. This subject has been explored in a number of books under such rubrics as 'audience studies', 'fandom' and 'spectator-ship' (see Bibliography). The title of one book – Barry Divola's *Fanclub: It's a Fan's World, Popstars just Live in it* (1998) – maintains that it is the fans who exercise power rather than the celebrities. Fans who murder celebrities exercise ultimate power over the objects of their obsessions.

Specialist studies have been made of fans in particular realms such as sport, movies, rock music, science fiction and comics. However, the audience for fine art tends to be smaller and older than for popular culture and therefore such phenomena as screaming teenage fans and groupies are not so evident. Power also tends to reside with dealers, curators and collectors rather than the gallery-going public. Nevertheless, as we shall see, the art audience is widening and becoming younger, and British artists such as Tracey Emin have developed a cult following among young art students. Emin is one of a number of fine artists who have 'crossed over', that is, they appear in the tabloids as well as the specialist art press. High attendance figures are also important to museum directors and curators mounting major exhibitions and so they try to please the public and are devoting more and more effort to publicity, marketing and sponsorship.

Of course, in the case of audiences there are degrees of involvement, which range from mild interest to fanatical obsession. Fans contribute to the glory of the celebrity but they also share in it. (Most fans will not be able to fulfil their own desires for fame and immortality but, vicariously, they enjoy the success of others.) The 'obscurity-to-fame, rags-to-riches' narrative of so many biographies and biopics has a perennial appeal. When individuals join huge audiences at sports matches and rock concerts and scream their heads off, they participate in emotional, collective experiences, which enable any personal problems or social concerns to be set aside. The most active fans band together and form clubs where they share a sense of belonging to a community or subculture. By acquiring autographs, posters and other memorabilia, fans enjoy the pleasures of collecting that wealthier individuals gain from assembling art collections.

Signing an autograph has been described as 'the definition of being a famous person'. Full-time, 'in-person' autograph hunters who acquire them for sale to dealers and collectors pester celebrities and some stars agree to provide multiple examples of their signatures to such hunters for prearranged fees.[29] The signatures of artists on drawings and paintings, of course, are also crucial in the realm of art as evidence of authorship.

Many fans are creative and produce visual tributes to their idols and some fans then give them to the celebrities concerned. Art by fans has been sold in an auction of Marilyn Monroe's effects and displayed in exhibitions devoted to the Beatles and Manic Street Preachers.[30] As we shall discover, several American and Australian artists depict celebrities in a manner very similar to that of fans.

The American Gary Lee Boas is a curious instance of a nerdish fan interested in all celebrities – from movie stars to presidents to porn actors – and in collecting images of them via instamatic cameras. Sometimes he photographed celebrities without knowing what they were famous for. His paparazzi-like hobby has lasted decades and so he has accumulated 60,000 photographs. In 1999, a selection of his images taken between 1966 and 1980 was published as the book *Starstruck*.[31] In February 2000, his photos were also exhibited in the New York art gallery Deitch Projects and in April 2001 at the Photographers' Gallery, London even though many of them are poorly composed and blurred. Another curious fact is that Boas' amateurish snaps have been admired and collected by some of the celebrities he has photographed – Warren Beatty, for example. Boas delighted in appearing in photos (taken by his friends) standing next to such stars as Dame Elizabeth Taylor and Ronald Reagan. He himself has become well known and hence has been described as a 'superfan-turned-celebrity'.

Jessica Voorsanger (b. 1965), an American artist living in London, employs various media to explore the subjects of celebrity and fandom in an amusing but thought-provoking manner. As a child in New York during the 1970s, family television shows and stars such as the actor/singer David Cassidy (b. 1950) fascinated her. She now thinks the longings of fans resemble unrequited love. Voorsanger's final MA exhibition at Goldsmiths College in 1993 was devoted to Cassidy and in the same year, she finally managed to meet him and video their encounter. Later exhibitions have included letters from celebrities written in response to Voorsanger's requests, plus photographs and videos of meetings with such figures as Richard Branson and Michael Owen. Like a relentless fan or journalist, she has rifled through the garbage of celebrities such as Bob Geldof and then presented her findings as art. The celebrity's exciting but frightening experience of being mobbed by shrieking fans, Voorsanger simulated in 1997 by hiring young women to form a *Fan-A-Gram*, which targeted pre-selected nonentities. More examples of her work will be cited later.

As Ilene Rosenzweig's 1994 book *The I Hate Madonna Handbook* and the Internet game 'Slap a Spice Girl' indicate, not all those who take an interest in celebrities are admirers. Indeed, many viewers are amused by the spectacle of celebrities behaving foolishly and take malicious pleasure in their failings and discomfort. Even off duty, entertainers can be entertaining. News reports of the sufferings, suicides and violent deaths of famous people can provide a frisson of horror or even sadistic pleasure; they add excitement to the humdrum lives most people lead and prompt a feeling of participation in momentous events.

**4. Hugh MacLeod, 'Happiness ...' (2001).**
Pen and ink cartoon published in the *Guardian*, 20 April 2001, p. 19.
© Hugh MacLeod/Gapingvoid.com.

Celebrities who produce cultural commodities need to develop thick skins because they can expect harsh as well as positive reviews from professional critics. The American artists R.B. Kitaj and Julian Schnabel were angered by the negative reviews they received from British writers. Furthermore, if celebrities decide to address controversial subjects such as politics, religion and sex, then they will arouse the attention of people who are not their fans: censors, the police, politicians, priests, puritans, and so on. Of course, it is often the case that shock tactics are deliberately employed by celebrities precisely in order to generate outrage and thus free publicity. The history of the avant-garde is also replete with examples of 'shock art'.

We all experience the discrepancy between our inner and outer selves; we all understand that a public persona or mask may be required to hold down a job or to fulfil a social role. However, the question then arises: 'is there a real, private, inner self that persists beneath the public masks or are we simply the sum total of all our masks?' Celebrities who are actors have to play a succession of mostly fictional characters. The better the actor, the more diverse roles he or she can play. Some viewers may not be able or willing to distinguish between the fictional character on screen or stage and the actual individual. This is because most fans are not familiar with the private person and so they tend to conflate the actor's role with the actor. (Also, many American movie stars, John Wayne and Robert Mitchum for instance, no matter what parts they played, always seemed to be themselves.) For example, actors playing fictional doctors in television series have received fan mail asking for medical help! Neal Gabler, in his book *Life the Movie* (1998), concludes that entertainment has now 'conquered reality'.

The error of equating individuals with the roles they play on screen is easily illustrated by the example of Rock Hudson (aka Roy Scherer, 1925–1985): Hollywood film studios repeatedly cast this tall, handsome actor as a tough, masculine, heterosexual lover while in private life he was a practising homosexual. Hudson spent his whole career trying to keep his sexual preference secret from his fans until he was dying of Aids and it was no longer possible. In 1992, the American independent filmmaker Mark Rappaport (b. 1942) produced a humorous video entitled *Rock Hudson's Home Movies* that employed a look-alike actor (Eric Farr) and clips from Hudson's Hollywood movies in order to explore the gay subtext of his career.[32]

The issue of persona raises quite complex conceptual problems regarding the nature of human identity and personality. Paglia, the American scholar who admires Madonna and Dame Elizabeth Taylor, and who became a minor celebrity herself during the 1990s, has explored this issue and has explained the term's origin as follows:

> *Persona* is the Latin word for the clay or wooden mask worn by actors in Greek and Roman theater. Its root is probably *personare*, 'to sound through or resound': the mask was a kind of megaphone, projecting the voice to the farthest tiers of spectators. Over time, *persona* broadened in meaning to include the actor's role and then a social role or public function … Western personality thus originates in the idea of mask.[33]

As we shall see, this issue is particularly relevant to the work of Cindy Sherman and Madonna, and to the art of Warhol and Yasumasa Morimura. It was also the subject of an exhibition held in Bologna in 2000 entitled *Appearance*.

While some celebrities have allowed themselves to be altered or 'made-over' – given new names and looks – by their managers and promoters, others have taken charge of the process themselves and created a fictional persona on a temporary basis in order to intrigue their fans. The Beatles' adoption of the identity of a fictional marching band – Sergeant Pepper's Lonely Hearts Club Band – is a well-known example. Sir Paul McCartney has recalled that they were fed up with being 'four little mop-top boys' and so he thought: 'Let's not be ourselves. Let's develop alter egos so we're not having to project an image which we know. It would be much more free. What would really be interesting would be to actually take on the personas of this different band.'[34] David Jones, who adopted the name David Bowie and then invented stage characters such as Ziggy Stardust and the Thin White Duke, is another example. Regarding the difference between the private person Jones and the 'media monster' Bowie, David Buckley has observed:

> Like most cultural icons, Bowie is supremely 'mythogenic'. Biographers who concentrate on 'revealing the real person behind the mask' are constantly missing the point: it's the myth that has far greater resonance and is far more intriguing than stolid attempts to identify some 'true' essence ... what Bowie did as a cultural icon was to interrogate those accepted stereotypes that have symbolic meaning, such as heroism and villainy, comedy and tragedy; those archetypes which help to form the narratives that underpin our culture. In becoming a hero, and a particular sort of hero – media-manipulative, cross-generic, pan-sexual – at that, he was playing around with the very fabric of how we make sense of what is around us.[35]

It seems that the public/private division exaggerated by celebrity-hood and the many fictional characters actors are called upon to play can result in split and multiple personalities. (Normally, someone with multiple personalities is regarded as mentally ill!) Fraudsters and hoaxers are also fond of adopting false identities and impersonating others (so-called 'identity theft'). Assuming a false identity – a new name, a different age or gender – is especially easy on the Internet and millions of web users have exploited this possibility for purposes of creative play, privacy or crime.[36]

Movie and music stars achieve distinctive looks by such means as body language, clothes, hair dye, wigs, make-up and various props. (One is reminded of the attributes the Gods of ancient Greece and Rome possessed to facilitate recognition.) The 1999 travelling exhibition *Rock Style: Music + Fashion + Attitude* confirmed the importance of specially designed costumes to rock and pop stars. As we shall see, certain fine artists have followed suit.

Some stars have gone to even greater lengths by changing their appearances, via bleaching agents and plastic surgery, in a more permanent manner. Michael Jackson, the American singer and dancer who has lived in the spotlight since childhood, is the prime example. It seems to observers that he has tried to change his appearance and racial identity from black to white. The American artist Jeff Koons, creator of a sculpture of Jackson, has expressed admiration for Jackson for his willingness to 'exploit himself'. In the fine arts, performance artists such as the Frenchwoman known as Orlan, are also willing to transform their bodies by means of surgical operations and in the case of the British 'living sculptures' Gilbert & George the merging between their private and public identities is so complete that observers cannot prise them apart.

Impersonation can be a source of amusement and income for non-celebrities. For example, individuals who happen by chance to resemble a celebrity can earn a living as a model impersonating that celebrity. In major cities, there are agencies that specialise in offering look-alikes for hire. The work of Alison Jackson, a British artist-photographer who makes use of such look-alikes, will be discussed later. Many fans also feel compelled to impersonate their idols by dressing up in similar clothes and imitating their mannerisms. In 1997, Devon Cass and John Filimon published a book entitled *Double Take: The Art of Celebrity Makeover* that provided advice to fans on how to copy their idols. Cindy Sherman is an American artist who is internationally known for 'film stills' in which she poses as unnamed, fictional movie actresses. She has also impersonated Marilyn Monroe. As already indicated, the relationship of her work to that of Madonna will be considered in Chapter 1. Morimura, a Japanese artist, also uses photography to record his impersonations of named actresses, while Gavin Turk, a British artist, is noted for sculptures in which he impersonates famous pop music and political figures.

To those watching from the sidelines, celebrities appear to be enviable individuals enjoying glamorous lifestyles, but, as we all know, there is a downside: the pressure to keep up, to be perpetually on display, the relentless demands of photographers and journalists, the lack of privacy, the fear of being stalked, the prospect of death threats and violent attacks from unstable individuals. We have only to recall the murders of John F. and Bobby Kennedy, Martin Luther King, Sharon Tate, John Lennon, Jill Dando, Rebecca Schaeffer and Selena Quintanilla, to realise that some pay the ultimate price for their fame. 'Celebrity slayings' was the theme of Time-Life's 1993 book *Death and Celebrity*. Some obsessives attack the famous in order to acquire instant notoriety even if this results in vilification and a prison term. Mark Chapman's only claim to fame, or infamy, is that he murdered Lennon in New York in 1980. Valerie Solanas is primarily remembered as the extreme feminist who shot and wounded Warhol in 1968. (She claimed he was 'controlling her life too much'.) In 1996, a feature film directed by Mary Harron was made about Solanas and the events leading up to the murder attempt. Rob Scholte (b. 1958), a Dutch art star, was another victim of attack. In 1994, an unknown assailant – possibly a jealous rival – bombed his car and Scholte lost both legs below his knees.

Although anyone can die accidentally, the trappings of celebrity lifestyles, which involve travelling in hired helicopters and aircraft – American soul diva Aaliyah Haughton died in a plane crash at the age of 22 in August 2001 – driving fast sports cars and motorboats, having access to exotic locations and swimming pools, drugs and alcohol in abundance, and so on, increase the risk of accidents, as does being driven by chauffeurs. The deaths of Princess Diana and Dodi Fayed in a car crash in Paris are generally thought to be due to the reckless driving of a chauffeur who was trying to outrun a pursuing pack of paparazzi. The British art critic Peter Fuller was also killed in a car accident while being driven by a chauffeur.

Furthermore, the pressure of living under constant surveillance tends to exacerbate any personal problems celebrities may have and this has often resulted in drug overdoses and suicides: Ian Curtis, Marilyn Monroe, Kurt Cobain, Michael Hutchence, Sid Vicious, Paula Yates, et al. Posthumous fame, of course, is frequently enhanced if a star suffers a premature death by accident, illness or design: Buddy Holly, who died in an plane crash, James Dean, who died in a car crash, and Jean Harlow, who died from uremic poisoning aged 26, are just three examples from the world of entertainment. In 1979, Marianne Sinclair documented this aspect of celebrity in her book *Those who Died Young: Cult Heroes of the Twentieth Century*. (Visual artists of the modern era who died prematurely include: Jean-Michel Basquiat, Pauline Boty, Helen Chadwick, Derek Jarman, Keith Haring, Eva Hesse, Piero Manzoni, Amedeo Modigliani, Blinky Palermo, Jackson Pollock, Stuart Sutcliffe and Robert Smithson.) During the 1980s, Larry Johnson (b. 1959), an American artist resident in Los Angeles, commemorated celebrities like the film actor Sal Mineo (b. 1939, stabbed to death by a stranger in 1976) who had 'gone to heaven' by superimposing their names on colour photographs of blue sky and clouds.

When someone decides to become a performer, they generally adopt a new, professional name, which immediately establishes a split between the private person and the public persona. If they succeed in becoming a major celebrity, time spent alone diminishes. Anonymity, solitude, unselfconsciousness, a private life are sacrificed for celebrity. As celebrities live increasingly in the spotlight, they may reach a stage where virtually everything happens on camera. Eventually, the private or personal identity may be overwhelmed by the public persona with the result that some celebrities seem unable to function as human beings unless there is an audience and camera crew present. They emote and confess even their fears and weaknesses to the camera. In one telling scene in the documentary *Truth or Dare* (aka *In Bed with Madonna*), Madonna chats to assistants during a make-up session. She tries to persuade her then consort, the film star Warren Beatty – himself no stranger to the camera – to join in, but he lurks in the background and remains silent. Later he remarked somewhat bitterly: 'she doesn't want to live off camera … why would you bother to say something if it's off camera?' Clearly, Beatty disliked being a bit-player in Madonna's movie; nor did he want to conduct his affair with her on camera and so he sought to preserve the public/private distinction. When artists such as Emin decide to make their life and sufferings into art, which is then displayed in public galleries, they voluntarily demolish the division between private and public.

Given that celebrities' rise to fame depends on a willingness to flaunt themselves in public, it is no wonder the media and the public are generally unsympathetic when celebrities start demanding privacy. It has been argued that, although Princess Diana suffered because of media pressure, she was complicit in the publicity process and used the media for her own ends whenever it suited her.

**5. Madonna in *In Bed with Madonna* (aka *Truth or Dare*), 1991.**
Mirimax Production Company. Publicity still courtesy of the British
Film Institute (Stills, Posters and Designs), and Rank Film Dists Ltd.

Sometimes the demand for privacy is motivated by a desire to
control the release of images because they are a valuable source of
income. For example, one celebrity couple – Michael Douglas and
Catherine Zeta-Jones – objected when unauthorised persons photographed their wedding because they had already sold exclusive
publishing rights for such images to a particular magazine. The
feeding frenzy of the paparazzi is not fuelled by a love of stars but by
the large fees they can obtain for their copyright commodities.

Some celebrities do manage to retire from the public arena by
becoming recluses. The film star Greta Garbo, the novelist J.D.

Salinger and the Pink Floyd musician Syd Barrett are three examples. Rich celebrities also buy ranches and estates with perimeter fences and 24-hour guards, so that they can live away from the public gaze but even there, they are usually accompanied by dozens of assistants, servants and bodyguards. Even then, privacy cannot be guaranteed because some employees will eventually sell their stories to newspapers. Furthermore, the strategy of retreat often fails because it inflames the curiosity of fans and the media. It can also make comebacks difficult when the recluses change their minds.

Although the vast majority of celebrities actively seek fame, some, as Shakespeare put it, 'have fame thrust upon them' by birth or accident. Examples include 'celebrity victims', that is, ordinary people who become celebrities reluctantly because of accidents of fate such as the kidnapping and murder of their children, or because they survive a train crash and then campaign for safety improvements. During the early 1960s, Warhol memorialised victims of car accidents and food poisoning in paintings based on newspaper reports and photographs. Scandals involving major politicians often transform lesser players into media celebrities; witness the 1963 Profumo affair that made Christine Keeler a household name in Britain. As we shall see, this scandal was the subject of a painting by the artist Pauline Boty.

Although royals and aristocrats are now politically much weaker than they were in the past, many of them still enjoy the status of celebrities in the eyes of the media. Their fame is undeserved because it is due to an accident of birth, not for anything they have accomplished. (However, they can turn this to advantage: at least one member of the British royal family – Prince Charles – has artistic inclinations and interests [watercolour painting and architecture], plus a concern for the environment, and has used his fame and wealth for positive ends. Other minor royals have run businesses in which they traded on their royal connections.) It is surely a sign of greater democracy and social progress that celebrities in the realm of entertainment – many of whom emerged from the working class – have largely eclipsed the upper classes of the past. Royals, aristocrats and members of the upper middle class used to constitute what was called Society. Cleveland Amory, writing about Society in America, asked: who killed it? A prime suspect was celebrity.[37] Nevertheless, one can point to examples of mergers between the two realms: the 1956 marriage of the American film star Grace Kelly and Prince Rainer III of Monaco, for instance. (Kelly [1929–1982] died in a car crash.) It is also the case that British celebrities of humble origin can be ennobled: witness the knighthoods bestowed on the pop music stars Bob Geldof, Elton John, Paul McCartney and Cliff Richard.

Since the Restoration of King Charles II in 1660, Britain has been unwilling to abolish the monarchy and so it currently survives as part of celebrity culture and the heritage/tourist industries. Celebrities resemble royalty in the sense that they too constitute a social elite. Major pop and rock music stars are called 'kings' and 'queens', and top performers are referred to as 'rock royalty'. Key members of London's art world have been described as an 'Artocracy'. Celebrities often have 'courts' of admirers and can found dynasties; witness the children of movie stars who also become stars; for example, Jane, Peter and Bridget Fonda, the daughter, son and granddaughter of Henry Fonda. Picasso had a head start as an artist because his father was a painter and a teacher of art, and some of Picasso's children have benefited from his surname (see below).

Celebrity can also rub off on those close to stars; relatives and associates can become celebrities in their own right: Jackie Kennedy, the wife and widow of President John F. Kennedy, Monica Lewinsky, the White House intern who provided personal services for President Bill Clinton, for instance. Would we now know anything about the art dealer Theo van Gogh if his brother Vincent had not taken up art, or of Dr Gachet if Vincent had not known him and painted his portrait? James Monaco has used the term 'paracelebrities' to describe such individuals.[38]

Deyan Sudjic has also cited Paloma Picasso (b. 1949), the daughter of two artists – Françoise Gilot and Pablo Picasso – as someone who successfully exploited her father's surname to brand perfume and other goods:

Paloma Picasso is an obligingly non-specific sort of celebrity. She is famous for nothing in particular ... If she is famous for anything ... it is for being Pablo Picasso's daughter. And it is that fact that allows her to be all things to all consumers. Manufacturers can be confident that the Picasso name is not going to offend people who don't like sport, or put off those who think that film stars are a bit too obvious. And her name is curiously free of any national inflection: not quite American, not quite European, but equally recognisable on both sides of the Atlantic. It's the kind of celebrity that could have been created in the test tube, precisely engineered for maximum market appeal, while retaining vaguely cultural overtones. Putting the Picasso name on your product is certainly enough to help it to stand out from the anonymous herd.[39]

In 1999, Paloma's wealth was estimated to be £350 million. Her value to commerce is a tribute to the fame achieved by her father. He was one of the few fine artists of the twentieth century who became an international celebrity on a par with leading movie and pop stars. One writer has even adopted the habit of calling celebrities with real achievements to their names 'Picassos'.

So-called 'celebrity endorsement' is now commonplace and occurs for commercial (endorsing products and services in adverts), charitable and political reasons. In all three cases, additional publicity ensues for celebrities so even their support for good causes is not entirely disinterested.[40] Often it seems celebrities assist charities in order to massage their images and to assuage their guilt at being so well paid and privileged. A minor redistribution of wealth substitutes for a more radical redistribution that would follow fundamental political change. Cash-strapped arts institutions such as the Serpentine Gallery in London organise gala dinners and hold auctions to raise funds. At one such event to mark the 30th anniversary of the gallery in June 2000, Charles Saatchi paid £100,000 for a Mini car Hirst had customised with multicoloured spots. Earlier, in 1994, Princess Di had put the Serpentine on the social map by attending a gala there wearing an eye-catching black dress intended to upstage Prince Charles' televised confession about their marriage. One of the Princess' friends was Lord Palumbo, the wealthy property developer and arts panjandrum. As we shall see, art stars are now willing to endorse commercial products for financial gain. (Even the names of dead artists, such as Picasso, are used to endorse products, such as new cars.)

It is evident from exhibitions that have been held around the world in recent years that more and more artists and curators have been taking an interest in celebrities and in the overlap between art, celebrity and religion. For instance, *Pin-Up: Glamour and Celebrity since the Sixties* (Tate Liverpool, March 2002–January 2003). The contents of some of these shows will be discussed in later chapters.

Much of the literature on celebrity culture by academics and journalists is highly critical. The American writer Cintra Wilson, for instance, has called it 'a massive swelling ... a grotesque, crippling disease'. Celebrity, she claims, 'is a virulent killer of fundamental human values'. She thinks it is now 'out-of-control' and that celebrities are 'over loved' and the common people 'under loved'. 'Fame', she rages, 'is a perverse deformity, an ego swelling as ludicrous as an extra sex organ, and the people that have it, for a huge part, are wilfully and deliberately fucked-up past the point of ever having anything sweet or human or normal about themselves ever again'.[41] There will not be space here to repeat all the complaints made against the celebrity system but those that seem applicable to the visual arts will be considered.

Wholesale condemnation of celebrity culture is also inappropriate because, as Tyler Cowen has argued, in democratic, commercial societies it has positive as well as negative effects. For instance, he maintains that the power of politicians has been curbed by the fact that they have to compete with entertainers who must please the public. Although 'leaders lose their stature and become another set of celebrities ... voters and other external forces, such as the media, have more control over politicians than ever before. Famous politicians are kept on a short lease ... [hence] the danger of political abuse and very bad outcomes is smaller [than in the past].'[42]

The cult of celebrities – who now include certain fine artists – is so entrenched and pervasive, it is hard to see beyond it, even though what humanity has constructed humanity can always demolish; however, some alternatives explored by artists since 1800 are described in Chapter 4. Finally, the conclusion reviews the advantages and disadvantage of celebrity art and artists. Answers will be sought to such questions as: 'can art survive in an era of entertainment and celebrity? Can art preserve a distinct identity or will it be condemned to a minor role in celebrity culture? Is high quality in art incompatible with celebrity? Can art perform a critical function in respect of modern idolatry?'

# 1

# Celebrities as Art Collectors and Artists

Celebrities in such realms as film, television and rock music are often highly creative individuals and so they have an affinity with fine artists. Some stars meet visual artists and, in certain cases, friendships and collaborations follow. Crossovers also occur: some film stars take up painting while some visual artists direct films. A number of leading actors have played the role of artists in films and this has encouraged them to make a close study of the life, work and methods of those artists. Examples include: Charles Laughton as Rembrandt in *Rembrandt* (1936); José Ferrer as Toulouse-Lautrec in *Moulin Rouge* (1952); Kirk Douglas as van Gogh and Anthony Quinn as Gauguin in *Lust for Life* (1956); Charlton Heston as Michelangelo in *The Agony and the Ecstasy* (1965); Ed Harris as Jackson Pollock in *Pollock* (2000).[1]

## Art Collectors and Patrons

Successful entertainers earn millions and so have large surpluses to spend and invest. Some decide to become serious art collectors. Furthermore, they generally acquire large mansions or apartments (sometimes several in different countries), which then need decorating and furnishing. Many Hollywood figures have vied with one another for high status by buying expensive art works, ceramics, furniture and designer-name goods in order to display them in their so-called 'celebrity homes' (those that are the subject of bus tours in Hollywood and television series).[2] In 1970, Paul Staiger (b. 1941), a West Coast painter, depicted the exteriors of celebrity homes belonging to such stars as Kirk Douglas and Randolph Scott in a photo-realist manner. His titles provided precise postal addresses. Today, emerging movie stars are more likely to keep their addresses secret because of the dangers posed by stalkers.

Notable Hollywood art collectors of the past and the present include: Michael Caine, Douglas Cramer, Tony Curtis, Kirk Douglas, David Geffen, Richard Gere, Alfred Hitchcock, Dennis Hopper, Sam Jaffe, Charles Laughton, Steve Martin, Jack Nicholson, Clifford Odets, Vincent Price, Sylvester Stallone, Billy Wilder and Edward G. Robinson.

Robinson (aka Emanuel Goldenberg, 1893–1973) was born into a Jewish-Romanian family that moved to the United States early in the twentieth century.[3] While growing up in New York, Robinson enjoyed collecting cigar bands (later he became a heavy cigar smoker), cigarette cards depicting baseball players and pictures of stage and music hall female stars. His interest then shifted to the visual arts and he began to collect reproductions of works by Remington, Rembrandt and Goya. He developed an ambition to become an actor and after succeeding on the New York stage, he received offers from Hollywood and, in 1931, he became famous for his role as the gangster Rico in the film *Little Caesar*. Much to Robinson's chagrin, he became forever identified with this character. Hal Wallis, the film's director, was also an art collector.

Once Robinson became a movie star, he discovered that fame and money did not satisfy his cultural needs. However, the money enabled him to afford genuine works of art and on every trip to major cities, he would visit public and private art galleries. In 1926, he bought his first oil painting in an auction. Soon, his taste fixed on impressionist and post-impressionist paintings. Robinson, a committed and discriminating buyer, established a substantial and valuable collection of pictures that included works by the Europeans Cézanne, Chagall, Corot, Degas, Delacroix, Matisse, Monet, Morisot, Picasso, Pissarro, Renoir, Rouault, Seurat, van Gogh and the American Grant Wood. (Wood was to become a friend.) Robinson sought advice from art dealers but he also visited artists in their studios; for instance, he met Matisse in Paris on the latter's 70th birthday and conversed with Chagall in Rome. In 1939, when Robinson was in Paris with his wife and son, he encountered Vuillard and since the artist was short of money, Robinson commissioned him to paint a family portrait. On a trip to Mexico, he visited Diego Rivera, the communist muralist, and bought some paintings. Rivera showed him watercolours by his wife Frida Kahlo and Robinson acquired several; thus, he appreciated Kahlo long before Madonna. (Rivera also arranged for the movie star to visit the exiled revolutionary Leon Trotsky in his closely guarded villa.) In 1947, Robinson purchased a painting by the British artist Walter R. Sickert from the Kaplan Gallery, London because it depicted him and co-star Joan Blondell in the 1936 gangster film *Bullets or Ballots*. The painting, entitled *Jack and Jill*, was probably based on a publicity still.[4]

**6. Walter R. Sickert, *Jack and Jill*, c. 1936–37.**
Painting, oil on canvas, 62 x 75 cm. Private Collection.

Robinson lived in Beverly Hills but instead of adding the usual swimming pool to his home, he built a gallery and opened it to art lovers and students twice a week. (Some Hollywood mansions have sculpture gardens.) In May 1953, the National Gallery of Art in Washington DC was pleased to mount an exhibition of 40 paintings from Robinson's collection. Robinson's first wife Gladys was an amateur painter and he himself took up the medium for private pleasure in later life. In 1956, when he was compelled to sell his beloved collection to meet a divorce settlement, it raised $3,250,000. Being a self-confessed 'art addict', he bought some pictures back and quickly established another collection, which included African sculptures. This collection was eventually sold for $5,125,000. Regarding his acquisitive urge, Robinson once remarked: 'I have not collected art, art collected me. I never found a painting, they found me. I have never *owned* a work of art, they own *me*. What people call my collection is this group of masterpieces that collected each other, and then very kindly allowed me to go into debt to pay the bills.'[5] Robinson's passion for collecting and appreciating visual art encouraged many of those around him to follow suit.

Vincent Price (1911–1993) was a tall, handsome American with a charming, extrovert personality and distinctive voice. He became famous for playing sinister but suave, humorous villains in horror movies but he also excelled on the stage, radio and television. Before his acting career took off, he was fascinated by fine art and its history.[6] Price came from an affluent, cultured, middle-class family in St Louis and became interested in the visual arts via reproductions in art books. He soon enjoyed seeing originals in the city's museum of art. His obsession with collecting art began at the age of twelve when he bought a Rembrandt etching for $37.50 and it persisted throughout his life. At the age of 16, his parents allowed him to tour European cities where he tirelessly explored museums, galleries and cathedrals. From then on, whenever he had any spare time, Price would haunt junk shops, private galleries and museums in order to increase his knowledge of art and its monetary value, and to hunt for bargains. In the 1960s, I encountered him at John Kasmin's gallery in London (he was often in England for films being shot at Elstree) and I remember being surprised to see a screen idol in the flesh and in a gallery because it had not occurred to me that movie stars might be interested in contemporary art.

Price studied English and the history of art at Yale University. As a young man, his secret ambition was to be either an artist or an actor. He tried his hand at practical art but discovered he had no aptitude for it; furthermore, he was colour-blind. He then undertook an MA degree course at the Courtauld Institute in London where he researched a thesis on Albrecht Dürer and the School of the Danube. While in London, during 1935, he attended openings of exhibitions by the Anglo-American sculptor Jacob Epstein, whose work was then outraging the public. Price abandoned the Courtauld when he was offered acting roles in historical dramas.

On his return to the United States, Price was a success on the New York stage. For one of his apartments, he commissioned the American artist Bernard Perlin to paint a mural of Adam and Eve in his tiny bathroom. He also bought a large oil painting of the revolutionary leader Emilio Zapata by the Mexican painter José Orozco. Like Robinson, whom he eventually befriended, Price moved from New York to Hollywood to appear in films. With his second wife Mary – a costume designer who was also an avid collector – he occupied various houses in Los Angeles and filled them with acquisitions. Many visitors, who included established artists such as Max Beckmann and Rufino Tamayo, and the teenage Dennis Hopper, saw his homes and art collection. During the early 1950s, at one home, Hopper painted abstracts and used a kiln the Prices had to make tiles. The works by de Kooning, Pollock and Richard Diebenkorn that Hopper saw there left a lasting impression.

Price's appreciation of art spanned many cultures and periods; he valued contemporary American art as well as the masterpieces of the past and so his ever-expanding collection was extremely broad ranging. It eventually included paintings by Afro, André Derain, Diebenkorn, Goya, Pollock (a small one), Mark Tobey and Maurice Vlaminck. Drawings, prints and watercolours especially appealed to Price partly because they were more affordable. Acquisitions included: lithographs by Honoré Daumier; a drawing of Adam by Modigliani; a drawing by Delacroix; a self-portrait drawing by Henri Matisse; a watercolour of a picador by Constantin Guys; and a lithograph of the Irish singer May Belfort by Toulouse-Lautrec. At one time, he even owned a handwritten book by Paul Gauguin attacking Catholicism. Price also collected tribal artefacts from Africa and North America (including a Benin bronze and a Native American carved totem pole), folk art and pottery, and pre-Columbian art from Mexico and Peru. Price's eye sometimes let him down: he once bought a 'van Gogh drawing' that turned out to be a fake.

During 1943–44, Price tried his hand at art dealing by opening The Little Gallery in Beverly Hills. One customer was Charles Laughton; he bought works by Morris Graves. Price later participated in a crusade to establish a contemporary art museum in Los Angeles. The Modern Institute of Art existed for two years – 1948–50 – before funding dried up. Price tried hard to raise the cultural level of Los Angeles and the movie community. Exasperated by the struggle, he told one reporter: 'You can sell 'em [the moneyed men who ran Hollywood] sin and sell 'em sex but when you try to peddle "culture" you run smack into a solid wall of stupid ignorance.'[7]

Once Price's support for the arts became widely known, he was asked to serve on many arts committees, councils and juries. In

1958, for example, he served on the jury of the Pittsburgh International Exhibition alongside Marcel Duchamp and Professor Lionello Venturi. The prizewinner that year was the Spanish painter Antoni Tàpies.

Price was not content to enjoy art by himself – he wanted the public to share his pleasure and so he proselytised on its behalf by giving public lectures, radio talks and by writing about it. Even today, the enthusiasm conveyed by his 1959 'visual autobiography', *I Like What I Know*, is highly infectious.[8] Other books and catalogues he wrote or compiled included: *The Drawings of Delacroix* (1961), *Contemporary Sioux Painting* (1962), *The Holy Bible Illustrated by Michelangelo ...* (1964) and *The Vincent Price Treasury of American Art* (1972).

A hugely popular television quiz show in America during the 1950s was *The $64,000 Question* (and *The $64,000 Challenge*). Price appeared on the show answering questions about art and he was joint winner twice. One of his contestants was his friend and fellow collector Edward G. Robinson. Between 35 and 50 million watched the programmes and Price was convinced they helped to increase public appreciation and knowledge of the visual arts.

During the 1960s, he wrote articles on architecture, junk sculpture, modern art, collecting, nudity in art, museums and art books for a syndicated column published in over 80 newspapers. In 1962, Price accepted a commission from the Sears Roebuck Company to select 15,000 original art pieces for sale to the public via the company's department stores. For several years, he toured the world buying art both old and new. (He persuaded Sears to give him a chequebook so that he could pay living artists immediately.) Mary Price established a frame-making workshop to ensure all purchases were well presented. The so-called 'Vincent Price Collection' was a tremendous success both financially and in terms of publicity for art and for Sears Roebuck. However, Price's promotion of 'department store art' did prompt some sour comments from one LA art dealer.

Earlier, in the 1950s, Price had donated 90 works to the East Los Angeles College, Monterey Park, to establish a 'teaching art collection'. The Junior College, located in a largely Hispanic district, has trained a number of artists and actors (Edward James Olmos, for instance), and it later opened a Vincent Price Gallery on campus devoted to preserving Price's legacy and extending his enthusiasm for the visual arts. The gallery has mounted a programme of exhibitions including, in 1983, one devoted to Price himself. It also maintains a website.[9] Price's contribution to the furtherance of the

**7. Andrew Macpherson, 'A member of Spitting Image
modelling film star Vincent Price', 1984.**
Photo © Andrew Macpherson, Los Angeles.

American public's understanding of the visual arts can hardly be
over-estimated.

Sylvester Stallone (b. 1946, New York, aka 'The Italian Stallion')
became a world-famous movie star during the 1970s and 1980s for
his action-man roles as Rocky the boxer and Rambo the Vietnam
veteran. He currently lives in Beverly Hills but during the 1990s, he
occupied a large mansion and estate in Miami worth $16 million. In
1997, Stallone's neo-classical-style villa overlooking Biscayne Bay was
profiled by the glossy magazine *Architectural Digest*.[10] Stallone has a
passion for architecture and building and spent a small fortune
remodelling the mansion. He was inspired by the baroque fantasies of
Gianni Versace (1946–1997), the Italian fashion designer to the stars

(and celebrity murder victim), a friend of his who had a home in South Beach Miami, and by interiors seen in Paris and Venice. Stallone was seeking 'warmth, boldness, pageantry and over-the-top myth' and told his Italian designer Massimo Papiri to 'Rococo me to the max'.

Photographs by Dan Forer revealed lavishly decorated interiors with allegorical ceiling frescos, ornate chandeliers and furniture, and many paintings and sculptures. Stallone's taste in art is eclectic: his collection included paintings by the nineteenth-century academic artists William Adolphe Bouguereau and Luis Ricardo Faléro, the British painter Francis Bacon, the American painters Leroy Neiman and Andy Warhol (both portraits of Stallone), and sculptures by Robert Graham, marbles of nude females by Jean-Baptiste Carpeaux, and a bronze statue of Eve by Auguste Rodin. Antique stone statuary was distributed among the tropical vegetation in the extensive grounds and next to the swimming pool was a bronze figure of Stallone as Rocky Balboa with one arm raised. The latter was created by De L'Esprie, an American sculptress who has received commissions from several movie stars.

Another sculpture of Rocky, this time with both arms raised, was created in 1980 as a film prop. It merits a digression because, although it represented a fictional character, it became a controversial public sculpture. In *Rocky I & II*, the boxer runs up the steps leading to the Philadelphia Museum of Art and raises his arms in triumph. In *Rocky III* (1982), a sculpture commemorating the triumphal moment is donated to the city and placed in front of the museum. Stallone's biographer Frank Sanello reports:

> When Stallone decided to let life imitate his art and donate the $60,000 statue by renowned sculptor A. Thomas Schomberg [b. 1943, a Colorado sculptor of athletes and public monuments], the City Fathers thought the gift was a publicity stunt, considered the statue kitsch, and told Stallone to take it back. The sculpture ended up unceremoniously lashed to a tree in the backyard of his Malibu home until other residents of the City of Brotherly Love mounted a drive to get their 'Rocky' back. A compromise was achieved. Schomberg's statue ended up in front of Philadelphia's Spectrum, a hockey, basketball and boxing venue. Embarrassed by the backlash against its good taste, the city's Art Commission allowed the sculpture to remain in front of the art museum during the first two months of *Rocky III*'s release ...[11]

**8. A. Thomas Schomberg, *Rocky*, 1980.**
Public sculpture, bronze, photographed outside Philadelphia's
Museum of Art. Photo courtesy of the artist and Cynthia Schomberg.

Danielle Rice, a curator of education in the museum, has argued that
the Rocky bronze proved popular because the movie character
portrayed reinforced the mythic vision of liberty as free enterprise
and therefore ideally suited the American dream of success.[12] When
*Rocky V* (1990) was made, the statue resumed its original position
and Stallone wanted it to remain there. He told the press that he and
Rocky had done more for Philadelphia and its tourist trade than
Benjamin Franklin. Rice reports that 'as a concession to tourism, the
city installed a concrete plate with "Rocky's footprints" at the top of

the museum steps, in the place previously occupied by the much-debated monument'.

Henry Rogers, Stallone's publicist, once arranged for a six-page article to appear in *Life* magazine about his client's interests in making and collecting art. The aim was to change the public's perception that Stallone was simply a crude Rambo character by showing that he was really a man of culture.

A number of Hollywood collectors specialised in the work of certain living artists and as a result developed friendships with them; Charles Laughton and Morris Graves, Tony Curtis and Joseph Cornell, Vincent Price and William Brice, for instance.

In 1970, the Otis Art Institute in California mounted an exhibition entitled *Hollywood Collects*, which featured art works owned by over 60 film actors and entertainment-industry figures. Each collector was represented by a single work; they included: George Cukor (a Georges Braque still life), Tony Curtis (a Joseph Cornell box), Kirk Douglas (a painting of a child by Picasso), Gene Kelly (a Mary Cassatt pastel of a child), Burt Lancaster (a gouache of a family by Fernand Léger), Gregory Peck (a Raoul Dufy oil painting of a circus), Vincent Price (a semi-abstract gouache by Mark Tobey), Jack Warner (a Salvador Dalí portrait of Mrs Ann Warner), and Billy Wilder (a painting of female nudes by Ernst Kirchner). The exhibition demonstrated that Hollywood collectors were catholic in their tastes, were willing to buy abstractions as well as figurative works, European as well as American art, established modern art and the latest contemporary trends. Henry J. Seldis, in his catalogue introduction, gave two reasons why Hollywood collected in addition to aesthetic pleasure, investment and the collecting mania itself: 'The high degree of visual-mindedness that the best film-makers have, along with the ennui that hits them between assignments, brings them into galleries the world over.'[13] Some film stars are even willing to accept roles in films they do not respect if they provide travel opportunities and thus the chance to explore museums and art stores in foreign lands.

Although New York still dominates the American art market, the auction houses Christie's and Sotheby's have branches in Beverly Hills and there are many private galleries serving the affluent citizens of Los Angeles, that is, those whose wealth derives from financial services and from the high-tech and entertainment industries.

Art dealers welcome celebrities and movie stars to their premises because, as Vincent Price once pointed out, stars have audiences and what stars do and buy is news.

Because celebrities are very busy and often ignorant about the art world and the monetary value of art objects, they generally seek advice from art advisors and dealers. However, problems can still arise. For instance, when Stallone bought art during the 1980s he relied on the advice of the art consultant Barbara Guggenheim. She obtained the Bouguereau plus a painting by the German Anselm Kiefer. However, Stallone soon became dissatisfied because the Bouguereau turned out to be heavily restored and the Kiefer began to fall apart and so he attempted to sue Guggenheim for $35 million. Furthermore, some advisors turn out to be unscrupulous. One such dealer – Tod Volpe, an expert on the American Arts and Crafts Movement – who assisted Hollywood's elite to 'accumulate competitively' during the 1980s became bankrupt and ended up in prison for fraud. He later wrote a frank account of the services he performed for such clients as Linda and Jerry Bruckheimer, Jack Nicholson, Joel Silver, Patsy and Steve Tisch, Barbra Streisand and Bruce Willis.[14]

In some instances, stars sponsor exhibitions of the work of their favourite artists in public museums while others sit on the boards of major art institutions. Former movie actress Jennifer Jones (b. 1919, aka Phylis Isley), was married to the rich businessman and philanthropist Norton Simon until his death in 1993. Since 1989, Jones has presided over the Norton Simon Museum in Pasadena which has art works by such famous names as Cézanne, Degas, Gauguin, Goya, Rembrandt, Rubens and van Gogh. Film star Gregory Peck is also a member of the museum's board of directors.

## Celebrity Art

Although this term does not appear in existing dictionaries of art, it can be found on many websites. It has two meanings: art works *depicting* celebrities; and art works *by* celebrities. Celebrity art in the first sense will be considered in Chapter 2. Celebrity art in the second sense frequently occurs on the Internet in relation to charity auctions. What happens is that fundraisers invite contributions from stars – drawings (even doodles), paintings and photographs – and then offer them for sale.[15] One suspects the famous signatures rather than the aesthetic merits of the works themselves attract buyers. (In

April 2002, Helen Clark the Prime Minister of New Zealand became involved in a scandal when it was revealed she had signed doodles and paintings sold at charity auctions, which she had not produced.) Some American collectors specialise in celebrity art. For instance, in 1999, the Jerry Gilbreath celebrity art collection was exhibited at the Pensacola Museum of Art in Florida. Gilbreath, a Mississippi attorney and businessman, owns art works by Ted Kennedy, Tennessee Williams, David Bowie and Donna Summer.

A surprising number of entertainment stars engage in or have engaged in creative activities such as drawing, painting and sculpting in their spare time.[16] Often they resort to it for therapeutic reasons: as a form of relaxation, as a hobby or pastime. It also appeals because they can work alone and thus exercise total artistic control. Some of them are sufficiently successful to exhibit and sell their work. They include: David Byrne, Rolf Harris, Kim Novak and Ronnie Wood (who all had art school training), Herb Alpert, Tony Bennett, Jeff Bridges, Charles Bronson, Pierce Brosnan, Richard Chamberlain, Tony Curtis, Miles Davis, Patrick Ewing, Peter Falk, Henry Fonda, Vincent Gallo, Jerry Garcia, Gene Hackman, John Huston, Holly Johnson, Piper Laurie, Joni Mitchell, Jack Palance, Anthony Quinn, Arnold Schwarzenegger, Jane Seymour, Sylvester Stallone, Jon Voight and Don van Vliet.

The reclusive American singer, musician, poet and artist Don van Vliet is an untypical example of a celebrity artist because first, he made a permanent switch from music to painting, and second, his paintings became highly respected in the art world. Van Vliet was born in California in 1941 into a working-class family and was christened Don Glen Vliet. His later adoption of the word 'van' was a tribute to Vincent van Gogh. During his childhood, the self-taught van Vliet was proficient in the arts of sculpture, painting and drawing and for a time he studied commercial art at the Antelope Valley College of Art. However, as a teenager his interest – like that of his friend Frank Zappa – shifted to rock 'n' roll. For 18 years, from 1964 to 1982, as Captain Beefheart, leader of His/The Magic Band, he composed and performed lyrics and rock music of a radical, difficult and dissonant kind.

Van Vliet recorded a number of albums and developed a cult following, which judging from the books and websites devoted to him persists to this day, but his musical career was a commercial failure. Furthermore, van Vliet had no ambition to become a rock star. Therefore, in 1982, the 41-year-old turned his attention to the art of painting. In fact, he had been making visual art and sketching on tour throughout the 1960s and 1970s and some was used to illustrate his record covers. Since the mid 1980s, van Vliet has mounted exhibitions in Europe and North America in private galleries and public museums. (He benefited from the revival of interest in expressionistic-type painting that took place in the 1980s.) Despite van Vliet's late start as a professional artist, sales, critical approval and reviews in major art journals followed. The artists Julian Schnabel and A.R. Penck became admirers and recommended him to the German art dealer Michael Werner who has galleries in Cologne and New York. Werner advised him to make a clean break with music, otherwise he would be perceived as 'a musician who also paints'. A retrospective of 40 of van Vliet's works toured in 1994.

Van Vliet has cited the action painter Franz Kline as an influence and his paintings – some figurative (primitivistic images of humans and animals) and some abstract (informal rather than geometric abstraction) – exemplify the instinctive, improvised character of the action painting of the 1950s: large format, rapid execution, imagery invented on the spot, brushwork left visible, thick pigment, an unfinished or provisional quality. There was in fact an overlap in terms of iconography, method and style between his music and his paintings. Van Vliet thinks all the arts derive from 'the same substance'.

Naturally, fans of Captain Beefheart swelled the visitors to exhibitions because they were curious about his visual output. On the one hand, his previous reputation as an avant-garde rock musician was bound to gain him media attention in the art world but, on the other hand, it could have prevented him from being taken seriously as an artist. In the event, his drawings and paintings were of sufficient originality and quality to overcome any fears on that score.

Ronnie Wood (b. 1947), the multimillionaire guitarist who has played in the Rolling Stones since 1975, is a keen spare-time artist albeit of a conventional, illustrational kind. He studied at Ealing College of Art during the early 1960s and resumed painting in the 1980s. Even while on tour Wood continued sketching. Naturally, he has depicted fellow musicians such as Chuck Berry, David Bowie, Bob Dylan, Mick Jagger and Annie Lennox. Most of his output consists of portraits but he is also fond of representing animals. An article about Wood and his pictures and prints of African wildlife produced on behalf of the conservation charity Tusk Trust has appeared in *Hello!* magazine. Distant Dreams Worldwide Holidays

**9. Don van Vliet,** *Crepe and Black Lamps,* **1986.**
Painting, oil on canvas, 148 x 122 cm.
Photo courtesy of Michael Werner Gallery, Cologne.

sponsored a trip to Kenya so that Wood could sketch endangered species in the Lewa Wildlife Conservancy. In 2001, Wood was commissioned by Lord Andrew Lloyd-Webber to produce a large-scale group portrait (15 x 8 feet) of a more pampered species, that is, 60 contemporary celebrities and powerbrokers inside The Ivy, a fashionable, expensive London restaurant. To qualify for portrayal in *London Dining*, celebrities had to eat at The Ivy at least once a week, which meant that Mr and Mrs Beckham were excluded. It is planned

**10. John Paul Brooke, 'Ronnie Wood with one of his paintings of Mick Jagger', 2001.**
Photo © John Paul Brooke.

to exhibit this epic painting in the Drury Lane Theatre and the Tate Modern gallery. One celebrity who sat for her portrait in Wood's Kingston-upon-Thames mansion was journalist Mariella Frostrup. In his studio, she noticed a series of works about the events of 11 September 2001, which Wood intended to auction in order to help the New York fire fighters.[17]

Wood has held numerous solo shows in galleries around the globe. One San Francisco gallery claims to have sold over $3 million worth of his paintings and prints. Reproductions of his art works can be found on many websites, in biographies and a limited edition book specifically about his creations.[18]

Anthony Quinn (1915–2001), the movie star with Irish and Mexican blood who grew up in poverty as an immigrant to Los Angeles and who had tremendous energy, virility and creative drive, is an interesting example of an actor-artist because some of his neo-fauve/expressionist paintings were based on his film and stage roles. For example, he depicted himself playing Paul Gauguin in *Lust for Life* (1956) and Alexis Zorba in *Zorba The Greek* (film: 1964, Broadway play: 1984). During the 1920s, Quinn's father cranked a camera in Hollywood's Zelig Studio. His father was accidentally killed while Quinn was still a child and so he tried many schemes to earn money. Since he had a talent for drawing, one was to copy in Crayola colours photographs of such idols of the day as Douglas Fairbanks, Pola Negri, Ramon Novarro and Rudolph Valentino and then to post them to the actors in the hope of a reward. However, only Fairbanks replied and enclosed $10.[19] At the age of eleven Quinn won a

**11. Anthony Quinn at work in his New York studio, 1980s.**
(The painting of Zorba was based on a photograph of him playing the role on Broadway in 1984.) Photo courtesy of Center Art Galleries, Hawaii.

statewide sculpture competition with a bust of Abraham Lincoln. One teenage ambition was to become an architect and he studied architecture at the Polytechnic High School. When he sought advice from the famous American architect Frank Lloyd Wright he was advised to correct a speech impediment because architects needed to enunciate clearly to clients. It was because of voice lessons following an operation on his tongue that Quinn became an actor instead of an architect.

While learning his craft, Quinn became friends with the legendary stage and screen actor John Barrymore (1882–1942) who, incidentally, had trained at the Art Students League in New York and worked for a time as a freelance sketch artist, and through him met the Los Angeles painter John Decker (1895–1947). Although Decker was a minor artist and is now almost forgotten, in his lifetime he was known as 'Hollywood's own artist'. He was a colourful, bohemian character with a humorous disposition and strange early life. His father had been a Prussian aristocrat, a von der Decken, and his mother hailed from San Francisco (Decker was born there). Decker was raised in England before World War I and learned to paint with Joseph Hacker, a London scenic artist, and he studied at the Slade School of Art with Walter Sickert. He also met an artist who taught him to forge modern masters such as van Gogh, Gauguin and Utrillo. During the war, Decker was interned on the Isle of Man as an enemy alien. Later, he spent time in Paris where he met Modigliani.

When Decker returned to the United States, he made a stab at acting and earned a living drawing caricatures of theatre and movie celebrities for such publications as *The New York Evening World, The New Yorker* and *Shadowland*. He moved to California in the early 1930s where he painted portraits, landscapes and still lives. Unfortunately, Decker paid little heed to sound techniques: he painted fast on plywood supports and used a quick-drying varnish that soon cracked. His cottage-style studio in Bundy Drive, Brentwood was a favourite gathering and drinking place for Barrymore, W.C. Fields, Gene Fowler, Thomas Mitchell (a film actor who was also an art collector) and their cronies.[20] One way in which Decker kept his many creditors at bay was by painting satirical portraits from memory of such stars as Clark Gable, Errol Flynn, Beatrice Lilly and Harpo Marx. The portraits also travestied the style of old masters. For instance, he portrayed W.C. Fields with puffed checks and red nose, dressed as Queen Victoria with the strutting dandy associated with Johnnie Walker whisky in the background. Fowler commissioned the portrait and hung it in his office where it was seen by many actors and writers. Decker also portrayed Barrymore wearing clown's rags while holding a sceptre, which was topped by a cabbage as a mocking symbol of sovereignty. The picture was entitled *The Vagabond King*. Harpo Marx he depicted as Gainsborough's *Blue Boy*.

In 1941, Decker painted some cartoon-style murals depicting Hollywood movie stars – Charlie Chaplin, Mae West, et al. – for the Wilshire Bowl Restaurant where they accompanied a cabaret about the golden age of film entitled *The Silver Screen*. Watercolour studies for the murals are preserved in the National Portrait Gallery in Washington DC.[21]

Later, in 1944, Decker went into partnership with Errol Flynn and opened a gallery in Los Angeles in order to 'make the finest paintings available to Hollywood folk'. Decker acted as the gallery's director.

Quinn bought several Deckers, as did Flynn, Joan Fontaine and Artie Shaw. However, Decker held some Hollywood art collectors in contempt because he thought they were ignorant and because they acquired paintings as status symbols. Quinn reports that Decker faked a Rouault and sold it to Billy Rose (1899–1966), a composer, actor and writer, for $15,000.[22]

Quinn resumed making art to fill the gaps between films and the long hours between takes while on location. He also designed jewellery and made sculptures and prints, and sold some works for thousands of dollars. Quinn never developed a style of his own – he borrowed styles from such modern masters as Matisse, Picasso and Henry Moore. In 1982, a library in the County of Los Angeles Public Library system was renamed after Quinn because he donated a personal collection of art works, photographs, scripts, memorabilia, etc. In the same year, he held a major exhibition at the Center Art Galleries in Hawaii; one of those who attended the opening was Marlon Brando. The exhibition sold out and raised $2 million. Quinn's paintings, along with those by other celebrities, were reproduced on Private Issue credit cards issued by Dean Witter, Discover & Co and exhibited aboard the cruise ship *Explorer of the Seas* owned by Royal Caribbean International.

While living in Italy, Quinn became friends with the noted sculptor Giacomo Manzù (1908–1991) who produced a bronze bust of Quinn as a gift; unfortunately, Quinn's wife thought the portrait resembled Gregory Peck more than her husband.[23] In his lifetime, Quinn established an art collection worth $2.8 million, which included a head by Rodin and a painting by Picasso.

During the 1990s, when Sylvester Stallone could not sleep, he resorted to painting in a former garage on his Miami estate. Painting, he has explained, he finds fun and therapeutic. He has painted abstracts but in 1997, he was working on a series entitled *Tribal Nights*, which featured crudely rendered faces of witch doctors and shamans. Stallone favoured lurid colour schemes, slabs of pigment and a direct attack with a palette knife. In fact, he once compared his slashing painting manner to fencing. Stallone has also remarked that some of his paintings were about how fame destroys celebrities. Earlier, in 1990, Stallone held a one-man show at the Hanson Galleries in New York. His pictures have fetched as much as $40,000 but he often gives them to charity auctions because he would feel 'somewhat tawdry' selling them because, after all, he was not 'a true starving painter'.[24]

Tony Curtis, in contrast, has no such qualms about selling his Matisse-style paintings and prints, and Cornell-style assemblages in boxes via such venues as the Catto Gallery, London. Indeed, the money from sales was useful when his film career was in decline. Curtis starred with Marilyn Monroe in *Some Like it Hot* (1959) and so it is no surprise that he has painted a portrait of her.

Some art galleries thrive on celebrity art. For instance, on the island of Maui, Hawaii, in the South Pacific, Gerard Marti established a 'rock 'n' roll' art gallery (the New York–Paris Gallery) specialising in art works by musicians. Later, in Lahaina, he established a gallery called Célébrités focusing on art works by and about famous entertainers. In 1986, the Yume Hotaka Celebrity Art Museum was opened in Hotaka, Japan. It is dedicated to art produced by people – actors, singers, film directors – who have talent in more than one sphere. The Modern Art Museum in Japan has also mounted a celebrity art exhibition.

Although celebrity art clearly has curiosity value for the fans of celebrities, many in the art world dismiss it as 'high-priced, limited-edition autographs, produced by people whose commitment to art is superficial'. And, according to Los Angeles critic Doug Harvey, most professional fine artists regard celebrity 'Sunday' artists as

> spoiled dilettantes who use the leverage of their wealth and fame to elbow themselves an undeserved portion of the scarce market shares, gallery space and media coverage. It's a small trough, and it's easier to generate interest for art made by

famous people than it is to generate fame for art made by artists
... Celebrity art makes for strong copy, it attracts attention.

However, he also acknowledged that, conversely, celebrity artists
'seldom get a fair shake (or any shake at all) from the serious art
press'.[25]

Rather than continuing with a general survey, four celebrities –
two American and two British – will be considered in detail: Dennis
Hopper, Madonna, Sir Paul McCartney and David Bowie.

## Dennis Hopper

Hopper, a slim, intense man with an adventurous and rebellious
temperament, was born in Dodge City, Kansas in 1936. His parents
were affluent but his childhood, spent among the flat farmland of
the mid-west, was rather lonely and so he sought refuge in vivid
imaginings and the fantasy worlds of the cinema. He avoided
schoolwork apart from art and recitation. As an adolescent, he took
art classes at the Nelson-Atkins Museum of Art, Kansas City, where
he was taught by the American regional painter Thomas Hart Benton
(1889–1975) who also taught Jackson Pollock. By 1955, he was
making heavily textured paintings influenced by European matter
art. In 1961, his artistic career suffered a severe setback when a
canyon fire destroyed 300 abstract paintings in his Bel Air studio.

In any case, during the 1950s, Hopper had turned to acting and
had been discovered by Hollywood while performing a Shake-
spearean role in a San Diego theatre. He then appeared with James
Dean in *Rebel Without a Cause* (1955) and *Giant* (1956). Hopper and
Dean became close friends and Dean too had tried his hand at
painting. After a dispute with a movie director, Hopper moved to
New York to study method acting, took up photography and became
involved in the art world at a time when the vogue for abstract
expressionism was giving way to happenings, neo-dada and pop art.
(Hopper thought the latter indicated 'a return to reality' and he was
often to use found objects in his own work even though he retained
a fondness for gestural marks.) While in New York, Hopper became
a 'gallery bum', that is he haunted the Museum of Modern Art until
he knew every work on display.

Hopper's versatility is demonstrated by the fact that he has been
a movie actor and director, a painter, sculptor and photographer,
and an art collector. He has also written essays for exhibition

catalogues about artists such as Bo Bartlett and Kenny Scharf. Furthermore, he has appeared in television dramas and commercials, and presented a television documentary about the interaction between advertising and art. In 1983, he devised a dangerous performance piece that involved him crouching within a circle of dynamite while it exploded!

Hopper has acted in over 100 films but is perhaps best known for his role as the long-haired biker and cocaine smuggler Billy in the counter-cultural film *Easy Rider* (1969), which he directed and also claims to have written, and his role as the sadistic drug dealer Frank Booth in David Lynch's disturbing film *Blue Velvet* (1986). The unexpected commercial success of *Easy Rider* enabled Hopper to direct an anti-illusionistic, intellectually ambitious and symbolic film entitled *The Last Movie* (1971). Shot on location in Peru, it was a movie about moviemaking, illusion and reality, and the impact of America on a foreign culture. Hopper has compared his film-editing, designed to foreground the medium itself, to that of modern painting: 'In a way, it's like an abstract expressionist painting, where the guy shows the pencil lines, leaves some empty canvas, shows a brush stroke, lets a little drip come down and says, "Yeah, I'm working with paint, canvas, and a pencil line."'[26] He has also acknowledged that the experimental films made with stock footage by the West Coast artist Bruce Conner (b. 1933) influenced both *Easy Rider* and *The Last Movie*. Although the latter won a prize at the Venice Film Festival, it was not a box-office success and Hopper's directorial career stalled for nine years.

During the 1960s and 1970s, Hopper mixed with artists from both the East and West Coasts, namely Wallace Berman, Bruce Conner, Allan Kaprow, Edward Kienholz, Roy Lichtenstein, Ed Ruscha and Andy Warhol, and with such art dealers as Walter Hopps and Irving Blum. His earlier friendship with the movie star and art collector Vincent Price has already been mentioned. Like Conner, Hopper made assemblages and in the early 1970s, Conner made three series of etchings, which he misleadingly entitled *The Dennis Hopper One Man Show*. When Warhol visited Los Angeles in the early 1960s to mount exhibitions of his paintings of soup cans and Elvis Presley at the Irving Blum Gallery, Hopper was one of those who welcomed him and who purchased canvases. (Warhol produced a portrait of Hopper, and Hopper took a photo of Warhol that was used on the cover of *Artforum* magazine in January 1964.) When Warhol attended a party Hopper arranged, he was delighted to meet such young male actors as Troy Donahue, Sal Mineo and Dean Stockwell. Hopper too produced some examples of pop art employing coca cola signs and images of American cars.

Warhol shot one of his first 16 mm films in Los Angeles. It was entitled *Tarzan and Jane Regained … Sort of*, and Hopper appeared in it. Hopper was impressed by the Marcel Duchamp retrospective held at the Pasadena Art Museum in October 1963, which he attended with Warhol. Hopper met Duchamp and ever since has been influenced by his use of readymades, his love of irony and his questioning of the concept 'Art'. Some of Hopper's works, such as the 1997 neon sign stating 'This is Art' – entitled *This is Art (Marcel's Dilemma)* – pay homage to the French dadaist.

Kaprow was famous from the 1950s for the mixed-media happenings he organised in New York. In 1964, he was in Los Angeles where, at various locations, he created *Fluids*: rectangular enclosures built from blocks of ice, which at night were illuminated with flares. Hopper called them 'ice palaces' and recorded their construction with his camera.

Another art dealer Hooper met during the 1960s was the Briton Robert Fraser (1937–1986). Fraser ran a gallery in London's Mayfair, which featured American pop artists such as Jim Dine and Claes Oldenburg. In December 1964, Fraser had also given the American assemblage artist Conner a show of sculptures and screened some of his films. In 1965, Fraser visited California to find eight artists for a mixed exhibition. He befriended Hopper and they visited Mexico to view examples of Mexican 'primitive art'. Fraser was a drug addict and introduced Hopper to cocaine. The show was held in London in January 1966. Entitled *Los Angeles Now*, it included works by Conner, Larry Bell, Wallace Berman, Ed Ruscha and sculptures by Hopper made from foam rubber. Laden with photographic equipment, Hopper crossed the Atlantic to see the exhibition and to experience Swinging London. He was most impressed and later recalled it was 'incredible, amazing … the most exciting time I'd ever seen, or seen since'.[27]

Being opposed to Hollywood's establishment, Hopper was also sympathetic to the radical political movements of the 1960s. In 1965, he participated in a civil rights march in Selma, Alabama and documented it with his camera. This is how he came to photograph Martin Luther King delivering a speech. In 1967–68, when the war in Vietnam was escalating, Hopper made a large-scale, sardonic, kinetic sculpture entitled *Bomb Drop* from Plexiglas, stainless steel and neon that was based on a bomb release mechanism from a World War II aircraft found in a junk yard.

Celebrities have access to celebrities in their own profession and in other professions; hence, one reason for the appeal of Hopper's photographs is that they feature such figures as Marlon Brando, Peter and Jane Fonda, Jasper Johns, Roy Lichtenstein, Paul Newman and Andy Warhol. As an actor and director, Hopper was also able to photograph stars 'behind the scenes', that is, on film sets and locations: in 1962, for example, he photographed John Wayne and Dean Martin on horseback during the making of the Western *The Sons of Katie Elder*. By including the tripod of a movie camera in the foreground, Hopper called attention to the staged character of the scene. Following President Kennedy's assassination in 1963, Hopper took a series of photos of the black and white television transmission of the President's state funeral. In *Apocalypse Now*, Francis Ford Coppola's 1979 film about the Vietnam War, Hopper was appropriately cast as a drug-addicted photojournalist.

Hopper's photos were not the snaps of an amateur. They were significant for their formal and compositional qualities as well as their content, and have been exhibited internationally; several anthologies of them have also been published. One of the latter – *Out of the Sixties* (1988) – is now an expensive collector's item. During 2001, signed limited edition prints of Hopper's portraits of Bill Crosby, Ike and Tina Turner, Paul Newman and James Rosenquist were offered for sale via the virtual gallery/Internet website Eyestorm.com.

Further recognition of Hopper's achievements was demonstrated by the film retrospective and exhibition – *Dennis Hopper: From Method to Madness* – held at the Walker Art Center, Minneapolis (and then touring) during 1987–88.[28] A second retrospective that focused more on his visual art was mounted by the Stedelijk Museum, a prestigious modern art venue in Amsterdam, in February 2001. The exhibition occupied eleven of the Stedelijk's rooms and a book/catalogue was published.[29] Another version of this show was held in Vienna.

Due to his association with leading American artists and his appreciation of visual art, Hopper became a keen and daring collector of contemporary art. In fact, during his lifetime, he has assembled three different collections because two had to be sold to meet divorce settlements. (Hopper has been married five times.) As already indicated, collecting art in Hollywood is something of a tradition. Artists whose work Hopper acquired have included Jean-Michel Basquiat, Keith

**12. Dennis Hopper, 'Peter Fonda and
Edward G. [Robinson]', 1964.**
Gelatin silver print, 61 x 41 cm. Photo © Dennis Hopper.

Haring, Roy Lichtenstein, David Salle, Cindy Sherman and Andy Warhol. (A painting of Chairman Mao by Warhol that Hopper owned suffered the indignity of being shot at while Hopper was drunk.) He has been included in a list of the top 100 American art collectors and his present collection is reputed to be worth several million dollars.

When Hopper held the first exhibition of his photographs in New York in 1986, he met Julian Schnabel, an artist who rose rapidly to fame during the late 1970s and early 1980s. The two men became friends and Hopper added one of Schnabel's trademark broken crockery relief paintings to his private collection. (Schnabel later painted a head and shoulders portrait of Hopper over broken plates.) In 1988, when Schnabel tried his hand at directing a film – *Basquiat* – he persuaded Hopper to play the role of the Swiss art dealer Bruno Bischofberger.

Tony Shafrazi was an art student at the Royal College of Art during the early 1960s and, while living in London, he became friends with Robert Fraser. During the 1980s, he followed Fraser's example by setting up as a New York dealer and gallerist at a time when a number of young artists – Basquiat, Haring and Scharf – were emerging from the graffiti street scene. Hopper has appeared in a group photo with Haring and Shafrazi, so he was obviously familiar with this milieu. Shafrazi has also mounted exhibitions of Hopper's photos and published books about them.

For many years, Hopper maintained a large studio in an old movie theatre in Taos, New Mexico, but he currently occupies a complex in Venice Beach, California. It consists of two condominiums designed by the fashionable, 'deconstructionist' architect Frank O. Gehry and a house designed by the iconoclastic architect Brian Murphy in 1987. Situated in an area with a high crime rate, the Murphy structure is built like a fortress with steel doors, walkways and stairs, plus a steel mesh roof. Inside, besides Hopper's art collection, there is furniture designed by Gehry constructed from crinkled cardboard. It is typical of Hopper that he should be willing to make his home in such a radical example of contemporary architecture.

One of the most famous and remarkable artistic monuments of Los Angles is the Watts Towers, designed and built by the folk or outsider artist Simon or Sam Rodia (1879–1965) during the period 1921 to 1954. The three towers, one of which is almost 100 feet tall, are made from steel, concrete, broken plates, bottles, shells and tiles, and are located in a black ghetto that was the scene of riots and burnings in 1965. In 1988, the towers appeared in a feature film directed by Hopper and starring Sean Penn and Robert Duvall as two cops. Sarah Schrank has commented:

> In a perverse case of art imitating life, the damaged Watts Towers [that is, damaged by bungled attempts at restoration] appear in the movie *Colors* (1988) ... which deals with gang violence in South Central. Gang members fleeing the scene of a drive-by shooting are chased through Watts by cops. The neighborhood is flagged for knowing viewers by a long shot of

the towers; the scene climaxes with the getaway car crashing into them and exploding, blowing both the towers and the gang members sky high. Hopper uses the Watts Towers metaphorically to show how the black community is torn apart by gang warfare, police violence, and drugs. With Hollywood special effects on his side, Hopper smashes and incinerates what the municipal government never could quite manage to: the towers and what they have popularly come to represent – black community. Then, in another twist, the towers appear once more in their former splendor at the end of the film.[30]

The social themes and iconography of *Colors* also prompted Hopper to produce, in 1991–92, a series of multi-panel paintings or 'joiners', which placed grainy black and white stills (printed on linen) excerpted from the movie alongside coloured, hand-sprayed graffiti writing.

As an actor, Hopper has often played psychotic killers. For example, in *Catchfire* (aka *Backtrack*, 1989), he played the part of a hit man called Milo hired by the Mafia to find and eliminate a female artist called Anne Benton – played by Jodie Foster – because she had witnessed a murder. (Hopper also directed *Catchfire* but after a disagreement over editing, he had his name removed from the credits and so the director's name became 'Alan Smithee'.) Benton is a conceptual artist noted for her slogan-type art displayed on moving electronic signs. This character is clearly based on the real American artist Jenny Holzer (b. 1950), author of such slogans as 'Abuse of power comes as no surprise' and 'Money creates taste', and in fact, Hopper engaged Holzer to make the art works used in the film. Slogans that appear in the film include: 'Protect me from what I want' and 'Lack of charisma can be fatal'. To trace Benton, Milo undertakes a crash course in contemporary art: he visits a gallery show of her work and buys a sign which flashes: 'Killing is unavoidable but is nothing to be proud of.' When he shows it to his Mafia bosses – Vincent Price plays Don Lino Avoca – one hood complains about the waste of money but another sees an investment opportunity because 'when the broad dies, the prices go through the roof'. In another amusing scene, Milo studies a conceptual art publication. Its convoluted language and philosophical conundrums strain his brain and he asks: 'What the fuck am I doing...?' Benton tries to escape her pursuers by moving to another city, assuming a new identity and finding work as an advertising copywriter, but Milo is now sufficiently knowledgeable to be able to recognise her style and so penetrate her cover.

Bob Dylan also appears in *Catchfire* in a cameo role as an artist who modifies abstract painted wooden constructions with the aid of a chainsaw. In addition, works of art by Botticelli, Bosch and Georgia O'Keeffe are briefly cited. It is highly unlikely that so many artistic references would have appeared in such an otherwise typical Hollywood thriller without Hopper's awareness of art from both the past and the present.

Hopper's visual awareness and pop sensibility made him sensitive to the signs and urban landscapes of cities, particularly those of Los Angeles. He photographed bikers, motorways, stained walls, torn posters, billboards and wall graffiti and admired the tall, crude, free-standing figures promoting restaurants and gas stations. Hopper's wealth enabled him to commission professional commercial artists to make replicas of 'Mexican' or 'La Salsa Man' and 'Mobil Man', and to paint photo-realistic representations of his billboard images (thus turning photos of billboards back into billboards).

Façades are common to both the urban environment and film sets. In 2000, Hopper began constructing a series of freestanding assemblages of such walls from wood, stucco, plastic sheeting, corrugated fencing and metal sheets. One was nine feet tall and 26 feet long. They exemplified the provisional, decaying aspects of a highly divided city. Jan Hein Sassen has described them as 'details from the city, selected by Hopper and reproduced for their inadvertent beauty. The reality of the city is now directly linked with the illusion of a film set.'[31]

During the 1970s and early 1980s, Hopper's self-destructive behaviour reached an extreme. He consumed huge quantities of alcohol and cocaine, assaulted two of his wives and so, for a number of years Hollywood studio executives regarded him as unemployable. Hopper claims that his over-indulgences in drink and drugs were crucial to the creative process – at least to begin with. Lynn Barber, a British journalist who has interviewed Hopper, noted his tremendous ambition to be a genius, but then commented: 'Unfortunately, he made the common mistake of studying the lifestyles of geniuses rather than the work – what one might call the If-I-cut-off-my-ear-I-will-paint-like-Van-Gogh delusion.'[32] Hopper himself told Barber that his motivation for making art was the hope that he could 'cheat death a little by leaving something that's going to last a little bit beyond your own time'.

For many years, Hopper had a reputation for being at the cutting edge in filmmaking and in his support for avant-garde art. However, Peter Biskind, the author of the book *Easy Riders, Raging Bulls: How the Sex-Drugs-and Rock 'n' Roll Generation Saved Hollywood* (1998), thinks that age and success have caused him to become conservative. According to the critic, Hopper appears on numerous television talk shows to promote such poor films as *Waterworld* (1995), wears expensive suits, plays golf, sides with the American gun lobby (actually he has worn cowboy hats and toted guns for many years), and votes for the Republican Party.

The disparate and discontinuous character of Hopper's output revealed by the Amsterdam retrospective makes it difficult to assimilate and evaluate. Films are often shot out of continuity and this characteristic applies to Hopper too in the sense that his artistic progress was often recursive and out of sequence. For instance, abstract expressionist phases in his painting occurred in 1982–83 and in 1994. His development was also staccato – occurring in bursts – because of the interruptions caused by movie acting and directing. Hopper's refusal to specialise may count against him after his death: will he be remembered as a talented film actor/director or as a gifted visual artist? What emerges from this summary of his career is that there was a fertile, mutually informing relation between his participation in movies and the visual arts.

## Madonna

On 9 December 2001, Madonna presented the annual Turner Prize cheque to the winner Martin Creed at Tate Britain, London. She was introduced as 'an art collector' rather than as a pop star or artist in her own right. Even though Madonna stated that such awards were 'silly' and uttered a swearword that attracted headlines the next day, her presence indicated a willingness to lend her fame and glamour to an event – transmitted live on Channel 4 Television – promoting contemporary British art, but it also signified a desire on her part to share in the fashionability of London's art scene. However, Shirley Dent, a critic of the event, claimed that 'celebrity is now the stuff art is made of' and that the prize ceremony captured 'a culture that has nothing to say for itself and is all sheen and celebrity'.[33]

Surprisingly, the highly effective brand name 'Madonna' was the so-called Material Girl/Queen of Pop/Madge's actual Christian name: Madonna Louise Veronica Ciccone was born in Bay City, Michigan

**13. Ismail Saray, 'Madonna and Martin Creed at the
Turner Prize event as seen on TV', 2001.**
Photo © Ismail Saray.

in 1958 and grew up near Detroit, the city famous for automobiles
and 'Motown' music. She was one of six children in a lower middle-
class, Catholic family. Her father was an Italian-American who was
college educated and worked as an engineer. Her mother, also called
Madonna, was French-Canadian. Madonna's childhood was marred
by the early death of her mother from breast cancer.

Madonna has recalled that her first exposure to visual art was via
paintings and drawings made by members of her family and via the
décor of the Catholic churches she attended.[34] Religious imagery was
later to become significant in terms of the iconography of her dress,
music videos and stage performances. The crucifix was a potent
symbol for her from early childhood. She has remarked: 'The whole
idea of the Crucifixion and the suffering of Christ is all kind of intertwined with masochism, and Catholicism is a huge part of my
upbringing, my past, my influence.'

Visits to the Detroit Institute of Art stimulated an interest in the
work and lives of two revolutionary Mexican artists: Diego Rivera
and Frida Kahlo. However, the arts that most attracted Madonna in
high school and college were dance, drama and jazz. She has claimed
that her interest in role-playing and gender bending developed early
when she dressed like a boy in order to attend gay clubs. Madonna
has a tolerant attitude towards homosexuality, admires drag queens,

works with gay dancers and has performed benefits for Aids charities; and some of her first fans belonged to the gay community. She has also flirted with lesbianism and sadomasochism. Madonna believes we are all to some extent bisexual.

In 1977–78, she moved to New York City to further her dancing career and supported herself by modelling nude for photographers and art students; photographs from this period surfaced in *Penthouse* and *Playboy* magazines in 1985. Short of money, she often visited New York museums such as the Cloisters (a branch of the Metropolitan Museum of Art) because they were free. In 1979, she spent time in Paris as a member of a disco stage show. Despite the fact that certain critics and even Madonna herself has admitted that her acting, dancing and singing abilities were only moderate, her career as a pop music singer and movie actress blossomed during the 1980s until she achieved huge commercial success and worldwide fame.

From 1985 to 1989, she was married to the American movie actor Sean Penn. In 1990, she toured the world with a show entitled *Blond Ambition*, which was the subject of a frank, backstage documentary film *Truth or Dare* (aka *In Bed with Madonna* [1991]) directed by Alex Keshishian. In 1996, she played the lead role of the Argentinian actress and wife of a dictator – Eva Perón – in the musical *Evita*. In May 2002, she played the part of Simone, a ruthless art dealer, on the London stage in the satire *Up for Grabs* by David Williamson. She currently lives in Britain with her second husband Guy Ritchie, a British film and video director, and her two children Lourdes Leon and Rocco Ritchie.

During the years spent in New York's East Village district, Madonna participated in the nightclub and art world's social scenes. She made friends with artists associated with the graffiti movement such as Norris Burroughs, Jean-Michel Basquiat and Keith Haring. Haring (1958–1990) had arrived in New York shortly after Madonna. His vibrant, primitivistic drawings of 'radiant babies' executed in subways and nightclubs quickly gained him a reputation and soon he was showing in art galleries. For a time Madonna used the expression 'Boy Toy' about herself and she wore a skirt decorated with Haring's designs and a top incorporating the words 'Boy Toy'. Haring was gay and died of Aids just as Madonna was busy with her *Blond Ambition* tour. When the show reached New York, Madonna made a dedication to her artist-friend on stage. She has recalled:

We were two odd birds in the same environment. I watched Keith come up from that street base, which is where I also came up from. I've always responded to Keith's art. From the very beginning there was a lot of innocence and a joy that was coupled with a brutal awareness of the world. The fact is, there's a lot of irony in Keith's work, just as there's a lot of irony in my work. And that's what attracts me to his stuff. I mean, you have these bold colors and those childlike figures and a lot of babies,

**14. Michael Putland, 'Madonna wearing skirt with Keith Haring designs', 1983.**
Photo © M. Putland/Retna Pictures Ltd, London.

but if you really look at those works closely, they're really very powerful and really scary.[35]

Provincial origins, ambition and energy were not the only things Haring and Madonna had in common; both sought to please a popular audience and to supply it with affordable merchandise. Haring's life, work and products posthumously continue via a website and online 'Pop shop'.

In the autumn of 1982, Madonna and Basquiat had a brief affair. Both attended the same clubs and parties, and were keen dancers. Basquiat was a jazz fanatic and had even played in an 'art-noise' band entitled Gray (named after the reference book *Gray's Anatomy* used by doctors and artists. One of those who played with Gray was the versatile Vincent Gallo, who is now well known as a painter, photographer, actor, film director and song writer). Both were physically attractive and sexual predators, and so had a succession of lovers. When they met, Basquiat was just becoming famous within the New York art world and he was ahead of Madonna but it was not long before she overtook him. (For more on Basquiat, see Chapter 5.) Madonna and Basquiat spent time together in Los Angeles where he was having an exhibition. They were guests in the beach house of Larry 'Go-Go' Gagosian, Basquiat's aggressive LA dealer.

However, the romance was doomed because their lifestyles were incompatible: Basquiat was a heavy drinker and drug user, he ate junk food and slept late, whereas Madonna was an early riser, ate health food, took exercise, and disdained drugs. Basquiat enjoyed chaos while Madonna preferred organisation. While both were hungry for fame and wealth, Madonna was much more self-disciplined and businesslike than Basquiat. She proved able to cope with the pressures of celebrity whereas they crushed Basquiat. Madonna ended the relationship because of the drugs and the risks of unsafe sex. Basquiat was naturally upset and demanded the return of some paintings he had given her.[36] According to Andrew Morton, a Madonna biographer, what Basquiat and Madonna shared was 'artistic courage'.[37] One could also cite the practice of appropriating motifs from both fine art and popular culture.

In 1992, four years after Basquiat's death, the Whitney Museum of American Art mounted a retrospective of his paintings; Madonna helped to fund it. She also recalled her affair with Basquiat when an exhibition of his work was held at the Serpentine Gallery, London in 1996:

He was one of the few people I was truly envious of. But he
didn't know how good he was and he was plagued with insecur-
ities. He used to say he was jealous of me because music is more
accessible and it reached more people. He loathed the idea that
art was appreciated by an elite group.[38]

Basquiat had admired Andy Warhol and they eventually painted
collaboratively. Madonna too met Warhol – she has recalled dining
in a New York restaurant with Basquiat, Haring and Warhol – and
was probably impressed by his 'business art' practice. She and Sean
Penn invited Haring and Warhol to their exclusive marriage
ceremony held in California in August 1985. As a wedding present,
Haring and Warhol created a silkscreen painting reproducing a front
cover of the New York Post with a photo of the betrothed, to which
Haring had added one of his radiant babies and a heart shape sign
of love. Four years later, Madonna gave an interview to Warhol's
celebrity magazine Interview.

Once Madonna's income permitted, she began collecting original
works of art. Peggy Guggenheim, the noted founder of a museum in
Venice and pioneer collector of Jackson Pollock and other modern
artists, served as a role model. Madonna purchased works by
Salvador Dalí, Fernand Léger, Tamara de Lempicka, Maxfield Parrish,
Frida Kahlo and the Scottish artist Peter Howson (b. 1958). Madonna
bought a picture of a boxer from Howson as a present for Penn.
(Howson has painted controversial portraits of Madonna in the
nude; they were unveiled in April 2002.) David Salle presented her
with one of his drawings. She also admired the art of Edward Hopper,
Picasso, Man Ray, André Breton and other surrealists. Madonna
owned a portrait of Dora Maar by Picasso, which she considered a
representation of Maar's personality rather than her appearance.
Picasso was an artist who changed his style a number of times and
thus served as a precedent for Madonna's own periodic reinventions.
A Man Ray photograph that Madonna hung in her office of Lee
Miller kissing another woman inspired her and encouraged the use
of lesbian imagery.

Madonna has stated that what primarily interests her in art are
'suffering, and irony and a certain bizarre sense of humour'. Her
interest – indeed obsession – with Kahlo (1907–1954) coincides
with the first characteristic because Kahlo is well known for her
injured and pain-racked body, and troubled marriage. Another
reason Kahlo appealed was that she often dressed like a man (as did

Lee Miller) and this reinforced Madonna's attraction to cross-dressing. In 1991, Madonna announced her intention to make a film about Kahlo's life in which she would play the lead. However, it appears she has missed the opportunity because in 2001 two Kahlo biopics were announced.[39]

As a woman, Madonna is conscious of both femininity and feminism. The special rapport she has with female artists was evidenced in the remark: 'We chicks have to stick together.' Partly due to Madonna's promotion of Kahlo, the artist became a posthumous celebrity not only in the domain of art history but also in popular culture.[40] The Madonna/Kahlo coupling that occurred in the mass media during the early 1990s prompted a critical response from Janis Bergman-Carton:

> The Madonna/Kahlo connection is principally a ploy by Hollywood publicists, art world entrepreneurs and Madonna herself to exploit an old and reliable advertising device, the artist/celebrity validation code. By this measure, Kahlo is considered a better artist (investment) because her work is collected by Madonna, and Madonna is considered a more serious and respected celebrity (investment) because she collects Kahlo's. The reciprocity resonates in box offices, museum coffers, record companies and the art market.[41]

However, Bergman-Carton also maintained that Madonna and Kahlo were critics of female stereotypes, that they seized 'control of their bodies in order to dramatise the ideological issues of gender representation' and challenged 'the social parameters of acceptable sexual behaviour'. Both masqueraded in costumes to 'manipulate cultural signs and refashion religious iconography in order to constitute identities so insistently fluid' that they refused 'a singular, essential self'.

When Madonna displayed Kahlo's disturbing painting *My Birth* (1932) in her New York apartment, she used it to test visitors: anyone who disliked it could not be her friend. In 2001, she loaned another Kahlo – *Self-Portrait with Monkeys* (1943) – to Tate Modern for inclusion in a surrealism exhibition.

As someone who has been photographed by fans and the paparazzi thousands of times, and who has posed for numerous professional photographers, it is hardly surprising that Madonna developed a close interest in the medium of photography. She collected images by Guy Bourdin, Tina Modotti, Weegee (aka Usher Fellig) and Edward Weston, and admired the work of Nan Goldin, Lewis Hine, Horst P. Horst, Inez van Lamsweerde, Lee Miller, Helmut Newton, Robert Mapplethorpe and Paolo Roversi. Photographers with whom Madonna has collaborated for portraits, family images, publicity shots, book and album covers, include Steven Meisel, Herb Ritts, David Lachapelle, Mario Sorrenti and Mario Testino. She claims 'a sort of artist-muse relationship' developed between her and Meisel, Ritts and Testino. Such photographers are highly paid and have become celebrities in their own right. (In August 2001, Meisel was honoured by an exhibition in the London art gallery White Cube 2 and in February 2002 Testino was honoured with a show in London's National Portrait Gallery. One critic called Testino a 'lick-spittle' because he produced such flattering images of his sitters.) Ritts was also commissioned to direct the 1989 music video 'Cherish'. There is little doubt that Madonna is now extremely knowledgeable about photography, that she is indeed a connoisseur.

Cindy Sherman (b. 1954), an American artist who takes pho-tographs of herself playing roles in fictional films and who has impersonated Marilyn Monroe, became of special interest to Madonna. This was due to the close parallels between their artistic projects: Madonna too adopted a series of roles and fictional personae that involved drastic changes of appearance. In her 1985 music video 'Material Girl', Madonna reprised the role of Monroe in the 1962 musical film *Gentlemen Prefer Blondes*. The British pop star David Bowie was also a key early influence on Madonna because he also adopted invented personae on stage and because of his penchant for androgyny.

Sherman became famous within the international art world during the early 1980s but Madonna was able to explore similar ideas in the much wider realm of mass culture. Naïve interviewers who assume that the life and psyche of an artist are directly expressed in their art often seek to equate the real Madonna with the parts she plays, with the content of the songs and stories she writes. However, although Madonna has used her experience of Catholicism, it is evident from interviews that she fully understands that art depends upon artifice, invention and masquerade, and the use of earlier art, social reality, literature, myths, etc., as well as personal experience. Art may reflect the emotions and personal lived experience of an artist or it may not. (A crime novelist does not have to commit a murder to write a convincing murder mystery.) She has stated, for instance, that the erotic tales in her book *Sex* (1992) are fantasies, which many people share but which are not necessarily her own. (Mae West wrote and appeared in a play called *Sex* in 1927, for which she was jailed and fined for 'indecency'.) Meisel provided the photographs of Madonna for this best-selling volume, which appeared at the same time as an album entitled *Erotica*.

Furthermore, the visual influences informing the book Madonna has cited as Man Ray's photographs, Warhol's films and the actress Ingrid Thulin in Luchino Visconti's 1969 movie *The Damned*. (Pier Paolo Pasolini is another European director who has inspired her because his films combined religious and sexual ecstasy.) She also wanted to imitate Sherman's chameleon-like disguises, only with 'a twist' and more aggression. 'I had fun' striking poses for Meisel, Madonna later recalled, 'the whole thing was like performance art'.

Another sign of Madonna's commitment to Sherman's work was her willingness to sponsor a show of Sherman's simulated film stills at the Museum of Modern Art (MoMA), New York in 1997. (She also sponsored a Tina Modotti show.) Darlene Lutz, Madonna's art dealer, brokered the arrangement and Peter Galassi curated the exhibition. Earlier, in 1995, MoMA had acquired a complete set (69 black and white prints) of Sherman's *Untitled Film Stills* (1977–80) for a reported $1 million. Madonna admitted to Vince Aletti in 1998 that, strangely, she did not own any of Sherman's images.

The pop star and the artist met in June 1997 at MoMA for a private conversation. The conservative critic Hilton Kramer was not impressed: 'As for their relationship, I think they eminently deserve each other. It is trash subsidising trash; the kind of make-believe art where you dress yourself up in various repellent costumes and props. Most kids get over that by puberty.'[42]

Projects such as those of Sherman and Madonna problematise the self's identity: is it fixed or fluid, is there one or many, is there a real, authentic private self behind the public masks stars adopt? Camille Paglia has remarked: 'Feminism says, "No more masks." Madonna says we are nothing but masks.'[43] However, Paglia herself believes 'there is a real person behind every text ... Man is not merely the sum of his masks. Behind the shifting face of personality is a hard nugget of self, a genetic gift ... the self is malleable but elastic, snapping back to its original shape like a rubber band.'[44] Rather than choosing one or the other, P. David Marshall has argued that there is a dialectical relationship between authenticity and assumed image that produces an enigma as far as fans are concerned:

David Bowie and Madonna ... transform and transfigure themselves, and through these reincarnations present a moving subjectivity and ultimately an enigma about their authentic selves. Their enigmatic quality is reinforced by the centrality of authenticity to popular music discourse. Their play with identity and image is often an ironic modality to the claims in rock for authenticity. Indeed, their claim could be construed as an appeal to an aesthetic in which the performer has the 'genius' to transform like the brilliant actor. The key to their continuing appeal is the continual deferral of the resolution of the enigma; the authentic self is never revealed completely.[45]

Richard Corliss has made a similar observation: 'the fascinating thing about Madonna is that she is all-real and all-fake – in other words, pure show biz'.[46] Ambiguity was a recurrent feature of Madonna's output and this stimulated the interpretive abilities of audiences and critics. Even the documentary *Truth or Dare* was ambiguous because viewers did not know what was planned and what was spontaneous. Madonna said of it: 'I like that confusion of is it real or not real? Is it life imitating art or is it art imitating life?'

Although Madonna has produced her fair share of dross, the detailed analyses of her finest music videos written by American academics testify to their complex content and memorable sounds and images. Such videos, which appeared on MTV (Music Television) from 1983, were crucial to her success and Madonna has claimed that 'every video I've ever done has been inspired by some painting or some work of art' (including photographs). For instance, the female surrealist painters Leonora Carrington and Remedios Varo influenced the dreamlike video 'Bedtime Story' (1995).

A number of writers have stressed the importance of the visual to Madonna and one has described her career as 'a succession of images'. Unlike Sherman's staged photographs, Madonna's images were not limited to stills. In her screen roles, her images were moving ones and in the *Blond Ambition* stage shows, the images were animated and three dimensional. As Madonna once remarked, these shows were different from conventional rock concerts because they presented a themed theatrical experience. Emotional, erotic and celebratory songs, combined with music, dance, costumes, lighting, sets and a highly athletic performance on the part of Madonna and her back-up singers and dance troupe at times induced a frenzy of pleasure in the huge stadium audiences. The rapport between star and public became palpable, and the physical distance between them seemed to contract. There are few art forms and artists capable of providing such exhilarating experiences and this is why Madonna has attracted so many loyal followers and remains a superstar.

Evidently, Madonna is no vapid pop singer, no creature of management. Indeed, she is an acute observer of trends in art, cultural and sexual politics, gender issues, fashion, film, music, photography and style. She evolved as an artist during the era of post-modernism, cultural pluralism and the vogues for appropria tion and gender bending; consequently she realises that being receptive to a wide range of cultures and new trends is crucial to her bricolage aesthetic and to maintaining her popularity. (Celebrities wanting a long career have to reinvent themselves periodically to prevent the public becoming bored. Furthermore, since stars and audiences change as they age and mature, makeovers are inevitable.) Madonna pillaged many different sources and then adapted what she borrowed to her own ends. While the academic Paglia has praised her (the two have much in common), the black writer bell hooks has criticised Madonna's appropriation of black culture and this, hooks claimed, caused many women of colour to hate her.

Celebrities can hardly avoid reflecting upon the phenomena of fame and fashion, and some use their art form to comment on it. For instance, in Madonna's 1990 song/video 'Vogue' she paid homage to Hollywood glamour and cited such stars as Marlene Dietrich, Greta Garbo, Marilyn Monroe and Ginger Rogers. One phrase from the lyric – 'strike a pose' – could almost be an instruc-tion from Cindy Sherman.

There is irony in the fact that Madonna, an extremely wealthy woman (her fortune was estimated in 2001 to be £149 million including the art collection valued at £14 million) who is a product and idol of the world's capitalist superpower, has admired several artists who were convinced communists (Kahlo, Rivera and Modotti). Of course, the example of Picasso demonstrates that wealth and Communist Party membership can be compatible, but the question remains: has Madonna any radical convictions? Her career has certainly been marked by some degree of subversion: by mixing sex and religion in her 1989 music video 'Like a Prayer' she attracted the condemnation of right-wingers and Catholics. Their campaign against her caused the cancellation of a contract to promote Pepsi Cola. In Toronto, police threatened her with arrest and prosecution for simulating masturbation on stage. Her boldness, self-confidence, energy, work rate and support for girl power empowered many young female fans during the mid 1980s. However, the subversive content and shock tactics recurrent throughout Madonna's career have generally remained within the limits tolerated by the music industry, and indeed considered essential to a feisty, rebellious image. A revolt into style, rather than politics, one may conclude.

Of course, Madonna's immense success would not have been possible without the help of a legion of other skilled individuals – art directors, choreographers, fashion designers, video directors, photographers, etc. – and without the backing of film, publishing, record and television companies. Madonna, a shrewd business-person, eventually founded her own production company – Maverick Records (although under the auspices of Warner Bros) – and was then able to choose which artists she wanted to collaborate with or to employ. The financial and technical resources she commands far exceed those of even the most commercially successful fine artists and this gives her tremendous creative freedom and power in the realm of culture.

Even though the main sources of Madonna's iconography and inspiration have been Catholic popular culture and the mass media of film, photography and music, it is also evident from the above summary that the fine arts of the twentieth century have been a sig-nificant influence. Furthermore, the best of her music videos surely merit inclusion in the collections of museums of modern art.

Warhol was one of the first fine artists to acknowledge the art/commerce nexus. Following Warhol, Madonna has remarked: 'what I do is total commercialism, but it is also art'.[47] In an online debate between Strawberry Saroyan and Michelle Goldberg about Madonna's career, the former defended Madonna's morphing of art and commerce because the notion of starving artists with no viewers was outmoded. Goldberg observed: 'Madonna's a great marketer, but is she a great musician? Shouldn't that matter?' She also expressed concern that fame was now its own artistic validation and that the market had become 'the ultimate arbiter of cultural worth'. Goldberg added: 'Madonna's celebrity tactics – self-conscious artifice and zeitgeist surfing – are now *everywhere*. Now it's just assumed that any famous person has meticulously constructed his or her image … That makes Madonna's metamorphic skills – her ability to shed personas like snakeskin – seem less remarkable.'[48] Goldberg also considered that, due to Madonna's influence, 'artistic output has become a by-product of fame instead of the reason for it' and that 'the current notion of celebrity *as* an art form that Madonna helped propagate has hideous consequences'. In response, Saroyan argued that 'the nature of celebrity has changed ... Being a modern celebrity does not necessarily mean being hollow or a sell-out. Instead ... it often means that there is a message at the core of one's art that is bigger than a particular project, movie or record.' Goldberg characterised contemporary celebrity as 'grotesque, soul-eroding' because 'hype replaces content as a measure of artistic success' and she sought a return to artistic integrity and authenticity. Saroyan riposted: 'To me, she is authentic and does have integrity.' According to reporter Dylan Jones, Madonna admires the British artist Tracey Emin because she is 'intelligent, wounded and provocative', and 'has something to say'.[49] This admiration is rather strange given that as artists they are opposites: Madonna represents artifice and manipulation while Emin embodies authenticity and self-expression. (Emin and Madonna have met – at the launch party for the opening of Tate Britain on 23 March 2000.) Perhaps Goldberg should look to Emin for 'authenticity'.

### David Bowie

Bowie's creative accomplishments, like those of Dennis Hopper, are hard to encapsulate because they are so diverse and extend across so many realms: song writing, composing, performing and producing rock and pop music (in many different styles), acting in films, music videos and plays, making and collecting visual art, writing art criticism, publishing, supporting young artists, and establishing Internet websites. (He once rightly described himself as 'a generalist' and has been dubbed 'a post-modern Renaissance man'.) Regarding his willingness to try new media and art forms, Bowie told biographer George Tremlett, 'If I thought another media would mean more to me, I would move into it'; hence his receptivity to the new medium of the Internet.[50] The experience of being exploited by several managers compelled Bowie to become astute at business.

Bowie (aka David Robert Jones) was born in 1947 out of wedlock into a lower middle-class family. He spent his early childhood in the poor district of Brixton, South London and his teenage years in the suburban environment of Bromley, Kent. His mother, a cinema usherette, enjoyed singing and his older, half-brother Terry was a jazz fan. Bowie has described his family as 'dysfunctional' and he feared mental illness because Terry developed schizophrenia and committed suicide. Although his only school leaving qualifications were for art and woodwork, Bowie had immense intellectual curiosity and became an autodidact. At the age of 13, he learnt to play the saxophone and listened to jazz and rock 'n' roll. He was soon performing on stage and appearing in skiffle and pop groups. A relentless pursuit of stardom followed but during the formative years of the 1960s, there were many false starts and failures.

Legend has it that Bowie attended art school – like so many other British rock stars have done – but this is not the case. He was, however, attracted to commercial art/graphic design and worked for six months for the Bond Street agency Nevendy Hirst as a 'junior visualiser'. The attention he has paid to the design of his appearance, stage costumes and sets, and record covers indicate that his early interest in art and design persisted throughout his career. Bowie may not have been to art school but he had an art student's sensibility and was willing to combine high and popular cultures. The challenge for Bowie was to retain his artistic integrity while at the same time achieving commercial success.

Ken Pitt, Bowie's first manager and friend was a cultured homosexual who had once studied at the Slade School of Art. He was impressed by Bowie's interest in literature and art. In 1966, Pitt visited New York to see Warhol and brought back a recording of Lou Reed and the Velvet Underground. Bowie was to be influenced by Warhol, especially his demonstration that stardom could be fabricated, by the Factory's transsexual 'superstars', by his philosophy of 'business art' and by the sound of Reed and the Velvets. Reed and Bowie were later to play music together. In 1971, Bowie wrote a song paying homage to Warhol (featured on the *Hunky Dory* album) and visited Warhol to present him with a copy. The lyrics included: 'Andy Warhol looks a scream, hang him on my wall, Andy Warhol Silver Screen, can't tell them apart at all.' Warhol was not amused. Other visual artists cited in Bowie's songs include Georges Braque and the American performance artist Chris Burden.

Bowie has been compared to a chameleon because, from the outset, his enthusiasms, musical tastes and self-image changed rapidly. He told one reporter: 'I spent all those formative teenage years adopting guises and changing roles. One moment I was a musician and performer, the next a mod, just learning to be somebody.'[51] His interests have encompassed Buddhism, the silent art of mime, dance (which he studied with Lindsay Kemp), Japanese culture and theories of the occult. Photographs of Bowie in mime mode show him with his face hidden behind a mask of thick, white make-up. When Bowie mimed on stage, backing tracks provided the sounds. One of the first films he acted in was a short called *The Image* (1967), directed by Michael Armstrong. Bowie played the part of a painter who copies a portrait from a photograph. Later, in 1972, he told a reporter: 'I'm just an image person. I'm terribly conscious of images and I live in them.' Appropriation, quotation and intertexuality were key characteristics of post-modern culture and in these respects, Bowie was a post-modernist.

Bowie was distinguished from the majority of British pop musicians by his higher intellectual ambitions, his awareness of the artifice involved in stardom, and his experimental, transgressive attitude to creation that echoed that typical of avant-garde art. When telling reporters about his influences, he would cite the cut-up writing technique of William Burroughs, Dada cabarets and collages, surrealist and German expressionist films, and the art of Dalí and Duchamp, just as often as records and musicians. (However, what Bowie ignored about the avant-garde were its revolutionary politics.) Pitt may have envisaged him evolving into an all round family entertainer, but Bowie had other ideas. Mediocrity was to be avoided at all costs and gradually he took control of all aspects of his career just as Madonna was to do later. In addition, he undertook numerous collaborations with other musicians whom he respected – Marc Bolan, Brian Eno, Robert Fripp, Lou Reed, Iggy Pop, Steve Strange and even Bing Crosby, with performance artists such as Klaus Nomi and Joey Arias – and mobilised the skills of people like the dancer Lindsay Kemp, the fashion designers Natasha Korniloff and Mr Fish, record producers, sound engineers, and even fine artists.

In 1969, the year Americans landed on the Moon, Bowie had his first hit record with *Space Oddity* featuring the fictional astronaut Major Tom. In Beckenham, Kent, Bowie organised a so-called 'Arts Lab' – a room above a pub where Bowie and his friends performed and held mini-festivals.

Bowie's reputation as a world-class singer/songwriter/composer was established in the early 1970s with such albums as *The Man who Sold the World* (1971), *Hunky Dory* (1971), *The Rise and Fall of Ziggy Stardust* (1972), and *Aladdin Sane* (1973). As mentioned in the Introduction, he was fond of adopting fictional personae and used costumes and make-up to realise these characters on stage where, Bowie once explained, he felt more like an actor than a rock musician. The periodic changes in Bowie's persona were designed to astonish and surprise his audiences, to renew their interest in him so that his career could be prolonged, and to save Bowie himself from boredom and repetition.

Although by now married to Angela Barnett with a son named Zowie, he claimed to be bisexual and delighted in androgyny and gender bending. While glam rock was fashionable, Bowie wore silk dresses, lipstick and mascara, and dyed his shoulder-length hair bright colours. Journalists were reminded of Hollywood stars such as Lauren Bacall and Greta Garbo. The camp look and swishy queen impersonation were marketing tactics designed to attract controversy and publicity, and they succeeded in doing so. They also contributed to the debates about sexual identity and the movement for gay liberation that occurred during the 1970s.

Humour and parody were part of the mix. David Buckley has claimed that Bowie made 'camouflage and misinformation part of his actual art', that he 'loves playing at being a rock star' and 'sending himself up'.[52] In 1971, Bowie informed John Mendelsohn that pop/rock music should not be taken too seriously, that it should be 'tarted up, made into a prostitute, a parody of itself. It should be a clown, the Pierrot medium. The music is the mask the message wears – music is the Pierrot and I, the performer, am the message.'[53] At this time, he compared himself to 'a Photostat machine with an image'. (This remark echoed Warhol's desire to be a machine and his practice of 'mirroring' the culture around him.) Bowie then described the pop-biz as 'an art form of indifference, with no permanent philosophy behind it whatsoever'.

His pop concerts, Bowie decided, were to be lavish, outrageous, theatrical spectacles and some were prefaced by screenings of surrealist films by Luis Buñuel and Salvador Dalí. The latter, wearing a shoulder cape (Bowie was also fond of capes), attended such a show held at the Radio City Musical Hall, New York, in 1973. No doubt, the Spaniard was checking to see what the new master of persona and publicity had to offer. To convince fans and journalists that he was now a star, Bowie played the part of one on tour: limousines, posh hotels, bodyguards, etc.

Bowie has always claimed to be apolitical but in the mid 1970s, he was accused of flirting with fascism. He foresaw and seemed to welcome the right-wing shift that was to occur in Britain and the United States during the 1980s and was, for a time, fascinated by the visual power of Nazi symbols and propaganda. He was aware of

Nietzsche's superman concept and no doubt could discern similarities between Hitler's mass rallies and rock concerts in which uncritical admirers worship a leader figure.

While Bowie was becoming a star, he naturally reflected on the process in his lyrics – witness such songs as 'Changes', 'Heroes', 'Star', 'Starman', 'Fashion' and 'Fame'. Success as a performer resulted in offers to appear in films. Notable film roles that Bowie has played include: the alien in Nicholas Roeg's *The Man who fell to Earth* (1976), a British soldier in Nagisa Oshima's *Merry Christmas Mr Lawrence* (1983) and an advertising executive in Julien Temple's *Absolute Beginners* (1986). Especially relevant to this book was his portrayal of Warhol in Schnabel's 1995 film about Basquiat. He also appeared in many visually striking music videos. 'Ashes to Ashes', made with David Mallet in 1980, for instance, is memorable for its beach scenes with a bulldozer and its solarised imagery, unnatural colours and black sky. In four minutes, Bowie played three characters: a Pierrot, an astronaut and an asylum inmate.

Bowie began to paint in 1975 and subsequently became a prolific visual artist. Besides paintings, he has produced lithographs, computer-generated prints, postcards and posters, and mixed-media constructions and installations, many of which can be viewed and purchased on numerous Internet websites including his own (BowieArt.com). Reproductions also appear in fanzines and on some of Bowie's album covers. Samples of the wallpaper he designed for Laura Ashley in 1994 are preserved in the collection of the Whitworth Art Gallery, Manchester.

In April 1995, he held his first solo exhibition, entitled *Davie Bowie: Paintings and Sculpture, New Afro/Pagan and Work 1975–1995*, at The Gallery in Cork Street, London.[54] It was organised with the help of his dealer friend Kate Chertavian. Until the rise of the East End, this street was the heart of London's commercial gallery system but Bowie had to hire the venue and pay for the catalogue himself. Such luminaries as Damien Hirst, Janet Street Porter and Jeremy Irons attended the private view. Many visitors were attracted to the show because of Bowie's fame and a Japanese collector and Charles Saatchi bought works. (In fact, all exhibits were sold.) In terms of aesthetic quality and artistic originality, the exhibition – consisting of acrylic paintings, computer prints, charcoal and chalk drawings, chrome-plated bronzes and mixed-media installations – was not an embarrassment but struck some observers as a display worthy of a promising art student. There were portraits, images of the Minotaur, ancestor figures and a black man and a white woman sharing a shower.

Holly Johnson, the Liverpool pop singer/star of Frankie Goes to Hollywood, who is also a painter, reviewed the exhibition for *Modern Painters*. Johnson, a Bowie fan, expressed admiration for his 'sampling' method and draughtsmanship but thought his use of 'primitive' African iconography combined with atomic bomb clouds teetered on the edge of bad taste and judged that some works 'did not come from the heart'.[55]

Since 1995, Bowie has mounted other one-man shows in Switzerland and Japan, and participated in numerous group exhibitions alongside internationally recognised artists such as Arman, Hirst, Eno, Patrick Hughes, Yoko Ono and Tony Oursler. Some of these

**15. David Bowie, *Afro-Pagan III*, 1995.**
Computer print, 107 x 76 cm.
© David Bowie, courtesy of Chertavian Fine Art, London.

shows were mounted to help needy art students and charities such as War Child. To assist the latter in 1994, Bowie donated a series of boxed prints entitled *We Saw A Minotaur* for auction and two years later he constructed, with the help of others, a triptych devoted to the Walker Brothers made from photographs, Formica, X-rays and a light box.

Another charity Bowie has supported is Art Against Addiction. (Bowie was once a cocaine addict.) He and the British painter Martin Maloney headed its committee and in February 2001 they persuaded Sotheby's to auction works on the theme of addiction by 73 artists to raise funds for the charity.

In 1995, Bowie collaborated with Hirst to generate some circular spin paintings, one of which was entitled *Beautiful, Hello, Space-Boy Painting*. (Another, macabre project they considered was the re-creation of the Minotaur by grafting a bull's head onto the body of a man.) Hirst's opinion of Bowie is not high: 'Bowie's trying to harness the power of art for his own good in his own work. And he's just failing miserably. He's basically trying to turn David Bowie the musician into David Bowie the artist. Which is just sick.'[56] A year later, Bowie devised an installation at London's Institute of Contemporary Arts for a conference about Artaud and Genet. The Italian critic/curator Germano Celant of the Guggenheim Museum in New York commissioned Bowie to produce a cyber chrome figure and mixed-media construction entitled *Where Do They Come From? Where Do They Go?* It was exhibited in the show *New Persona/New Universe*, held in Florence in 1997. Tony Oursler (b. 1957), an American artist noted for weird installations in which images of talking heads are superimposed via miniature video projectors onto mannequins and sculptures, supplied projections of Bowie's face. Oursler's projections of faces onto giant eyeballs and deformed animals were featured in the promo video made for the 1997 song 'Little Wonder' and appeared in the 'Earthling' tour stage show. Laurie Anderson and the South African artist Beezy Bailey have also collaborated with Bowie to generate drawings and paintings.

Although Bowie's paintings reflect several art-historical influences – surrealism, outsider and 'primitive' art – expressionism is the most prevalent. (For example, his 1976 painting *Child in Berlin*, executed while Bowie was staying in the German city, closely resembles an Edvard Munch.) This applies to most of the art produced by celebrities, presumably because expressionism is subjective, imaginative, direct and fast, and suits their mercurial temperaments and short attention spans. Given the demands of their main professions, one cannot imagine stars spending months or even years on an objective painting of a nude model in the painstaking manner of, say, Euan Uglow.

Many of Bowie's images are portraits of his present wife Iman and friends such as Iggy Pop and, of course, himself. Artists who have produced portraits of him include Derek Boshier, Peter Howson, Sir Paul McCartney and Jessica Voorsanger. Boshier depicted Bowie as the Elephant Man, a role he played on the Broadway stage in 1980. As an American teenager, Voorsanger was a Bowie fan and she witnessed his performance from the third row of the stalls. Decades later she included Bowie's face in a painting entitled *The Davids* (2001), which featured portraits of eight famous men with the same Christian name: Beckham, Cassidy, Soul, etc. Furthermore, there are several websites featuring Bowie portraits created by devoted fans who are not trained artists.

Since Bowie is a wealthy superstar, he maintains several houses and apartments in Europe and the United States, which he adorns with his personal collection of art and furniture. He visits antique fairs, shows in private galleries and sales at auction houses such as Christie's. Bowie began collecting in the early 1970s when he acquired books illustrated by Arthur Rackham, Aubrey Beardsley and Kate Greenaway, art nouveau glassware by Galle and Lalique, designs by Erté, and art deco artefacts. Since then, he has bought examples of old masters – Rubens and Tintoretto – and contemporary artists such as Frank Auerbach, David Bomberg, Gilbert & George and Damien Hirst. In 1994, Bowie bought a painting by Peter Howson depicting a rape during the Bosnian war that had proved too controversial for the Imperial War Museum.

During the 1990s, Bowie founded 21 Publishing Ltd, which specialises in art books, and added to the discourse of writing about contemporary art by serving as a contributing editor to *Modern Painters*, the British magazine established by the critic Peter Fuller in 1988. *Modern Painters* has published interviews between Bowie and the American artists Julian Schnabel and Jeff Koons (a photograph of Bowie and Koons in the artist's New York studio appeared on the front cover of the magazine's spring 1998 issue) and the British artists Damien Hirst and Tracey Emin. He has also written about Jean-Michel Basquiat and the erotic, figurative painter Balthus. Bowie shows an informed understanding of the work of these artists but since he mainly admires them, adverse critical judgements tend to be avoided. His writings – which vary from plain journalism to more poetic, stream-of-consciousness texts – have also been published in Warhol's *Interview* magazine, in the *Guardian*, the *Evening Standard*, *Dazed & Confused* and *Q Magazine*.

During the 1990s, Bowie became excited by the World Wide Web, which he discovered via his son's interest in computers. Bowie has recalled:

> Through the photo-manipulation package Photoshop, I began working with digital images and when I discovered e-mail, I began to realise that the Net might influence my professional life. It allows for a kind of playfulness that appeals to me – the fun of exchange ... The first site I built was an art site, initially to display only my own works ... Then I expanded the site to showcase other people's work [including art students], people who didn't have gallery representation and could make their address a website. Anyone wanting to buy could get directly in touch with them. [Bowie took no commission on sales.] It seemed a good way of disseminating not just digital art, but work by sculptors and painters. The site became Bowieart.com and is slowly but surely expanding [he then established Bowie Net] ... We get a lot of feedback from users because their comments aren't edited before going on the site ... I love the chat rooms, because you get to hear what people genuinely think. The communication between me and my Web audience has become more intimate than it's ever been ... it is a new positioning of what the artist is, it is demystification.[57]

Bowie was also intrigued by the delivery and creative potential of the Internet and envisaged releasing new music via it, which fans could download and then play around with. The business potential of the Internet has also attracted his attention: in 2000, he entered into a co-branding arrangement with an American bank to establish BowieBanc.com, an online bank.

Bowie will be primarily remembered for his inventive self-transformations, for his contributions to pop music, fashion and movie acting rather than for his paintings and art criticism. However, as in the cases of Hopper, McCartney and Madonna (and Bryan Ferry, Brian Eno and John Lennon), the influence of the visual arts on the character of his work is too important to be ignored.

## Sir Paul McCartney

McCartney (b. 1942, aka Macca) was born during World War II into a working-class family and so his access to books and fine art was limited. However, he was curious and quick to learn, and the architecture and public art gallery of Liverpool provided visual stimulation that many other British towns lack.

As a child, McCartney was fond of the cartoon character Rupert Bear and his drawings of Rupert have appeared in exhibitions devoted to the art of the Beatles, which have also included portraits of McCartney by artists such as John Bratby and Sam Walsh. His early enthusiasm for drawing continued after he joined the Beatles: he produced caricatures of John Lennon and people they met. Many of his later portraits or faces resemble painted caricatures. At the age of eleven, McCartney was awarded a book token as a prize for a school essay and used it to buy an illustrated volume on modern art. A few years later, he received another prize for a painting depicting St Aidan's, a modern church in Liverpool.

Unlike two other members of the early Beatles, Lennon and Stuart Sutcliffe, McCartney did not attend Liverpool's art college and this caused a sense of inferiority. He studied at the Liverpool Institute High School for Boys, a grammar school, where English literature was one of his main subjects. During the 1950s, he was diverted from academic study by guitar playing, rock music, pictures of Elvis Presley and a growing interest in the visual arts. He once attended a university lecture on the modern architecture of Le Corbusier. McCartney learnt more about art through his friendships with Lennon and Sutcliffe (who admired the paintings of Nicolas de Staël) and, once in Hamburg, he learnt about photography, design and fashion through contact with Sutcliffe's German girlfriend Astrid Kirchherr (a photographer) and her design school friends Klaus Voorman and Jürgen Vollmer.

In 1963, after the worldwide success of the Beatles, McCartney found himself living in London as an eligible bachelor with time and money to explore the city's social and cultural life. He extended his awareness of the visual arts by befriending a number of artists and art dealers.[58] They included three young men – John Dunbar, Peter Asher and Barry Miles (a bookseller) – who, in 1965, decided to open a gallery and bookshop devoted to contemporary experimental art and literature. It was situated in Mason's Yard in the West End and called Indica. The gallery showed tendencies such as kinetic and op art, and artists such as Christo, Takis, Julio le Parc, Barry Flanagan and Yoko Ono. McCartney gave practical help and was a regular customer. Through his friends, he encountered the work of the Beat writers, William Burroughs, John Cage, electronic music, etc. Some aspects of avant-garde poetry and music influenced the music and lyrics McCartney created for the Beatles.

During the 1960s, in Swinging London, the realms of pop music, fashion, photography, graphic design and pop art flourished and converged.[59] For instance, Robert Fraser, a dealer who promoted both British and American pop artists, was also friendly with members of the Beatles and the Rolling Stones. (On one occasion he was handcuffed to Mick Jagger after they had been arrested on drug charges.) He also knew Hollywood actors such as Marlon Brando and Dennis Hopper, and Italian film directors such as Michelangelo Antonioni. McCartney met Fraser in 1966 and gained an informal art education by visiting his gallery and his apartment. For instance, McCartney became familiar with the work of such British pop artists as Clive Barker, Allen Jones, Eduardo Paolozzi, Richard Hamilton and Peter Blake. One evening Fraser and McCartney watched Warhol's film *Empire* together. McCartney was encouraged by its 'nothingness' to acquire a film camera and to shoot some experimental home movies.

Fraser arranged for Blake and his then wife Jann Haworth to be commissioned to create the cover design for the Beatles' 1967 *Sergeant Pepper* album, which was to become the most famous sleeve of the decade. Blake and Haworth discussed ideas with Lennon and McCartney and then assembled a three-dimensional, mixed-media installation that was photographed by Michael Cooper. The cover, of course, is noted for its crowd of famous heroes, both male and female, living and dead, mostly represented via photographic cut-outs. (There are even waxworks of the Fab Four.) Because of this collaboration, Blake became one of McCartney's friends, a fellow painter with whom he could discuss technical issues even though Blake favoured a 'tight' approach to painting while McCartney favoured a 'loose' approach.

McCartney was also involved in the design of the next, so-called 'White Album', created by Richard Hamilton, an artist often considered a founding father of pop art. The Beatle visited Hamilton's home and studio in Hornsey, North London, to view work in progress. Hamilton wanted to provide a sharp contrast to the complex, colourful composition of *Sergeant Pepper*, and so he devised a plain, all-white sleeve. However, inside was a poster made from a collage of personal photos of the Beatles that they had lent Hamilton.

In 1969, Lennon married an avant-garde, Japanese-American visual artist – Yoko Ono – and in the same year, McCartney too married a woman – Linda Eastman – who was skilled in a visual medium, that is, photography. Lennon and Ono made films together and mounted several well-publicised art exhibitions in London during the late 1960s, which McCartney must have seen and so increased his awareness of Ono's *oeuvre* that had its origins in the Fluxus movement.

McCartney began collecting art by purchasing a small drawing by Jean Cocteau. René Magritte, the Belgian surrealist painter of visual puns, was an established modern artist but he became even better known during the 1960s because of exhibitions and books. McCartney became an enthusiast and Fraser took him to Paris to meet Magritte's dealer Alexandre Iolas. McCartney then bought several Magrittes and Fraser later managed to acquire a Magritte painting of a big green apple with the words 'au revoir' written across it, which he left in McCartney's London home for him to find. So pleased was McCartney with the picture that the image of an apple became the logo of the organisation the Beatles founded in the late 1960s. In 1966, McCartney bought a kinetic sculpture by the Greek artist Takis from the Indica Gallery and a relief of the Guggenheim Museum by Hamilton from the Robert Fraser Gallery. He also com-missioned Blake to paint *Monarch of the Glen*, a variation on Sir Edwin Landseer's original. Items of furniture, such as a cupboard and a piano, McCartney had decorated/customised by artists Peter Simpson and David Vaughan.

Linda also helped McCartney to expand his personal collection. For instance, she bought him relics such as Magritte's easel, table and spectacles, and drawings by Tiepolo. What appealed to McCartney about the latter's draughtsmanship was the way he could represent a nostril with simply a squiggle of ink.

Linda, who came from a wealthy American family, had studied the history of art at the University of Arizona and later specialised in photographing rock stars. (She died from breast cancer in 1998.) At the age of 40 – 'life begins at 40' – McCartney was looking for something fresh to do and so he started painting. It was an ambition he had harboured for many years but had hesitated because of his lack of art school training. (But then, he had no formal musical training either.) Through Linda, McCartney met her father Lee who was a New York lawyer and art collector. Lee owned works by the French impressionists and by the American abstract expressionists. As a result, McCartney came to admire artists like Mark Rothko, Philip Guston, Robert Motherwell and Willem de Kooning, the Dutch-American who was one of the leading action painters of the 1950s. As his lawyer, Lee Eastman knew de Kooning personally and in the late 1970s arranged for Paul and Linda to visit the artist's studio in Amagansett, Long Island. In 1983, Linda photographed the two artists, wearing hats and beads, sitting side-by-side facing the camera in a garden with a dog for company. During one visit, McCartney expressed his desire to paint and de Kooning encouraged him to begin. De Kooning also gave Linda and Paul one of his 'pulls'

**16. Linda McCartney, 'Paul McCartney with Willem de Kooning, East Hampton', 1983.**
Photo © 2002 the Estate of Linda McCartney.

(that is, a print of what looked like a purple mountain made directly from the surface of a wet oil painting using a sheet of newspaper).

When McCartney commenced painting, circa 1982–83, he had no notion what kind of work he wanted to produce, only an itch to play with pigments, brushes and palette knife. Inspired by de Kooning's stress on freedom and his improvisational approach using house painters' brushes, Paul decided to trust his instincts, to try whatever took his fancy, to invent and discover imagery during the process of painting. McCartney even bought materials from the same art supplies source, the Golden Eagle paint shop, which de Kooning used. He also attempted to render the colour of the sand on a Long Island beach. Later, he told reporters that he only paints when in the mood and that, unlike professional artists, he never undertakes commissions or sells his paintings.

He made both abstract and figurative paintings but most had in common lyrical, painterly, expressionistic characteristics – drips, splashy brushwork, marks and lines scratched in paint, vibrant colours, crude drawing – that owed something to abstract expressionism and the German neo-expressionism fashionable in the 1980s. He painted faces and landscapes but avoided the objective recording approach associated with naturalism and photo-realism because he thought precision yielded wooden results. Dreams and the unconscious were crucial to the surrealists and at times they were a source of inspiration for McCartney's lyrics and melodies, and this applied to the imagery of certain paintings too. McCartney believes a common creativity informs both music and visual art, both sounds and colours, and sees no reason why an artist should be limited to one or the other.

The iconography of some pictures included masks and Celtic motifs. They were symbolic or allegorical and their style recalled that of Marc Chagall and naïve art. Often his subjects were autobiographical, that is, they included famous people he had met, such as Warhol and Queen Elizabeth II. McCartney, of course, had met the Queen at a royal command performance and discovered that she liked to crack jokes. In 1991, he produced three humorous portraits of her based on a magazine photo, one coloured grey, one blue and one green. (McCartney, one presumes, is not a republican, otherwise, he would not have accepted a knighthood.) About the Queen, he has remarked: 'in some ways I felt a bit sorry for her, because she is trapped inside her celebrity. My celebrity, unlike royal celebrity, carries with it freedom ...'[60]

McCartney also portrayed those close to him such as his first wife Linda (especially after her death in 1998) and Lennon. Although the style of *Yellow Linda with Piano* (1988) is heavily indebted to the work of Henri Matisse, it is one of his best, most controlled and carefully composed portraits. In a profile view self-portrait dated 1989, McCartney impersonated Elvis Presley singing into a microphone. A sardonic portrait of David Bowie showed him vomiting.

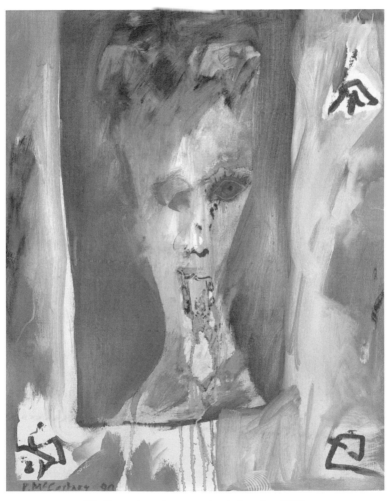

**17. Sir Paul McCartney, *Bowie Spewing*, 1997.**
Painting, oil on canvas, 50.5 x 41 cm. © Sir Paul McCartney.

In May–July 1999, an exhibition of 73 of McCartney's paintings selected from over 600 was held at the Kunstforum Lÿz, Siegen, Westphalia, Germany. It then travelled to several other venues including the Arnolfini Gallery, Bristol and the Walker Art Gallery, Liverpool (May–August 2002). Wolfgang Suttner, the show's organiser, had taken an early interest in McCartney's pictures and had visited McCartney's Sussex studio to view them. McCartney favoured Suttner over other curators precisely for this reason. He suspected that curators who wanted his pictures sight unseen were seeking to capitalise on his celebrity status instead of the artistic merit of his work. Knowing the movie star Tony Curtis, McCartney was also wary of the celebrity-who-paints syndrome and this is why he had been reluctant to exhibit his work. He finally decided to do so in order to receive some feedback.

The rock star realised that he had taken a risk by moving beyond his field of expertise and by exposing his paintings to public scrutiny, and that he was likely to receive adverse criticism for doing so. To head off criticism, McCartney told reporters that although he took painting seriously, he did not claim to be anything more than 'a dedicated amateur'. (McCartney often makes self-depreciating remarks as a defence mechanism.) It is clear that McCartney enjoys the activity of painting and that it serves a therapeutic function for him. Many of his paintings are characterised by exuberance, humour and pleasure.

Everything A-list celebrities do interests the news media and so it is no surprise that McCartney's exhibition received extensive press coverage (300 reporters attended a press conference given by McCartney when the show opened in Germany) and that 37,500 people visited the show. A year later, a major publisher was also happy to publish a glossy book about his paintings.[61] The book has over 200 colour plates of McCartney's pictures and photographs by Linda showing her husband at work in his studio. There are also essays by the artist Brian Clarke, the curator Suttner and by Barry Miles, and an interview with McCartney. Even if no gallery or publisher had expressed interest, McCartney was wealthy enough to have hired a gallery and paid for a book himself. Although a few old, unknown painters have been discovered and fêted, the art world generally prefers young artists who have been to art school and older ones with established reputations. Consequently, if McCartney had not been a world-famous celebrity it is unlikely that his paintings would have been noticed by the art world. While not without aesthetic qualities, they contribute nothing new to the trajectory of contemporary art. Nor do they match McCartney's earlier achievements as a songwriter and singer/performer in the Beatles. There is little doubt, however, that they have curiosity-value for Macca's millions of fans.

Another sign of McCartney's commitment to the arts, the needs of the entertainment industries for trained personnel and the fostering of creativity is the financial and moral support he has given to the 'fame' school, the Liverpool Institute of Performing Arts (LIPA), which was conceived in 1989 and opened by the Queen in 1996. McCartney himself donated £1,000,000 and used his celebrity status to gain additional help from such luminaries as David Hockney, Mark Knopfler, Eddie Murphy, Jane Fonda and Ralph Lauren. LIPA took over the refurbished 1825 neo-classical building in Mount Street that McCartney's old grammar school had occupied until 1985. McCartney has taught some master classes at LIPA. Its multi/cross-disciplinary ethos accorded with McCartney's own attitudes and achievements.

LIPA prompts the question: should new institutions of higher education in Britain have to rely on private rather than state initiatives? (Its funding was a mix of private and public.) Unfortunately, the most recent press reports about LIPA have concerned a management crisis, accountability shortcomings and staff resignations.

# 2

# Artists Depict Celebrities

Throughout the centuries, artists have been commissioned to depict in portraits and statues the famous, the rich and the powerful. This has continued into the modern era, with the difference that the famous now include celebrities from such fields as fashion, movies and sport. The artists, who now include cartoonists and photographers, are also free to criticise and satirise (unless they live in countries ruled by dictators) as well as to flatter. A whole book would be required to explore the above in detail and so this chapter will concentrate on images of modern celebrities by fine artists. But first, a historical digression is necessary.

### Waxworks and Halls of Fame

A significant new development in the popular appreciation of the famous was the emergence of exhibitions consisting of waxwork figures and tableaux. In 1770, Philippe Curtius, a German-born doctor and skilled modeller, opened a waxwork exhibition in Paris, which attracted royal visitors. Marie Grosholtz (b. 1761, Strasbourg), later known as Madame Tussaud, became his pupil and, after training, she modelled the figures of Rousseau and Voltaire from life. During the Terror of the French Revolution, she was assigned the grisly task of taking death masks from the heads of victims of the guillotine.

When Curtius died in 1794, Madame Tussaud inherited the waxworks show and, in 1802, she transferred it to England. For 30 years, the exhibition toured the country until, in 1835, a permanent display was established in London. Madame Tussaud died in 1850 but her attraction was continued and expanded by her descendants.[1] The current museum in Marylebone Road, opened in 1884, attracts nearly 3 million visitors annually. Today, besides London, there are Madame Tussaud's waxwork shows in Windsor,

Amsterdam, New York, Las Vegas and Hong Kong. The Tussaud's Group Ltd, Europe's leading celebrity-themed attraction developer and operator, manages them.

Waxwork figures take as long as six months to model in clay and cast in wax and cost £30,000 each. (Animated ones may cost £100,000.) They are life-size and as life-like as possible; faces are made from wax and bodies from fibreglass; genuine human hair is used and figures are dressed in real clothes, which have often been donated by the person being represented. Good lighting is important and some figures are enclosed within theatrical sets. The modeller's aim is an illusion that might, for a moment, deceive the eye and part of the frisson of such figures is the sense of the uncanny that they arouse. This feeling is probably due to the indeterminate status of waxworks, halfway between life and death. Salvador Dalí, who enjoyed viewing waxworks in the Musée Grevin in Paris, once described them as 'spectral and macabre'. The softness of wax when heated appealed to him because of the metamorphosis that ensued and melting wax figures reminded him of the decomposition and liquefaction of corpses.

Clearly, the millions of tourists and children who visit waxworks every year find pleasure in getting close to the famous, walking amongst them and looking them in the eyes, even while knowing that they are only effigies. Visitors enjoy having their photographs taken next to them. The gruesome contents of the Chamber of Horror, which had its origins in the relics of the Terror of the French Revolution, are especially popular.

Managers of waxworks make no distinction between heroes, celebrities and criminals: they feature royals, prime ministers, film stars, pop singers and groups, sports men and women, murderers, and so on; fame and notoriety are the only criteria for entry. To encourage repeat visits and to refresh displays, there is a turnover of figures as some personalities fade into obscurity while others emerge into the spotlight. Most living celebrities agree to be portrayed in Madame Tussaud's. One of the few to decline an invitation was Mother Teresa who said her charitable work in India was important, not her person.

Fine artists who have been represented in London's Madame Tussaud's include Pablo Picasso and David Hockney. Although the artists who create waxworks take photographs and measurements of their subjects and undertake months of work, the effigies have been criticised for failing to achieve convincing likenesses.[2] The public does not know the modellers' names and the latter eschew any personal expression or artistic licence in their sculptures. Fine artists who are portraitists know that copying external appearances does not necessarily capture a sitter's personality or character. Exaggeration may be needed to endow the figure with life; witness Rodin's famous Parisian statue of the writer Balzac. Increasingly, waxworks seek to overcome this problem by enlivening their effigies of rock and pop music stars by such means as animatronics.

In the 1990s, the fashionable, post-modern, Japanese-American photographer Hiroshi Sugimoto (b. 1948, Tokyo) was commissioned by the Deutsche Guggenheim Museum in Berlin to create a portfolio of large, black and white photographs entitled *Portraits*, which was

**18. Madame Tussaud's, 'Waxwork of Picasso', 1985.**
Photo © Madame Tussaud's.

subsequently exhibited in Europe and the United States.[3] Sugimoto left Japan in 1970 to study in Los Angeles where he was influenced by minimal and conceptual art. Strangely, the subjects of Sugimoto's portraits were not living human beings, but waxworks depicting historical figures likely to have been modelled from paintings: Henry VIII and his six wives, Shakespeare, Rembrandt, Napoleon, et al., hence the paradox of photographic records of people who lived before the age of photography. (Sugimoto's fascination with dioramas and wax museums dated back to 1976.) A major piece was a 25-feet-long, five-panel photograph of a waxwork tableau (fabricated by Mexican workers) of Leonardo's mural *The Last Supper*. Sugimoto found the tableau in a museum in a small Japanese town.

Sugimoto also took photographs of more recent figures almost certainly modelled after photographic portraits: Oscar Wilde, Winston Churchill, Queen Elizabeth II, Princess Diana, et al. Most were shot in London's Madame Tussaud's. Each wax figure was dramatically lit and isolated against a dark background to covey the impression that they were vivid portraits rather than representations of representations of representations. Sugimoto amalgamated three media – painted portraiture, wax sculpture and photography – and, since different historical moments were conflated, an ambiguous sense of time. His working assumption was that all representations are a blend of fiction and reality.

In Los Angeles, the city that has been the main centre for American film production, a museum has been established to celebrate the history of Hollywood – the place – and to preserve cinema, radio, television and recording arts memorabilia: the Hollywood Entertainment Museum. It has interactive facilities that enable visitors to pretend to make up, etc. The United States is also home to many so-called Halls of Fame. The first – the Hall of Fame for Great Americans – was the brainchild of Henry Mitchell MacCracken, Chancellor of New York University, and is located in the Bronx, New York. It was dedicated in 1901 and consists of an open-air colonnade (designed by the architect Stanford White) lined with bronze busts (created by leading American sculptors) and tablets commemorating 102 distinguished Americans. They include several presidents, the inventor Alexander Graham Bell, the writers Edgar Allan Poe and Harriet Beecher Stowe, the black educationalist Booker T. Washington and the painter James Abbott McNeill Whistler. Parties of schoolchildren are taken to view the memorial but otherwise it is little visited.

Other Halls of Fame tend to be devoted to particular categories of people such as clowns, cowboys, women of achievement, baseball stars, pro-football players, inventors, teachers and leaders of business. (On the Internet, there is even a Hall of Fame devoted to cynics.) In Cleveland, Ohio, a Rock 'n' Roll Hall of Fame was opened in 1995. When a new celebrity is added to the collection a so-called 'induction' ceremony takes place and the celebrity, if living, is invited to attend. Most Halls of Fame contain documentation, images and relics of exceptional individuals who, one presumes, are intended to act as role models for other Americans and future generations.

### Images of Popular Entertainers

Let us turn now to artists who have depicted or referenced entertainers. Henri Toulouse-Lautrec (1864–1901), a painter who came from a French aristocratic family, was one of the first fine artists to depict popular entertainers, namely, the cabaret and circus performers, dancers and singers of the café concerts, circuses and music halls of Montmartre, Paris. Some of them – Aristide Bruant, Chocolat, Jane Avril, La Goulue, May Belfort and Yvette Guilbert – were celebrities in the 1890s. Managers of the places of entertainment were so pleased with his images that they commissioned him to design posters, examples of which are now preserved in applied arts museums.[4] As mentioned earlier, the American movie star Vincent Price acquired some of Toulouse-Lautrec's images of entertainers for his private collection.

After Toulouse-Lautrec's death, his art became more widely popular and details of his bohemian lifestyle became known. Later, a biopic directed by John Huston (*Moulin Rouge*, 1952) was made. José Ferrer starred as the dwarf-like, alcoholic painter who haunted the Moulin Rouge and the brothels of Paris. A musical film entitled *Moulin Rouge*, directed by Baz Luhrmann and starring Nicole Kidman, was released in 2001. John Leguizamo played the minor role of Toulouse-Lautrec.

A living British artist who continues Toulouse-Lautrec's practice of sketching and painting people and animals is Maggi Hambling (b. 1945). In the early 1980s, she produced a series of paintings of the brilliant British comedian and sad clown Max Wall (1908–1990, aka Maxwell George Lorimer).[5] Hambling responded to her subject with painterly verve and human sympathy but static portraits of Wall resting in a melancholic mood could hardly compete with his dynamic stage performances or with film footage of them. However, one of her 1981 portraits of Wall is of particular interest because it depicts him seated with his feet up while behind is a dark silhouette. The latter represents Wall's stage character 'Professor Wallofski' (a weird, spidery figure with long hair, black tights, white socks and oversized boots who performed a silly walk); thus, the private man and one of his public personae appear in the same picture space.

Hambling, a butch, chain-smoking extrovert, is also relevant to the theme of this book because she became a minor television celebrity during the 1980s when she appeared on a Channel 4 arts quiz programme called *Gallery*. George Melly, the jazz singer and pop art historian, was also a panellist and they became close friends. Both

**19. Maggi Hambling, *Max Wall and His Image*, 1981.**
Painting, oil on canvas, 167.6 x 121.9 cm. © Tate, London, 2002.
Tate Britain collection. Photo courtesy of Tate Enterprises Ltd and the artist.

delighted in humour and were attracted to drag and vaudeville. Melly recalls that while making the programmes, they were never sober and that someone complained he was helping to 'change a painter into a performer'.[6] Of course, Hambling painted Melly's portrait, which is now in England's National Portrait Gallery. Another famous but deceased person Hambling has represented is the playwright Oscar Wilde. This time her medium was sculpture: a public monument to him in the form of a bronze head emerging from a granite sarcophagus was unveiled in Adelaide Street, London, in 1998. It was entitled: *A Conversation with Oscar Wilde*. Unfortunately, critics thought it 'grotesque' and 'tacky'.

A short distance away in Leicester Square is a 1981 bronze sculpture of Charlie Chaplin dressed in his famous role as a tramp. It is by the sculptor John Doubleday (b. 1947) who trained at Goldsmiths College. Other famous people Doubleday has sculpted include the Beatles, Nelson Mandela, Dylan Thomas and the fictional detective Sherlock Holmes.

Another living British artist who has depicted entertainers is the Yorkshire sculptor Graham Ibbeson (b. 1951) who trained at Trent Polytechnic and the Royal College of Art. Known as 'the people's sculptor', Ibbeson has produced public monuments of trapped miners and Jarrow Marchers as well as bronze statues of the comedians Eric Morecambe (for Morecambe Bay), Stan Laurel and Oliver Hardy (for Ulverston), and the movie idol Cary Grant (for Bristol). Grant (1904–1986, aka Archibald Leach) was born and grew up in Bristol before moving to the United States in 1920.[7] Ibbeson's figures are generally vivacious and executed in an academic/naturalistic style; consequently, ordinary people find them accessible and commissions are normally the result of public demand. To meet the needs of private collectors, Ibbeson has also generated editions of cold cast bronze statuettes around 30 cm high depicting such British comedians as Norman Wisdom, Tony Hancock and Benny Hill. They are for sale at affordable prices via the artist's website.[8]

Even abstract artists have been known to reference film stars for their publicity value. In the late 1950s, William Green (b. 1934) was a student at the Royal College of Art. For a short period, he became a minor media sensation because of his bizarre, experimental working methods: he was an abstract artist, a 'brutalist' action painter influenced by Jackson Pollock and Yves Klein, who used to disturb and transform the surfaces of bitumen-laden boards placed on the floor by dancing on them and riding bicycles over them. He also poured acid on them and set them on fire. Ken Russell filmed Green in action for a television news programme and a Canadian film crew recorded him; magazine and press photographers also photographed him. Sarcastic articles appeared in British and French newspapers, and the British comedian Tony Hancock parodied his bicycle riding in the 1961 film *The Rebel*.

Green himself was not averse to using marketing methods to promote his career. For instance, in December 1959, he held a one-man show at the New Vision Centre, London entitled: *Errol Flynn Exhibition*. The catalogue's cover reproduced a photo of the movie star who had just died. However, the show itself did not contain any paintings depicting Flynn. Green told one reporter that he had been thinking of Flynn while working on his abstractions. Dennis Bowen, director of the gallery, remarked: 'Flynn's name is good publicity, it will bring people in.' Other famous individuals intrigued Green: he produced a photo-static print of a negative image of Elvis Presley and another abstract work referred, in its title, to the French emperor Napoleon.

Green's fame or notoriety was of the 15-minute variety. Although his career prospects looked promising when he left the RCA, he spent the next 25 years in obscurity earning a living by teaching. He vanished so completely from the art scene that he was rumoured to be dead. Then, in 1993, he was rediscovered by an art dealer and a curator and became briefly famous again. A solo exhibition Green held at England & Co in March 1993 again used the name and image of a film star as a promotional device. This time the star was Susan Hayward. Seventeen bitumen and varnish paintings on display, dated 1992 and 1993, had titles bearing her name. What remains a mystery is whether the considerable media exposure Green 'enjoyed' as a young man contributed to his retirement from the fray.[9]

## Pop Artists and Movie Stars

Since pop art was defined by its reworking of images appropriated from popular culture, it was inevitable that pop artists would depict many celebrities, especially those from the realms of movies and rock/pop music. (Most pop artists collected photos, which they pinned up on walls to form multi-image collages.) For instance, the death of the teenager's idol James Dean in September 1955 in a car crash prompted artistic memorials by the American artist Andy

Warhol and the British artists Geoff Reeve, John Minton and Tony Messenger.

Gerald Laing (b. 1936) was a mature student at the St Martin's College of Art in 1963 when he made a series of works based on grainy newspaper photographs of European film stars such as Anna Karina and Brigitte Bardot. David Mellor comments:

> Laing took the photographic screening process that reproduced their faces and fame for publications, and then produced over sized images of them in paint. This technique ... atomised the photographic referent, blowing it up, in the case of Jean-Luc Godard's star, *Anna Karina*, to twelve feet high ... Laing's investigation of the materiality of the star's photographic apparition was parallel to Warhol's silk-screened paintings of image-scavenged stars ... Laing dwelt on a theme of publicity and the consumption of these star personages, through the industrial surfaces of reproduction – an area in English art that only had a pre-history in Sickert's coarse-textured paintings of the nineteen-thirties. Interviewed in the *Evening Standard*, Laing said, 'We don't know Brigitte Bardot – we know her through the newspaper image.' The face of Brigitte was pro-motional, monochrome, alien in its grille of information; Laing's strategy was utterly unlike [Peter] Blake's, who in *Girly Door* (1959), undertook to familiarise the spectator with the intimate, domestic scale experience of the 'sincere fan' and pin-up collector.[10]

Bardot, of course, was France's riposte to America's 'sex goddess' Marilyn Monroe. (The two stars appeared side-by-side in Peter Phillips's 1961 painting *For Men Only – Starring MM and BB*.) Super-imposed on Bardot's face was a perfect circle that enclosed her most crucial features. When adding this device, Laing had in mind Kenneth Noland's abstract, 'target' paintings and the geometry governing the composition of Renaissance figurative drawings and paintings.[11] Later, in 1968, Laing produced an edition of 200 silkscreen prints of the painting. In the prints, the circle was coloured pink. In 2001, Laing painted another version of the 1963 canvas but from a photo of Bardot as she is today. (She is now widely known as a supporter of animal rights.) He plans to exhibit the old and new paintings side by side. In addition, in 2001, a poster of the 1963 painting was issued by the British furniture chain store Habitat.

**20. Gerald Laing,** *Brigitte Bardot,* **1963.**
Painting, oil on canvas, 183 x 124.5 cm.
Private collection. © Gerald Ogilvie-Laing.

Blake's *Girly Door*, mentioned by Mellor, included pin-up photos of the female film stars Gina Lollabridgida, Shirley McLean, Elsa Martinelli, Kim Novak and Marilyn Monroe. The latter was also to appear in Blake and Haworth's famous LP cover for *Sergeant Pepper's Lonely Hearts Club Band* (1967).

### Marilyn Monroe

As is the case with so many models and movie actors, Norma Jeane Mortenson or Baker (1926–1962) adopted an invented name for professional purposes. This practice immediately opens a gap between the private person and the public persona. Monroe certainly became dissatisfied with the dumb blond role she was so often called upon to play. (One of Monroe's precursors and role models was the platinum blonde and Hollywood star Jean Harlow, whom the British artist Peter Blake celebrated in a 1964 painting.) While Monroe enjoyed the adulation she received as a star, she came to dislike being treated as a thing: she once remarked: 'A sex-symbol becomes a thing, I just hate being a thing.' Two of Monroe's marriages were to celebrities in different spheres of achievement – Jo DiMaggio (baseball hero) and Arthur Miller (prize-winning playwright) – and her lovers included the Kennedy brothers and the French actor Yves Montand.

Monroe became world-famous during the 1950s when her blend of sensual allure and childlike innocence and vulnerability entranced both male and female cinemagoers. De Kooning, a leading abstract expressionist, is well known for a series of paintings of archetypal but monstrous women executed in an aggressive manner. One, dated 1954, is entitled *Marilyn Monroe*. The artist, apparently, did not set out to paint her portrait; her image emerged unbidden during the act of painting. This work revealed more about its maker than its subject. De Kooning, it would seem, feared women.

One of the best known and erotic images of Monroe stemmed from the 1955 Cinemascope film *The Seven Year Itch*: in one scene, Monroe stood on a subway grate and an updraught of air billowed her skirt up to reveal her bare thighs and white nylon panties. (Many still photographs of the moment taken on location in 1954 were published.) The following year, a team of three British intellectuals who had been members of the Independent Group – Richard Hamilton, John McHale and Jon Voelcker – selected this image for their display of pop culture icons created as part of the Whitechapel Art Gallery's exhibition *This is Tomorrow*. In 1996, the Japanese artist Yasumasa Morimura produced a staged photograph of himself posing as Monroe with billowing skirt (see Chapter 3). Later, in 2000, the British pop artist Clive Barker produced small editions of bronze sculptures based on the same image of Monroe but this time emerging like a genie from a bottle of Coca Cola.

In 1958, the noted American photographer Richard Avedon (b. 1923) took a series of photographs of Monroe dressed and made up as earlier sex symbols of the screen such as Lillian Russell, Theda Bara, Clara Bow, Jean Harlow and Marlene Dietrich. Monroe posed in reconstructed period settings to convey a sense of historical authenticity. Some photos were produced exclusively for *Life* magazine and when they were published, Monroe's husband Miller supplied an introduction. These somewhat incestuous pictorial

**21. Clive Barker, *M M 10*, 1999.**
Bronze sculpture (one of 12 variations), 35.9 cm high. © Clive Barker.
Photo courtesy of the artist and Whitford Fine Art, London.

impersonations anticipated the later practices of Cindy Sherman, Madonna and Morimura.

When, in August 1962, it was reported that Monroe had died from an overdose of sleeping pills (conspiracy theorists have since claimed she was murdered in the presence of Bobby Kennedy[12]), Andy Warhol responded by making a series of silk-screen paintings of her, or rather of a black and white publicity photograph of her taken by Gene Kornman for the 1953 film *Niagara*. (Warhol had never met Monroe but death was a subject that appealed to him and which seemed to dominate the news during the early 1960s.) Warhol frequently used other people's photographs even though he constantly carried a camera and took thousands himself. Images taken in street Photomat booths also formed the basis for many of his painted portraits. Since childhood, he had been collecting images of celebrities that interested him and his archive included many of Monroe. The silk-screen technique facilitated fast, serial/multiple production and enabled Warhol to cash in on current events even when he was personally unmoved by them: he was like a mirror because he reflected America back to itself.

Dyed hair and heavy make-up are two of the means by which actresses alter their natural appearance in order to adopt the mask that constitutes the characters they play and their personas as stars. Warhol made this even more evident by using garish colours, which were applied to the canvas before the silk-screened image. He intensified and simplified the hues of Monroe's hair (yellow), lips (red), eye shadow (green and blue) and flesh (pink); her face was placed against plain backgrounds of orange or reflective backgrounds of gold and silver; in this way, the image became much more two-dimensional and poster-like; a surface without depth. Clearly, it was Monroe the public icon disseminated by the mass media that concerned Warhol, not the troubled, private individual Norma Jeane.

Warhol was to produce further paintings and prints of Marilyn in 1964 and 1967. In some paintings, the same image was repeated in rows across the canvas so that the result resembled a sheet of postage stamps or photo-booth strips; in one painting, Monroe's lips were singled out for multiplication. Repetition signified the vast quantity of images of Monroe in circulation and their photomechanical and assembly line character. In an essay on the theme of repetition in Warhol's *oeuvre*, William V. Ganis remarked: 'Warhol's art makes the standard, stereotyped and repeated intensely perceptible.'[13] A monochrome painting with six images of Monroe included the word 'six-pack' in its title, which served to highlight the fact that Warhol regarded her image as a consumer product comparable to cans of beer. However, not all of Warhol's images of Monroe were identical because colours and ink registration were deliberately varied. Such permutations embodied the 'difference within sameness' that typifies mass culture products and Hollywood genres.[14]

**22. Andy Warhol,** *The Six Marilyns (Marilyn Six-Pack),* **1962.**
Painting, silk-screen ink on synthetic polymer paint on canvas,
109 x 56 cm. Collection Emily and Jerry Spiegel. © Andy Warhol
Foundation for the Visual Arts/ARS, NY and DACS, London 2002.

Warhol, of course, was an artist fascinated by the phenomenon of fame and by celebrities whom he delighted in meeting and being photographed with. For instance, a photograph taken in 1979 inside the upmarket club Studio 54, shows Warhol alongside Truman Capote, Jerry Hall, Debbie Harry and Paloma Picasso. During the 1960s, many famous individuals made a point of visiting the New York Factory studio where Warhol held court. Accompanied by an entourage, Warhol would also attend exhibition openings, fashion shows, receptions, nightclubs, restaurants and parties virtually every day in order to be seen and to encounter even more famous people. Warhol freely admitted he had 'a social disease'. He enjoyed the fact that he could read a magazine featuring celebrities and know everyone in it.

His pictorial pantheon eventually encompassed an extraordinarily wide range of well-known people: Muhammad Ali, Marlon Brando, Troy Donahue, James Cagney, Warren Beatty, Dennis Hopper, Natalie Wood, Elizabeth Taylor, Liza Minnelli, Jackie Kennedy, Elvis Presley, Truman Capote, Mick Jagger, Beethoven, Franz Kafka, Lenin, Mao, Richard Nixon (with the caption 'vote McGovern'), Princess Diana, David Hockney, and even his chief European rival, the German artist Joseph Beuys.

During the 1970s, Warhol adopted the dubious but lucrative business practice of making painted portraits of wealthy individuals from instant snaps he had taken with a flash Polaroid camera called the Big Shot. Some of his subjects, like the fashion designer Yves Saint Laurent, were well known. In effect, he degenerated into a facile society portraitist exploiting his own celebrity status – 'you too can own a Warhol' – and offering clients the benefit of his celebrity-image production line – 'you too can be a star'.[15]

Monroe's impact was international. In the year of her death, the German artist Wolf Vostell produced a work about her, as did the Italian torn-poster artist Mimmo Rotella. Both artists employed found images of Monroe with damaged surfaces. In 1965, Richard Hamilton generated a mixed-media work (oil and collage on photo on board) entitled *My Marilyn* (Ludwig Collection, Aachen), which featured twelve photographs by George Barris of Monroe, wearing a bikini, posing on a beach with the ocean behind her. (Hamilton also produced various silk-screen prints of the same subject.) What is striking about this sequence of publicity shots is that Monroe, who was powerful enough to control the release of her own publicity images, has defaced most of them with crosses and scratches during a selection session. She has ticked the one she wants to be used. Hamilton was intrigued by the cancelled and damaged prints because of the contrast between the hand-made marks and the photo-mechanical images, and because the crossings out seemed to presage Monroe's death by her own hand. Ironically, an 'X' can also signify a kiss and Monroe was fond of blowing kisses at the camera. Hamilton added painted passages, which in one instance erased Monroe's face and body so that she was reduced to a blank silhouette. Monroe's manipulations of her own image could not, of course, survive her. After her death, photographers and fine artists manipulated it. Several other American movie stars appear in Hamilton's pop paintings: Bing Crosby, Patricia Knight and Claude Rains.

As art critic David Kirby has observed, 'Marilynmania' has grown stronger in the decades since her death at the early age of 36.[16] In October 1999, 1,500 items of her personal property were sold at Christie's, New York for $13.4 million. The sale was televised and the auction catalogue subsequently became a collector's item. A pre-auction travelling exhibition of Monroe's effects attracted crowds of admirers some of whom were so emotionally overcome they shed tears. CMG Worldwide manages Monroe's estate. Over 170 companies have licensing agreements enabling them to use her image in books and commercials, and on products, yielding revenue estimated to be $1 million per annum. An early Warhol of Monroe sold during the 1990s for $17.3 million. Almost any relic or photo of Monroe, it seems, now has a market value, even paintings by amateur artists, that is, those by fans of Monroe who gave their work to her when she was alive.

Furthermore, new generations of artists continue to reference her. As already mentioned, Morimura dressed up in drag in imitation of Monroe in order to be photographed. In 1999, the art dealer Emily Peterson, concerned that most representations of Monroe had been devised by men, organised a group exhibition in New York entitled *Marilyn Monroe X-Times: Through Eyes of Women*, which contained specially commissioned works about Monroe created by such female artists as Jane Dickson, Robin Tewes, Ellen Driscoll and Shonagh Adelman. An earlier work featuring Monroe by the British feminist artist Margaret Harrison is described in Chapter 5.

Kirby also notes:

This year [2000] New York artist E.V. Day riffed on the idea of the blonde bombshell in two installations. For the Whitney Biennial, Day re-created the white halter-top dress that Monroe wore in the 1955 film *The Seven Year Itch*. Day portrayed it as if in mid explosion, with bits of fabric suspended in the air by a network of wires. The Whitney acquired the piece for its permanent collection. Meanwhile, over at the Chelsea gallery Henry Urbach Architecture, Day gave a similar treatment to a silver-sequined sheath that resembled Monroe's 'Happy Birthday, Mr. President' gown. The Day dress sold for $28,000.

If Monroe had lived until 2001, she would have been 75 years old. In recognition of this fact, the Hollywood Entertainment Museum mounted a special exhibition of Marilyn memorabilia entitled *Happy Birthday, Marilyn* (June–August 2001). On display were artefacts such as dolls, comic books, postcards, playing cards, and some of her costumes, plus photographs by Bert Stern, Douglas Kirkland and Milton H. Greene, and art works by Ted LeMaster, Earl Moran and Steve Kaufman. Dr Jan-Christopher Horak, the museum's curator, was assisted by a group of dedicated collectors called Marilyn Remembered.

Given the intense and continuing public interest in Monroe, it is no wonder that she has been dubbed 'the most celebrated of all actresses' and 'the world's most famous sex object'. The latter description has prompted critiques and biographical studies by feminists.[17] Monroe, or rather her public image, seems to have achieved immortality. Her cult is unlikely to diminish because of reruns of her films and because so many collectors, dealers and merchandisers have an interest (profit) in maintaining it.

Movie directors are not nearly so popular, as subjects, with artists as movie stars. R.B. Kitaj (b. 1932), an American painter fascinated by cinema and montage, is an exception. In 1970, Kitaj was teaching in Los Angeles and preparing a painting, which he later destroyed, about Hollywood. During his preparation, he sketched and photographed such leading directors as George Cukor, John Ford, Henry Hathaway, Jean Renoir and Billy Wilder. Kitaj greatly admired Ford's Westerns starring John Wayne, and managed to see Ford (1894–1973) shortly before he died. Years later Kitaj painted *Amerika (John Ford on his Deathbed)* (1983–84, Metropolitan Museum, New York), a broadly executed canvas which has a profile view of Ford in bed surrounded by the ghosts of several characters from his movies, most notably Sergeant Quincannon, played by actor Victor McLagen, from the Cavalry trilogy (1948–50). Another Kitaj painting that pays homage to two film directors with whom he felt an artistic affinity is *Kenneth Anger and Michael Powell* (1973, Ludwig Museum, Koblenz). Kitaj knew them both personally; indeed he arranged for them to meet.[18]

## Pauline Boty and *Scandal*

The British painter Pauline Boty (1938–1966) was a member of the British pop art generation that emerged from the Royal College of

Art in the early 1960s. Many of her paintings depicted famous individuals from the worlds of culture, politics (President Lincoln and Fidel Castro), sport, movies (Monica Vitti and Jean Paul Belmondo) and even crime (the Chicago mobster Big Jim Colosimo). Boty was a proto-feminist who, in 1964, painted *It's a Man's World I*, which featured portraits of such male luminaries as Frederico Fellini, Marcello Mastroianni, John Lennon, Ringo Starr, Einstein, Lenin, Proust, President Kennedy, Elvis Presley, the matador El Cordobes and the boxer Muhammad Ali. Male military power and the threat of violence were represented at the top by an American bomber.

Boty greatly admired Monroe and was upset by news of her death. Boty had impersonated the star in art school reviews and later paid homage to her in the painting *The Most Beautiful Blonde in the World* (1964).

In 1963, the British establishment was rocked by a sex and security scandal. The media revealed that John Profumo, a married man (his wife was the British stage and film star Valerie Hobson) and Secretary of State for War in the Conservative Government of Harold Macmillan, had shared the same mistress as the Soviet naval attaché Eugene Ivanov. The two models/prostitutes involved in the case – Christine Keeler and Mandy Rice-Davies – became instant celebrities, as did their mentor Stephen Ward, an osteopath and socialite. Ward was also an amateur artist who made portrait sketches of the people that he met to ease social contact. In a memoir published in 2001, Keeler claims that Ward was a Soviet spy.[19] He was so devastated by the public exposure and prosecution for acting as a pimp that he committed suicide before the end of his trial. Profumo was forced to resign for lying to the House of Commons about his affair with Keeler, while she served a prison sentence for perjury.

This potent subject obviously intrigued Boty because she painted a picture about it at the time (*Scandal*, 1963) in which a naked Keeler sits provocatively astride a copy of an Arne Jacobson chair (an image derived from a famous photo by Lewis Morley) and gazes sideways at the viewer. Above Keeler, there is a frieze of portraits showing Profumo, Ward and two of Keeler's West Indian men friends Lucky Gordon and Johnnie Edgecombe. The picture can be interpreted as a tribute to the sexual powers that attractive young women – Boty included – wield over men. However, Keeler's life after 1963 was highly stressful because she became a public curiosity and a sexual trophy.

**23. Pauline Boty, *Scandal*, 1963.**
Painting lost.

Keeler even excited artists in France: witness Jean-Jacques Lebel's 1963 painting and collage on a wooden panel entitled *Christine Keeler Icône*, which features two photographs of Keeler in the nude. A British film – *Scandal* – directed by Michael Caton-Jones, was made about the Profumo affair in 1989. Joanne Whalley-Kilmer starred as Keeler and John Hurt played Ward. Keeler disliked the film because she thought it distorted the truth but she attended its premiere because she was paid £5,000 to do so.

During the early 1960s, Boty became a minor celebrity in her own right. She and her collages were featured in a television arts documentary directed by Ken Russell and, due to her youth and beauty, photos of her appeared in the press. She was also invited on television chat shows and she acted on the London stage and in television dramas. However, Boty was one of those artists who suffered a tragically premature death (she developed leukaemia and died in 1966 at the age of 28). Two decades of obscurity followed until interest in her life and art revived during the 1990s. Critics find it difficult to evaluate her work because her career was cut short and because it is hard to separate the art from her engaging personality and legend.[20]

## Pop Artists and Rock/Pop Musicians

Many pop artists in Britain and the United States during the 1950s and 1960s were enthusiastic followers of jazz, skiffle, rock and pop music and so they represented performers they admired or who made a splash in the media. As documented in my book *Cross-Overs*, artists such as Derek Boshier, David Hockney, Peter Blake, Richard Hamilton, David Oxtoby, Martin Sharp, Ray Johnson, Robert Stanley and Andy Warhol depicted such groups and stars as La Vern Baker, the Beach Boys, Sammy Davis Jr, Bo Diddley, the Everly Brothers, the Lettermen, Buddy Holly, Cliff Richard, Elvis Presley, Jimi Hendrix, Frank Sinatra, the Rolling Stones and the Beatles.[21] In most instances, the artists did not paint portraits of their subjects from life but from photographs. In Blake's case, he hoped that his images would appeal to the pop star's fans as did the publicity stills and fan magazines they habitually collected.

A few of Blake's paintings were responses to the experience of being a fan. For instance, in 1961, he painted a self-portrait in which he held a Presley fan magazine and wore a blue denim outfit adorned with badges, including one featuring Presley, even though at that time he did not like Elvis. In addition, between 1959 and 1962, he produced a painting entitled *Girls with their Hero*, which depicted British female fans, some hysterical, of Presley amidst the discs and the mass culture images of him that they had to make do with because Elvis never performed live in Britain. Blake says he has 'retired from art' but he is still active and at present, he is planning 'a shrine to Elvis'.

Michael Jackson (b. 1958), the American dancer and singer, became one of the world's most famous pop music stars during the 1970s and 1980s. Since then, he has been called 'The King of Pop' but also 'Wacko Jacko' because of eccentricities such as childlike behaviour and messianic delusions.[22] In 1988, Jeff Koons, the American master of kitsch art (that is, art that copies or simulates kitsch), directed Italian ceramicists to create a porcelain sculpture in a neo-baroque style from a publicity shot he supplied. It was to be one of a new series of ten works entitled *Banality*. The sculpture, *Michael Jackson and Bubbles*, was a life-size portrait of Jackson holding his pet chimpanzee. While Jackson reclines on a bed of roses, the chimp rests on Jackson's lap. (Due to his association with Jackson, Bubbles became the best-known chimp in the world. On his ranch, Neverland, Jackson kept a variety of animals in a private zoo.) Four casts were made: an artist's proof and an edition of three; two casts are now in the public collections in Greece and California; another was sold via Sotheby's New York to an anonymous buyer in May 2001 for $5,615,750.

**24. Jeff Koons, *Michael Jackson and Bubbles*, 1988.**
Ceramic, edition of three, 106.7 x 179 x 81.3 cm.
Santa Monica: The Broad Art Foundation.
Reproduced courtesy of the Jeff Koons Studio, New York.

Jackson was one of Koons' role models because of his abilities to manipulate and seduce audiences. (Two other entertainers depicted by Koons were Buster Keaton and Bob Hope.) Koons' statue proved controversial because the snow-white porcelain of the face made it seem that the Afro-American entertainer wanted to become a white person. (Jackson, Koons claimed, had to become white in order to appeal to white, pubescent, middle-class American girls.) However, Jackson fans have argued that he has never wanted to deny his race, and they claim that his skin lightening creams and numerous plastic surgery operations were needed to overcome the skin disorder Vitiligo. No matter, Koons approved of self-transformation whatever the cost. He believed the artist's duty was to communicate and entertain, and Jackson was brilliant at both. It was also the artist's duty to exploit the masses but that required self-exploitation too: Jackson had not been content with what nature had provided in terms of his appearance and so had taken charge of his own evolution; the result was an artificial body.

In the light of the above, one might have expected Koons to have depicted Jackson in a dynamic pose dancing on stage or in one of his memorable music videos rather than as a static figure. Jackson is off duty but he is shown wearing heavy make-up and an elaborate costume of glistening gold. His chimp has a matching outfit – one of 20 – designed by Jackson's personal costume designer. Koons presents Jackson as an ostentatious ornament. A curator at the San Francisco Museum of Modern Art, which owns one of the sculptures, commented: 'Koons' use of ceramic points directly to the hollowness and fragility of celebrity status.' Another curator, Doreet Levitte Harten, has described the sculpture as 'grotesque' and thinks there is 'something obscene and perverse' about it. She feels 'a sense of horror is inscribed in the lascivious surfaces of the sculpture'.[23]

In 1990, Jackson commissioned a portrait from Brett Livingstone Strong (b. 1953), an Australian-born artist living in Los Angeles. A Japanese executive from the Hiromichi Saeki Corporation then offered Jackson $2.1 million for it providing he appeared at an unveiling press conference and opened a new entertainment complex in Tokyo that the executive had developed. Jackson did attend the unveiling ceremony but not the entertainment centre opening. Clearly, the unprecedented price for a portrait of a living person reflected Jackson's fame and his promotional value rather than the aesthetic value of the painting itself, which was a neo-academic portrayal of the star holding a book, hence its title The Book. Strong is also a sculptor and has created a bronze statue of John Lennon and monuments dedicated to John Wayne and President Ronald Reagan.

The ranch house at Neverland was decorated with several portraits of Jackson. When, in 1993, police raided his home in search of evidence of child molestation they encountered 'a two-storey-tall painting by David Nordahl … the surreal portrait depicted a beatific Michael in a swirling firmament of cherub-faced children'. Next, they came across 'five other paintings showing Jackson surrounded by adoring youngsters'.[24] Jackson was not tried on the charges of child abuse in a criminal court but he paid $26 million to the parents of one boy to end their civil action against him.

While the black/Hispanic painter Jean-Michel Basquiat enjoyed success in the United States and Europe as an artist during the early 1980s, he moved in predominantly white circles and had affairs with white women. In terms of the visual arts, the artist Basquiat most respected and wished to emulate was Warhol rather than earlier Afro-American artists. Basquiat did not want his work categorised as 'black art' but many of his personal heroes were blacks who had achieved fame as entertainers, sportsmen and revolutionaries. For instance, he admired the jazz musicians Charlie Parker, Miles Davis and Dizzy Gillespie, the boxers Jack Johnson, Sugar Ray Robinson, Joe Louis and Muhammad Ali, and the revolutionary leader Toussaint L'Overture. Images and references to them appeared in many of Basquiat's drawings and paintings.

Basquiat was a fast and productive artist. He often had several paintings in progress at once and liked to work on the floor while sitting or standing on his canvases. He listened to bebop while he painted and surrounded himself with a wide variety of source materials from which he borrowed images, diagrams and quotations in a promiscuous fashion. (His direct, improvisational method echoed that of jazz.) In the three-part painting *Horn Players* dated 1983, for instance, crudely rendered, cartoon-like figures of two black jazz musicians – one holding a saxophone and one holding a trumpet – appear along with such hand-printed words as 'Dizzy Gillespie', 'Charlie Parker', 'ear', 'feet', 'soap', 'larnyx' [sic], 'teeth', 'alchemy' and 'ornithology'. The latter term referred to the fact that the saxophone player Parker (1920–1955) was nicknamed 'Bird' and was the creator of the bebop anthem *Ornithology*. Basquiat was fond of repeating words, misspelling them and crossing them through. (Crossing out was paradoxical because the words remained visible 'under erasure' and, as Basquiat noted, they attracted the viewer's attention.) In this canvas, Parker's name appears seven times in a column. They are all crossed through and then the whole column of names is cancelled with two large white brushstrokes. The

**25. Jean-Michel Basquiat, *Horn Players*, 1983.**
Acrylic and mixed-media on canvas, 244 x 190.5 cm.
Santa Monica: The Broad Art Foundation, photo Douglas M. Parker Studio,
reproduced courtesy of the Estate of Jean-Michel Basquiat, New York.
© ADAGP, Paris and DACS, London, 2002.

symbolism is self-evident. Both Parker and Basquiat were drug addicts and both died prematurely because of their habits.

As is well known, a number of leading rock and pop music stars died young through accidents, illness or self-destructive behaviour. They include: Marc Bolan, Jeff Buckley, Kurt Cobain, Alma Cogan,

Ian Curtis, Nick Drake, Marvin Gaye, Jimi Hendrix, Buddy Holly, Michael Hutchence, Brian Jones, Janis Joplin, Jim Morrison, Otis Redding, Sid Vicious and Gene Vincent. Fine artists have commemorated almost all of them. Three examples will be considered.

Ian Curtis (1956–1980), the lead singer and songwriter of the Manchester band Joy Division that achieved cult status in the late 1970s, suffered from epilepsy and depression. In May 1980, at the age of 23, he hanged himself. His death prompted the American artist Julian Schnabel to paint a memorial on black velvet entitled *Ornamental Despair* (1980). The painting included a grieving figure quoted from the cover image of Joy Division's album *Closer* (1980). Schnabel chose not to represent Curtis but his absence: one half of the painting consisted of a decorative frame enclosing an empty space.

Kurt Cobain (1967–1994), a singer, guitarist and visual artist (drawings and paintings), co-founded the band Nirvana in 1986. He was one of the leading figures in the grunge music and fashion scene, based in Seattle, which became fashionable in the United States during the late 1980s. Cobain married the singer Courtney Love in 1992 and they had one child. Unusually for a rock star, Cobain distrusted fame because much of it, he thought, was false and he felt guilty about possessing it. He was also an unhappy individual who suffered from depression, stomach pains and an addiction to heroin. In 1994, at the age of 27, he committed suicide by firing a shotgun at his head. (However, there are those who think he did not take his own life and who allege that he was murdered by society or on the orders of his wife.)

Much of the work of the Los Angeles artist Sandow Birk (b. 1965) had dealt with contemporary social and political events and so Cobain's death appealed to him as a subject. In his painting *The Death of Kurt Cobain, Seattle* 1994, he depicted Cobain's gruesome, faceless corpse lying prone on a floor splattered with his blood and brains. A halo floats in mid air and a landscape is visible through a large window in the background.

Birk had been a fan of Nirvana and grunge music, but he was taken aback by the excess of teenage grief that followed news of Cobain's death and by the fact that he was being treated as a saint (hence the halo) even though he had been a drug addict who had killed himself in a horrendous manner. Above all, Birk wanted to convey the ghastly reality of the event.[25]

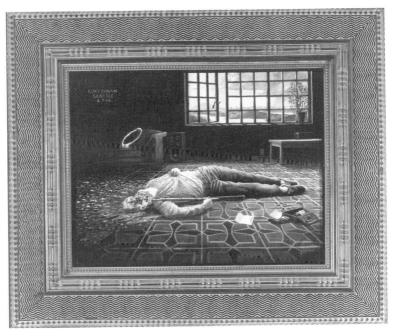

**26. Sandow Birk, *The Death of Kurt Cobain, Seattle*, 1994.**
Painting, oil and acrylic on canvas, 35.5 x 46 cm (unframed).
Los Angeles: collection of Michael Solway and Angela Jones.
© Sandow Birk. Photo courtesy of the artist.

In order to make his picture as accurate as possible, Birk relied on photos of the murder scene published in *Time* magazine and newspaper accounts by crime reporters. However, the composition, mood and illusionistic style of this picture were derived from another source: Henry Wallis' 1856 pre-Raphaelite painting *The Death of Chatterton*. Thomas Chatterton (1752–1770) was a British, eighteenth-century child prodigy poet who committed suicide at the age of 17 by poisoning himself with arsenic because of poverty and artistic failure. Wallis' painting was executed in the very attic in Gray's Inn, London, where Chatterton died. It was one of the first romantic representations of the 'tragic early death of a neglected genius in a bohemian garret' variety. Birk added an elaborately designed frame to his *Death of Cobain* painting in order to strengthen the reference to Victorian art. When the painting was exhibited in San Francisco and in a touring show, it elicited strong but varying reactions from viewers: horror, outrage, tears and laughter.

Sid Vicious (1957–1979, aka John Ritchie) was another rock musician who died prematurely. An ex-member of the British punk band the Sex Pistols, he overdosed on drugs in New York shortly after being indicted for second-degree murder. His victim was his lover Nancy Spungen (1958–1978) whom he was accused of stabbing. Both Spungen and Vicious had been consuming hard drugs while staying at the famous Chelsea Hotel. Their short, pathetic lives were later made into a docu-drama type movie – *Sid and Nancy* (1986) – directed by Alex Cox and starring Gary Oldman and Chloe Webb.

In 1993, the young British artist Gavin Turk (b. 1967) created a life-size human figure from wax and fibreglass, added real clothes and a replica pistol, and placed it in a glass case. The sculpture, entitled *Pop*, was remarkable for the number of images of celebrities referenced and the layers of meaning implied. Turk depicted himself impersonating Vicious as he appeared when firing a gun at the audience after singing Frank Sinatra's *My Way* in Julien Temple's film *The Great Rock 'n' Roll Swindle* (1980). Vicious in turn reprised Elvis as he appeared repeatedly (a strobe-light effect) in Warhol's 1963–64 screen-printed paintings based on a promotional still of Elvis acting the part of a gun-toting cowboy in the 1960 Western *Flaming Star*. Julian Stallabrass has commented: 'In this work the artist appears as a combination of handed-down stars, each with strongly negative as well as positive aspects to their personas; charismatic, but also abject.'[26]

Clearly, in this instance, Turk was expecting viewers to be well informed, to possess a wide knowledge of both fine art and popular culture. By including himself in the sculpture, Turk blended artist and pop icon. He seemed to be asserting: 'Pop culture is part of my identity and heritage. I can use the magical power of art to transform myself into a pop star.' In terms of its form, Turk's sculpture was conservative rather than radical. In fact, his deliberate imitation of the hyper-realistic figures found in waxwork shows was an attempt to gain for art the kind of popularity enjoyed by Madame Tussaud's.

In an interview, Turk explained that one reason why Warhol appealed to him is that the American artist became mainstream by making 'being a fan' a key theme of his work. Warhol was fascinated and interested in others and by depicting them in an impersonal, quasi-mechanical fashion he directed attention away from himself. (This argument ignores the fact that Warhol produced many self-portraits.) Turk thought Vicious had been in love with the image of being a rock star and had behaved in a violent and self-destructive

**27. Gavin Turk, *Pop*, 1993.**
Sculpture, glass, brass, MDF, fibreglass, wax, clothing, gun,
279 x 115 x 115 cm. London, Saatchi Gallery. © Gavin Turk.
Photo Hugo Glennınning, courtesy of Jay Jopling/White Cube, London.

manner as so many of them had done before him. Turk added: 'I was
looking at Sid in terms of a kind of cultural phenomena and also a
kind of tourist place, a kind of framing device.'[27]

The critic Brian Sewell judged *Pop* to be 'clever whimsy, utterly
ephemeral' but he also described it as a 'multiple pun on pop art,

pop music, pop star and pop gun'.[28] Another critic, Richard
Dorment, thought Turk was 'a Wizard of Oz figure, substituting self-
aggrandisement for substance, peeling away the layers of bluff and
hype that go into the creation of modern celebrity'. He added that
within the small but sophisticated audience of the art world, Turk
had 'already achieved the status of a cult figure'.[29]

## Elizabeth Peyton

Another artist who depicted celebrities, both living and deceased,
during the 1990s was Elizabeth Peyton (b. 1965), an American artist
based in New York, who trained at that city's School of Visual Arts.
She rapidly gained an international reputation for her drawings,
paintings and photographs. Like Warhol, who was a formative
influence, she mostly used existing images culled from the mass
media as starting points. Peyton began by depicting historical
figures such as Queen Elizabeth I, Louis XIV, Napoleon and Ludwig
II of Bavaria; she then painted rock music performers such as John
Lennon, Johnny Rotten (aka John Lydon), Sid Vicious, Kurt Cobain,
and the Britpop stars Liam and Noel Gallagher of Oasis, and Jarvis
Cocker of Pulp. (Cocker, incidentally, attended art college [St
Martin's] and has a strong interest in the visual arts; he has
presented programmes about 'outsider art' on Channel 4 Television.
Like Cobain, he has expressed scepticism about fame.) Other
subjects included: Oscar Wilde and Bosie (Lord Alfred Douglas)
holding hands, Brian Epstein, Leonardo DiCaprio, the German film
director Rainer Werner Fassbinder, the British royals Princess Diana
(as a teenager), Prince William and Prince Harry, artists such as
David Hockney (as a young man) and the Chapman brothers Dinos
and Jake.

Peyton has also painted and photographed friends and acquain-
tances, such as her American art dealer Gavin Brown, and then
exhibited the results alongside her celebrity pictures as if they were
just as famous and significant. Critic Christopher Miles was
prompted to remark: 'The genuine interest of her paintings of
unknowns shows the persona power of her celebrity subjects to be a
crutch she doesn't need.'[30]

Rather than copying her source photographs slavishly, Peyton
interpreted them intuitively, imprecisely, in a self-consciously
amateurish fashion. In her watercolours, paint drips remained and
her oil paintings were executed as if they were watercolours with

**28. Elizabeth Peyton, *Rainer Fassbinder*, 1995.**
Ink on paper, © The artist, courtesy Sadie Coles HQ, London.

thin, semi-transparent washes and with broad brushstrokes left visible. Colours were sweet and sour, and often exaggerated so that, for instance, her young, pale, thin, male subjects were endowed with red lips as if they were wearing lipstick. Some critics thought Peyton's works 'too illustrational' but others praised her painterliness and 'flamboyant palette'. Most of her portraits were small and this, combined with the personal handling, implied that they were the efforts of an admiring teenage, female fan or a high school student rather than a mature artist. Paradoxically, they were intimate portrayals of public figures.

Peyton deliberately adopted the standpoint of a fan but critics were convinced she genuinely admired the celebrities she depicted, that her work was a 'clear, life-affirming statement of private desires'. Critics also argued that she was attempting to capture and preserve moments of youthful beauty before age and decay intervened. According to fellow painter Martin Maloney, she presented her subjects as 'effete dandies' and one art historian characterised her work as 'fin-de-siècle wan dandyism'. Another writer commented that she 'turned scowling youths into pert cherubs'.

In an article on the lingering presence of extended adolescence in contemporary art, Gean Moreno perceptively summed up Peyton's project:

All lollipop boys, rendered by Peyton, bereft of interiority, ripe for the betrayal all celebrity is bound for, basking in the warm light of androgyny. Princes William and Harry ... [she] adoringly turns these royals into fragile pop princelings. Her boys are ethereal, angelic even, and like angels, they belong in stratospheres to which we'll never have complete access. She traffics in those seditious images that are engrossing because when we look at them we find our desire mirrored. But beyond this, Peyton commingles the protagonists of her boy hagiography with boys from her own life, irrevocably fuzzying the rigid mathematics that make the accessible banal and the distant flamboyantly exotic. Like a teenager, she looks to blur the line between her immediate environment and the fantasy world she has slowly woven out of magazine spreads and album covers. Hers is an exercise in memorialising that last stop on the road to growing up. This is what infuses her entire endeavour with a romantic melancholy. Everything in Peyton's work revolves around an effort to keep forever the fleeting beauty not of media darlings, but of the moment in which they embodied the very things we recklessly desired.[31]

Jon Savage, the British expert on punk, also praised in print Peyton's willingness to paint straight boys who were not afraid of being feminine/androgynous. He added:

Pop is one of the only safe havens for those of non-mainstream sexuality and gender. Men have to be feminised because purchasing power in the music industry is still located in young women. The androgyny that you can see in Liam Gallagher ... is also, according to anthropology, one of the hallmarks of the shaman: the performer healing through his own sickness ... Peyton is careful to emphasise male tenderness, beauty, bonding, femininity. These qualities are desired not only by the ardent fan but also, secretly, by the protagonists themselves –

sick of an archaic gender system that requires men to be tough, peer-pressured, unfeeling. It's my experience of Oasis that their persona masks vulnerability and intelligence ...[32]

In another thoughtful article concerning the role of emotion in contemporary painting, Jacqueline Cooper maintained that Peyton was 'infatuated with the cult of the beautiful personality', and that she 'focused on the idea of celebrity as the dominant currency of cultural exchange and used the genre of portraiture to reveal its face'. Furthermore, that she overlaid 'amplified emotional content on the coolly disseminated images of pop culture'. However, Cooper also judged Peyton's works to be 'passive portraits' that 'remain conservative as they politely resist challenging the establishment from which they are appropriated. Instead, the work prefers to reflect on the residue of radicalism traditionally seen as embodied in adolescence, but tragically consumed and rendered impotent by the entertainment industry.' What Peyton did, according to Cooper, was 'preserve and aggrandize the fragile countenances' of her celebrities so that her paintings 'mummified perfection' and became 'death masks'. She concluded that Peyton's project was 'non-critical and often fictitious'.[33]

Peyton herself, in an interview, complained about the alienating obscurity of so much contemporary art and then explained that she hoped to make works about the experience of being fascinated by other humans that would be as accessible to teenagers as the music papers they enjoyed reading. Certainly, Peyton's drawings and paintings of pop idols were aesthetically pleasurable and accessible but this does not mean that fans could afford them.[34] However, it should be said that articles about Peyton and reproductions of her works did appear in mass circulation magazines such as *American Vogue*, *ID*, *Elle* and *Jane*, as well as in art books and magazines.

## Sam Taylor-Wood and Sir Elton John

Taylor-Wood (b. 1967) was trained at Goldsmiths College in the late 1980s and then gained an art world reputation for her films and panoramic photographs of affluent people posing in posh interiors. She is married to the art dealer Jay Jopling and so, naturally, exhibits in his London gallery. She also regularly mixes with celebrities in other fields. For instance, she is a friend of the British pop star Sir Elton John (b. 1947, aka Reginald Dwight) who is a keen collector of twentieth-century photographs, many of which depict celebrities. His substantial collection includes images by such artists as Chuck Close, Nan Goldin, Man Ray and Andres Serrano, and part of it has been exhibited at the High Museum of Art in Atlanta (2000–01). In the past, he has collected cars, glassware and antiquities. He has also bought works by such British artists as Damien Hirst, Gary Hume, Marc Quinn and Taylor-Wood. In 2000, John appeared along with 20 other cultural icons (such as musician Alex James and actors Richard E. Grant and Ray Winstone) in a giant photomural (900-feet long x 60-feet high) that Taylor-Wood devised to wrap around scaffolding while the façade of the London department store Selfridges was being restored. Three, 360-degree photos were taken with a revolving camera in Peacock House, Holland Park, combined into one and then transferred on to thin plastic to protect the mural from the weather. The poses of the figures referenced famous works of art from the past and recent movies. Elton John, whose image above

**29. Sam Taylor-Wood and Sir Elton John with Selfridges' photomural in background, 2000.**
Digital photo published on the Internet.

the store's main entrance was 40-feet high, attended the unveiling ceremony on 8 May. While Selfridges – which now has its own art gallery called Inside Space – was delighted to benefit from an association with fashionable art and celebrities, Taylor-Wood was pleased by the business sponsorship and the opportunity to make such an ambitious, high profile, public work of art. The photomural, entitled *XV Seconds* (because the exposure time of each of the three photos was five seconds), was visible from May to October and seen by millions passing along Oxford Street. Taylor-Wood has explained that she was inspired by the Parthenon's marble frieze and that her subjects were 'modern day gods' adorning 'a temple of shopping'. Elton John was a particularly apt choice because he is known as 'the god of shopping' due to his lavish spending habit.

Taylor-Wood's interest in pop music stars is long-standing. At school, she painted gouaches of Bob Marley and her work has since featured Marianne Faithfull, Courtney Love and Kylie Minogue. In addition, she has made a film for a stage act of the Pet Shop Boys and directed a music video for Elton's song 'I Want Love'.

Journalists have profiled Taylor-Wood not only because of her art and famous friends but because she pluckily continued to work while having a child and suffering from breast and colon cancer.[35] (Overcoming adversity is a favourite theme of celebrity journalism.) When Andrew Billen interviewed her, he was so impressed he remarked: 'Never mind her celeb friends, she has her own star quality.'[36]

## Julian Opie and Blur

Opie (b. 1958) studied fine art at Goldsmiths College from 1979 to 1982, the same art college that Damien Hirst and Graham Coxon of the Britpop band Blur (founded 1989) attended in the late 1980s. (Two other members of Blur had Goldsmiths connections: Damon Albarn studied music part time and Alex James studied French.) Therefore, it is not surprising that both Opie and Hirst have produced art and music videos for the pop group. In 2000, Opie designed the cover of the *Best of Blur* album, which had four separate portraits of the musicians rendered in a highly schematic and decorative manner: flat, bright colours, simple black outlines. There is a tradition in Britain of fine artists collaborating with pop musicians who have been to art school and producing record sleeve designs for them.[37] Opie's procedure was to start with photographs, use a computer to simplify them and then output the results in a variety of media such as paintings, sculptures, wallpaper and animated films. For some years, Opie's art had been moving in a pop/consumer goods direction: reducing to essentials, using modules, issuing multiples and selling via mail order catalogues.

Some viewers of the Blur portraits were reminded of pictographs, children's book illustrations and the Tintin cartoons of Hergé. Essentially, Opie extended what Warhol did in his paintings of Monroe: turn a photograph into a graphic pop icon. Opie is fascinated by the

**30. Julian Opie,** *Four Portraits of Members of Blur,* **2000.**
Cover design for the *Best of Blur* CD.
© Julian Opie and courtesy of EMI Records.

terse language of signs found in the urban environment and seeks a similar 'universal' system. An exhibition of Opie's work held at the Lisson Gallery in February 2001 included large paintings of Albarn and James. The critic Jonathan Jones dismissed this show as 'contemporary British art at its worst' and he thought the Blur portraits were 'smugly celebratory' (he did not rate Blur's music either). However, the album cover portraits – also reproduced on posters and the official Blur website – were functionally effective because they fulfilled their promotional purpose and proved popular with the band's fans.[38]

## Images of Diana and the Exhibition *Heaven*

Lady Diana Spencer, later Diana Princess of Wales (1961–1997), may be described as the ultimate celebrity. From the moment Prince Charles began to court her, she was subjected to intense media attention. As his betrothed and wife, she was expected to sit for official portraits. Charles himself commissioned Susan Ryder to portray Diana in the absurdly flamboyant dress she wore for the wedding ceremony in St Paul's in 1981. In August 1998, BBC1's arts strand *Omnibus* transmitted an informative television programme entitled *The Art of Diana*, directed by Sarah Aspinall, that examined the dozen commissioned portraits by such painters as David Hankison, Douglas Anderson, June Mendoza, Emily Patrick and Bryan Organ.[39] Also featured were the paintings created by André Durand (discussed below) about Diana before her death. The official portraits veered between the staid and the saccharine, and therefore revealed little of Diana's vivacity or the emotional turmoil within. Lord Snowdon's studio photographs of Diana were discussed and compared to the more informal shots taken by supermodel photographers such as Mario Testino (one of Madonna's favourites). One dreads to think how many hours of her life Diana wasted posing.

The programme also traced the history of the various images, roles and personae that evolved during Diana's life – from virgin teenager, to fairytale bride/princess, to mother of two, to betrayed wife and victim of a repressed royal family, to Angel of Aids/Mother Teresa figure, to international fashion model and sexy celebrity, to Queen of Hearts/the People's Princess – as embodied in still photographs, film and television clips. It demonstrated that she gradually gained control over the image-making process until she achieved the kind of glamour and manipulative power over the media characteristic of major movie and pop stars. One interviewee remarked that Diana was 'the last of the silent film actresses'. Realising the power of images and publicity, Diana proved far more effective in her use of visual media than the rest of the royal family and so she upstaged them and transformed the public's conception of the monarchy in the late twentieth century. Finally, the programme considered paintings and sculptures produced after her death by such artists as Mark Kostabi and Kumiko Shimizu that treated her, Warhol fashion, as a pop icon.

Diana's sudden, violent death on 31 August 1997 prompted an avalanche of grief in Britain and in many nations around the world. (That grief was surely partly fuelled by guilt: the paparazzi would not have been hounding her if it had not been for the fact that millions of readers bought the newspapers in which their photos appeared. Thus, every fan of Diana was complicit in her death.) It was not long before demands were made for memorials to be erected and entrepreneurs began to generate commemorative merchandise, and hundreds of fans and fine artists began to produce paintings and sculptures about her. Mark P. Costa, for instance, produced a bronze and marble sculpture entitled *Princess Diana Ascending a Staircase* (presumably to heaven) in 1997. In Moscow, in July 2001, the Georgian monumental sculptor Zurab Tsereteli (b. 1934) unveiled an academic style, two-metre high, bronze statue of Diana holding a bouquet of flowers. Destined for a 'Museum of Modern Art' Tsereteli has established in Moscow, it was characterised by one reporter as 'a cross between Catherine the Great and a Georgian Milkmaid'.[40] Collectors of Tsereteli's sculptures have included President George Bush, Prime Minister Margaret Thatcher, Pope John Paul II and Robert DeNiro!

André Durand (b. 1950), a Canadian artist of Irish and French extraction who was trained in Paris and is based in London, has stated that Diana became his muse in 1981 and since then he has created several paintings about her. To gain a likeness he worked from photographs because he only met Diana once before her marriage to Prince Charles. The so-called 'Windsor Series' also includes pictures of Charles and sons William and Harry. Durand has been described as 'the only man alive to portray the royal family in situations more bizarre than their troubled reality'. He has remarked that he 'likes to have fun and make beautiful pictures'.

Durand is a commercially successful portrait painter noted also for a stream of allegorical, mythological and historical pictures executed in an exaggerated Italian Renaissance style. His melding of ancient and contemporary imagery is an attempt to bridge the gap between past and present, and the divide between high art and popular culture. His practice is theoretically justified by a neomodernist manifesto, which asserts: 'Neomodernism precedes and supersedes post-modernism.'

In 1987, Durand depicted Diana in the middle of a complex composition entitled *Votive Offering* in which she pays a hospital visit to the first female American Aids sufferer. In 1996, he showed Diana standing alongside Mario Molino, of the Italian Da Mario Restaurant, London, as Molino presented her with a special pizza entitled 'Pizza Diana'. This was also the title of Durand's painting. (Rather than being paid in money, the artist asked for £15,000 worth of food!) In the same year, Durand painted *Eclipse*, in which Diana was represented as a Roman goddess dancing on a crystal ball floating in the ocean. One of Durand's friends, the publicist Max Clifford, had suggested the idea of Diana dancing – and an ancient relief sculpture in Berlin of a Spartan woman supplied an iconographic source.

A second, more elaborate version of this painting, started within days of Diana's death, was entitled *Fortuna*. It showed Diana half-naked, with her breasts exposed and her hair blowing in the wind, enveloped in a swirl of blue drapery, in the guise of the Roman goddess of chance, fate, luck and fertility. One of her symbols was a sphere. Fortuna guided ships on voyages and this is why Durand employed an ocean setting with crashing waves, leaping dolphins and basking hippocampi (seahorses with fishy tails) and Triton, another mythological god who rides the waves on the backs of sea creatures and carries a twisted conch shell. The picture is very similar in content and style to the academic painting *The Birth of Venus* by George Spencer Watson (1869–1934) in the collection of the Russell Cotes Art Gallery, Bournemouth.

**31. André Durand, *Fortuna*, 2000.**
Painting, oil on canvas, 203.2 x 203.2 cm. London: artist's collection.
Photo © Camera Press/André Durand.

In September 2000, Durand's exuberant confection was unveiled at the Stanley Picker Gallery, Kingston University where he had been an artist-in-residence. Koo Stark, an actress, photographer, former consort of Prince Andrew and minor celebrity, performed the unveiling ceremony. Predictably, the 'topless' representation provoked consternation, condemnations and intense media interest. Durand argued that his use of the Princess reflected the heavenly status she had achieved in her lifetime. He added: 'Diana is an icon for the new millennium, regardless of what is said about her personality. She is an inspiration to me and to others ... she had goddess status and *Fortuna* reflects that.'[41] An article about Durand and *Fortuna* appeared in *Hello!* magazine and the website devoted to his work received thousands of hits.[42]

In 1999, Art Studio Demetz, an Italian workshop that specialises in ecclesiastical art, carved an over life-sized sculpture, *Lady Diana as a Madonna*, from lime wood and then coloured it. Demetz is represented by artist Luigi Baggi who employs the curious slogan 'Daily life work to become really art'. The carving was specially commissioned for the exhibition *Heaven: An Exhibition that will Break your Heart* (Düsseldorf Kunsthalle and Liverpool Tate Gallery, 1999), devised by the Israeli curator Doreet Levitte Harten. Although carved by hand, the artisans who made the figure were not interested in personal expression and originality – indeed, apart from the face, the statue conformed to a type that could be ordered by customers via a catalogue. (The Catholic Church, which once commissioned art from the finest artists in Europe, now tolerates kitsch.) This statue made explicit the desire of so many to treat the Princess as a saint, as a religious icon to be venerated. (Of course, some of the time she had behaved in a saint-like manner via the humanitarian acts she performed and the charities and good causes she had supported.) Diana, attired in long red and blue robes, clasped her hands together piously and gazed up towards heaven above. Pace Oscar Wilde, one would have to have a heart of stone not to laugh at this sentimental figure, which according to critic Richard Cork was 'strangely pallid, wholly lacking the charisma exerted by Diana herself'.[43]

When the sculpture was displayed in Liverpool, it upset the Christian pop singer Cliff Richard, a local bishop, an ex-Member of Parliament and leading art critics. The figure and the exhibition were condemned as 'deeply offensive, frivolous, an exercise in vulgarity, tasteless, shallow, meaningless, empty, infantile ... artists should hang their heads in shame ... they have become technological giants but remain moral pygmies ... the British art establishment is scraping the bottom of the barrel ... a disgusting blasphemy against the human mind'. However, reports of the controversial nature of the exhibits in the press did have the positive effect of boosting attendance.

**32. Luigi Baggi,** *Lady Diana as a Madonna,* **1999.**
Sculpture, painted lime wood, 69.5 x 186 cm.
Producer: Demetz Factory. Photo courtesy of Luigi Baggi.

The complainers seemed unwilling to admit the truth of the exhibition's premise:

> Celebrities, supermodels and pop stars are now idolised and adored as once were saints and angels and many worship at the graves of the famous, at pop concerts, clubs and fashion shows … physical perfection is now suffered for and valued more highly than spiritual perfection. Glory has become glamour, innocence has become youth, virtue is money, and paradise is a beach holiday … in *Heaven* the famous are graced and the glamorous are blessed … salvation is found in shopping malls and paradise is promised in tourist resorts … [it] shows the crossover of religion and popular culture in art.

These descriptions of contemporary society may be unpalatable but they are surely indisputable. A more valid objection to the show would have been the absence of any art overtly critical of celebrity culture.

Koons' Michael Jackson ceramic also featured in this exhibition plus a large wall painting in acrylic of the word 'glamour' by the Swiss artist Sylvie Fleury, and a Renaissance-style picture by the 'new academy' Russian artist Olga Tobreluts of the baby-faced American film star Leonardo DiCaprio. (DiCaprio, it may be remembered, played the role of a penniless young artist in the Hollywood disaster epic *Titanic* [1997].) Tobreluts employs computers to combine images from the past and the present. In this instance, she superimposed DiCaprio's visage on a Saint Sebastian painted by Antonello da Messina in 1475. Her desire was to see the faces of her contemporaries in the features of old portraits. Another tender portrait of DiCaprio was supplied by Karen Kilimnik, an American, self-taught artist.

Kilimnik (b. 1955), like Peyton, established an international reputation during the 1990s despite the fact that her early work was considered so dismal no art school would admit her. In 1992, she constructed a mixed-media installation based on 'The Hellfire Club' episode of the cult British 1960s television series *The Avengers*. Her later writings, drawings and paintings were deliberately tentative and resembled the jottings in a teenage girl's journal. Besides DiCaprio, she has depicted Princess Di (wearing her low cut black dress), the models Twiggy and Kate Moss (the British painter Gary Hume has also created an image of Moss based on a fashion photo), Alicia Silverstone, star of the movie *The Crush* (1993), and the British actor

Hugh Grant.[44] Her portraits, according to Jonathan Jones, 'capture the madness of fandom – the illusion that we know this person – by tapping into the devotional use of icons in orthodox Christianity'.[45]

**33. Karen Kilimnik,** *Twiggy at School in Cambridge,* **1977.**
Detail of painting, water-soluble oil colour on canvas, 51 x 41 cm.
© Karen Kilimnik. Photo courtesy of Emily Tsingon Gallery, London.

Art critic Adrian Searle was not impressed by the art and the argument of *Heaven*: 'No one seems to notice how badly it [the Koons] is sculpted, how wretched it is, or how feeble the idea it is to have pin-up pop stars and fashion models transformed into Renaissance painted icons ... I think I'm going to vomit.'[46]

Further artistic reactions to the deceased Diana appeared in the exhibition *Temple of Diana,* curated by the British artist Neal Brown, held at the Blue Gallery, London in July 1999. This show included works in several media by Tracey Emin, Harriet Guinness, Chantel

Joffe, Justin Mortimer, Adam Nankervis, Hugo Rittson, Klaus Whener, Caroline Younger and Alison Jackson (her images will be discussed in Chapter 3). Critic Jonathan Jones thought the artists were too adulatory and their works tame, apart that is from Jackson's, which he found had the redeeming quality of irony. The show, he considered, was 'an example of artists reaching out to popular culture only to expose the smallness of their own parameters'.[47]

A more critical approach to the subject of Diana was revealed in March 2000 when the left-wing, British artist John Keane (b. 1954) mounted an exhibition of paintings and prints at Flowers East Gallery, London, featuring images of her plus two rich and powerful men: Rupert Murdoch, Australian-born media mogul and Charles Saatchi, famous art collector. Only their heads and shoulders were portrayed and Keane clearly used photos as his sources. Many paintings were smeared and streaked horizontally as if they had been scraped across with the edge of a board while the paint was still wet. Some portraits showed his subjects blinking in order to evoke multiple associations: 'from the mild invective suggested by a play on the word itself, through the implication of blinking in a power struggle as giving way, and to the actual imagery of closed eyes and their suggestion of vulnerability and even death'.[48] In the case of Diana, her closed eyes could signify death, or the reaction of a woman protecting herself from camera flash, or her famous downcast glance. In *Untitled* (oil and collage, 1999), Keane depicted a strained-looking Diana flanked by images of crowds applauding. In *A Bigger Killing* (oil on canvas, 1999), a very similar image of Diana was juxtaposed against Murdoch with his eyes open and a ruthless expression on his face. This juxtaposition and the exhibition's title – *Making a Killing* – made it obvious that Keane considered Diana had been the victim of the kind of media Murdoch owned and profited from. Saatchi was included in the show because he was an exploiter of art.[49] Keane explained to one reporter that he depicted powerful individuals in order to wrest back a bit of control: 'It's a sort of voodoo deal, where you make an image of your demon.'[50]

Meanwhile, the collectable, gift, souvenir and memorabilia industries churned out numerous Diana products such as replica Di sunglasses and decorative plates with her smiling face on them. Indian restaurants in London hung Bollywood-style portraits of her on their walls to curry favour with diners. The painter D. John Brown retailed insipid watercolours of the island in a lake on the Althorp family estate, Northamptonshire, where Diana is buried – *Diana –*

**34. John Keane, *A Bigger Killing*, 1999.**
Painting, oil on canvas, 90 x 168 cm.
© John Keane, photo Gareth Winters,
courtesy of Flowers East Gallery, London.

*Her Final Resting Place.* The estate also has a Diana Museum, which opened in July 1998, containing relics such as her toys, school reports and the ludicrous wedding dress designed by Elizabeth Emanuel. Diana souvenirs are sold in the Museum's gift shop but Earl Charles Spencer insists they are 'tasteful'. He does not want Althorp to become as tacky as Graceland, Presley's shrine in Tennessee.[51]

However, by the second anniversary of Diana's death, interest in her had declined and some Britons were regretting their 1997 emotional outburst. The official Diana Princess of Wales Memorial Fund dropped the idea of a garden in Hyde Park with a 300-feet statue. Instead, a bland, low-level water feature, an 80-metre stone moat, by the American landscape designer Kathryn Gustafson has been decided upon. In addition, the Royal National Rose Society announced, in July 2001, a £20 million scheme for a six-acre rose garden in remembrance of Diana in St Albans.

Since Diana was no longer around, the paparazzi, royalty voyeurs and the media switched their attention to Prince Charles and his mistress Camilla Parker-Bowles and to the handsome Prince William who is already a heart-throb as far as many young women are concerned. When William marries (assuming he is heterosexual), no doubt the media will respond with the same frenzy they showed during Diana's lifetime.

## Celebrity Art

Numerous images of celebrities in the forms of original drawings and paintings, prints and posters are currently offered for sale via galleries and auctions advertised on the Internet, hence the label 'celebrity art'. They are bought, one suspects, by people who are more interested in the celebrities represented than in the art itself. In the main, the images are naturalistic in style, copied from photographs and of low aesthetic quality. Those who produce such images include: Scott Bateman, Michael Bell, Aaron Binder, Richard Hawkins, Jon Hul, Claude Julian, Cindy McLachlan, Marilyn Michaels and Ron Suchiu. Bell, an American, offers a 'Celebrity Prints' series for sale that includes portraits of Frank Sinatra and Elvis Presley but he has also represented New York gangsters such as John Gotti, once head of the Gambino crime family, whom he calls a 'Mobstar'. In the case of Gotti, Bell claims that his art work immortalising this 'Man of Honour' was intended to benefit Gotti's supporters and to help him get a new, 'fair' trial. (Gotti was tried in 1992 and sentenced to multiple life terms for several murders. He died in prison in 2002.) Curiously, Bell does not distinguish between real and fictional gangsters: he has also depicted Al Pacino as the Godfather, Robert DeNiro as a Goodfella, and James Gandolfini as Tony Soprano, star of the acclaimed television crime series *The Sopranos*. Of course, as far as most consumers of the mass media are concerned, fact, fiction and faction all appear side-by-side and so the differences between them tend to be elided.

## Relics and Shrines

Art, religion and celebrity culture may seem to be three separate, autonomous realms whereas in fact, they overlap. For instance, the cult of sacred figures and idolatry (the worship of objects or totems representing or associated with the cult figures); the presence of temples and shrines dedicated to the cult figures that require regular visits, pilgrimages and rituals such as candlelight processions; the wearing of images or symbols of the cult figures on the body. Although most examples cited will be derived from the Christian religion, the observations have a wider application because they are characteristic of many religions and cults around the world. Jan Koenot and Rogan P. Taylor are two writers who have explored the subject of the overlap between rock music and religion at greater length.[52]

Ecstatic experiences can be gained in crowded religious gatherings and in rock music concerts or while watching sporting contests. In black American culture, the gospel singing and music associated with church services has profoundly influenced pop music. Works of fine art are normally addressed to individuals and small groups rather than to mass audiences but many writers have compared the hushed and reverential atmosphere of art museums to that of churches. (Fine artists specialising in the mode of performance art can reach mass audiences if their work is popular enough. Laurie Anderson is an example: she gave stage performances to theatre audiences and issued best-selling records.) Millions of people attend museums on Sundays rather than church services and find in art spiritual experiences that earlier generations found in religion. Of course, some museums of art possess altarpieces and icons that were previously displayed in churches.

In the realm of art, the equivalent to the cults of Christian saints and martyrs are the cults of dead artists such as van Gogh, Kahlo, et al. The equivalent of healers and prophets are artist-shamans such as Joseph Beuys and Yves Klein. In the realm of celebrity culture, the cult figures are the major entertainers, especially those who died prematurely. The appeal and power of images and statues of the latter has already been discussed. Such representations clearly resemble the painted icons of Jesus, Mary and others found in Catholic churches; the highly stylised character of icons also accords with the simplified images of celebrities such as those of Monroe by Warhol (who was a practising Catholic) and of Blur by Julian Opie. In 1993, the artist Kathleen Kondilas (b. 1948) made explicit the connection between the icons of the Church and the icons of the media by combining an image of Monroe with that of a Byzantine Madonna and child.

Fanatical fans of top sportsmen and women venerate them as if they were gods. For example, Manchester United supporters used to refer to the French footballer Eric Cantona (b. 1966) as 'God' or 'Eric the King'. Cantona was a brilliant but hot-tempered striker who played for United from 1992 to 1997. He also painted abstractions and aspired to be a poet and philosopher. After he retired from English soccer, he turned to acting in movies and playing beach football: a Renaissance man, no less. The fans' street humour and hyperbole inspired the Manchester painter Michael J. Browne

**35. Michael J. Browne,** *The Art of the Game,* **1997.**
Painting, oil on canvas, 304 x 243 cm.
France: Collection of Eric Cantona. © Michael J. Browne.

(b. 1963) to produce a large canvas entitled *The Art of the Game* in which Cantona, wearing a red toga, was portrayed as Christ resurrected. The painting, which was based on sketches and specially taken photographs, was also a post-modern, historicist pastiche of two famous Italian Renaissance works by Piero della Francesca (*Resurrection*, c. 1472) and Mantegna (*Triumph of Caesar*, c.1486). Robin Gibson has remarked:

As well as Cantona's perceived divinity, the allegory relates more specifically to his triumphant return to redeem the misfortunes of Manchester United in 1995–6 after a fate worse (in football terms) than death – a year's suspension for kicking a jeering fan at Selhurst Park. Piero's sleeping sentries who should have been guarding the tomb are replaced by the slightly more watchful figures of Cantona's team-mates ... Phil Neville, David Beckham, Nicky Butt and Gary Neville ... Browne transforms Julius Caesar into the team's manager Sir Alex Ferguson [background, top right]. On one level, this painting is an elaborate satire on the excessive adulation afforded to modern football players ... [but] no mere satire would be worth the hundreds of hours of work that Browne clearly put into this painting, and his genuine admiration both for Cantona and for two great masterpieces of art shines through with touching transparency.[53]

The figures in Browne's hyperrealist picture are static and dressed in historical costumes; consequently, there is no depiction of the game of football or Cantona's skill on the ball. This bizarre, tongue-in-cheek canvas was first exhibited in April 1997 in Manchester City Art Gallery; some Christian leaders were offended by the representation of Cantona as Christ and the painting was attacked in print as 'tasteless' and 'idolatrous'. One journalist thought 'the deification of a mere sportsman' was the sign of 'a decadent age'. Bryan Appleyard identified a crisis of modern times – the end of the hero – and a crisis in art too, hence Browne's reliance on irony and borrowed, historical imagery.[54] Ferguson defended the painting by arguing that footballers are 'people's heroes'. Three years later, when displayed in a show at London's National Portrait Gallery, supporters of 'the reds' visited it. They admired and analysed the painting, while paying scant attention to other exhibits.[55] Cantona owns the painting and is rumoured to have paid £75,000 for it.

At certain times in history, and in certain religions still, the representation of deities has been forbidden or there have been outbreaks of iconoclasm (image breaking). One reason for these phenomena is surely the fact that when someone venerates an image there is uncertainty about what is being worshipped: is it the object itself (as in a modern art museum) or the personage being represented? What is common to religious icons and celebrity images is the belief that they are vehicles or channels to the persons depicted; they bring viewer and idol closer together.

Collections of relics were a feature of medieval Christendom. They included such items as fragments of the true cross, the image of Christ's face on Veronicas, or his body on the Turin Shroud, and the blood and bones of saints and martyrs. Relics were often stored in specially designed jewelled caskets called reliquaries. Clerics in charge of cathedrals were keen to establish a collection of major relics because they attracted masses of pilgrims and therefore revenue. (Arguably, pilgrimages were the tourist industry of the Middle Ages and the depositories of relics were the forerunners of public art galleries and museums.) Pilgrims often left votive offerings – the result of a pledge, or vow or thanks for some divine intervention – in the form of jewelled mementoes, and those who visited Canterbury Cathedral took home with them souvenirs in the form of tin lead, purse-shaped ampullae containing holy water that had been in contact with the blood of the martyr St Thomas. These were worn on the body. For most Christians, the image of Christ on the cross, or just the cross itself, is a powerful symbol and many of them wear small crosses around their necks to publicise their religious affiliation and as personal security devices. (Madonna, the pop singer raised as a Catholic who, in the eyes of the Church, has committed many sins, often wore several at once.) Fans of celebrities also adorn themselves with tattoos and wear T-shirts screen-printed with images of their idols or pin badges on their chests.

Contacts with icons and relics were considered by believers to be beneficial because miracles were associated with them and they were thought to have powers of health and protection. Even today, ill and disabled Catholics visit Lourdes in the hope of cures. Virtually every year there are press reports about a statue in a Catholic country, which is manifesting strange symptoms such as bleeding or weeping and is immediately credited with miracle-working properties.

Relics associated with celebrities include their personal possessions such as clothes, letters and musical instruments and, in the case of painters, items such as brushes, tubes of pigment, palettes and easels. Such relics are sold in prestigious auction houses and collected assiduously by fans and preserved in private collections but also in such public places as Hard Rock cafes, Halls of Fame, memorial museums, and secular shrines such as Graceland. In the case of artists, the equivalent to a shrine is the artist's home or studio that is preserved intact after the artist's death and becomes a tourist attraction.

In the 1999 exhibition *Heaven*, real celebrity relics were displayed: a bustier decorated with jewellery, plastic toys, medallions, etc., worn by Madonna in the film *Desperately Seeking Susan* (1985), and a glittering bejewelled glove thought to have been worn by Michael Jackson at the 1984 Grammy Award Ceremony. In addition, there were simulated relics such as three satin scarves supposedly stained with Elvis' sweat – Elvis used to throw such scarves to his audiences so that they could own some trace of his body – made by the American artist Jeffrey Valance in 1993. (Valance, ironically, was brought up as a Lutheran, and Martin Luther was opposed to the cult of relics.) Since there were many fake relics in Europe during the Middle Ages, it seems only appropriate that there should be simulated celebrity relics in our own time.

Certain stage costumes worn by stars are particularly well known and sought after by collectors. For instance, the Union Jack flag mini-dress worn by Geri Halliwell when she was Ginger Spice was sold at a 1998 charity auction in London for £36,200 and is now in the collection of the Hard Rock Hotel, Las Vegas. In demand also are the kitsch, white, jewel-encrusted jumpsuits with high collars, wide belts and bell-bottom trousers worn by Elvis Presley during the 1970s when he was overweight and in decline. Bill Belew of Hollywood designed over 60 such suits and many are preserved in Graceland. In 1992, the painter Alexander Guy (b. 1962, Scotland) depicted one, bloated and empty, hanging in the position of Christ on the cross. (Presumably, the body of Elvis had already ascended to Heaven.) Drips of blood ran down from where the hands would have been. The oil painting was entitled *Crucifixion*. No doubt, some Christians found the equation of Elvis' martyrdom (his artistic degeneration and his premature death from food and drugs binges at the age of 42) with that of Christ blasphemous or at least in poor taste.

Also displayed in *Heaven* were documentary photographs by Ralph Burns taken during several annual Memorial Day ceremonies held at Graceland. The photos revealed that some Elvis fans own mannequins of him, others deposit flowers and hold candlelit vigils, others wear T-shirts bearing his image and carve inscriptions or write messages to him on a Memorial Wall, and others impersonate him. Finally, there are fans who think he still lives. Those who believe this is literally true clearly share the Christian belief in resurrection.

Guy Gilbert, a documentary filmmaker, made a series of films in 2000 for BBC2 television on the subject of the fanatical fans of dead rock stars who venerate them by visiting their places of death, graves or secular shrines. He filmed 17 such places in Britain and the United States. Identification with a rock star usually occurs during a fan's

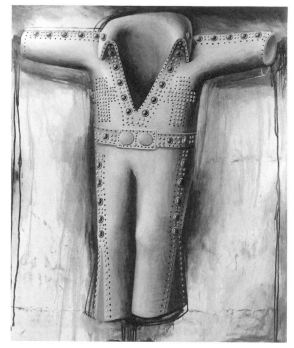

**36. Alexander Guy,** *Crucifixion,* **1992.**
Painting, oil on canvas, 208 x 175 cm. Glasgow: collection of Gallery
of Modern Art. © Alexander Guy. Photo © Glasgow Museums.

youth and is a response to the aesthetic and emotional impact of the
performer's music and appearance. Once the star is dead, that
experience can be revisited repeatedly via sound and video
recordings but the star's absence means that such moments are
tinged with nostalgia and sadness. As Tim Cumming noted in an
article on Gilbert:

> what they [the fans] feel is, I think, the most basic of emotions
> – grief for what has passed and what can never return ... And
> what they hear in the music of their idol is a voice from the
> burning bush, something ancient and eternal. With the songs
> as their guide, the faithful come to pay homage to keep
> themselves young and their dreams alive.[56]

Some dedicated fans establish, in their homes, private shrines to
their idols. In 1991, the Californian artist Joanne Stephens (b. 1933)

created a seven-feet tall, mixed-media assemblage/altar/shrine entitled *Homage to Elvis*. Stephens describes it and explains how it came about as follows:

> The altar rests on a 1960s' TV console cabinet with a vignette of black and white Elvis in front of a barn, singing to cattle (both a comment on audience and also the fact that he was 'just a farm boy at heart'). Also, the altar is lit with lights projecting from 45 rpm gold records … when the knob on the TV is turned on the voice of Elvis crooning 'Love Me Tender' and other such songs recorded on a continuous tape from an old scratch 33 record [is heard]. What motivated my interest in the subject: my local thrift store called to say they had a bunch of Elvis memorabilia and was I interested? I went and bought some, including the Mexican-plaster statue of Elvis. I was not a 'fan' as such, even though he was of my generation. I proposed to do a satirical presentation: mock-glory, dusted with the gray dust of age. But as I worked I played the old record to put me in the mood. I succumbed to his magic. It took hold of the work, which can still be read as satire; the angels singing with him, the urns dripping jewels, (to signify the wealth brought to him) the screaming girls on the pedestals … but in the end, regardless of initial intent, it became – a 'Homage to Elvis'.[57]

Stephens' assemblage was included in the 1994 travelling exhibition *Elvis + Marilyn: 2 × Immortal*, and was praised by critics and reproduced in the Sunday *New York Times* Arts and Leisure section.

While some fine artists pretend to be fans of the celebrities they represent, others are genuine followers. The Australian-born artist Kathy Temin (b. 1968, Sydney) now resident in New York, for example, has admired the television actress and pop music performer Kylie Minogue since 1987 when Kylie appeared in the internationally-popular soap opera *Neighbours*. (Temin and 'the pop princess' are the same age.) For the *Art>Music: Rock, Pop, Techno* exhibition held in Sydney in 2001, Temin devised a bright pink installation entitled *My Kylie Collection* which featured Kylie magazines, books, jigsaw puzzle, compact discs and photographs plus furniture, mirror tiles, rugs, synthetic fur, etc., intended to evoke a teenage girl's bedroom. A video monitor played Kylie's music videos and a computer linked to a website about her enabled viewers to keep track of her weekly activities. Temin also displayed a number of two-

**37. Joanne Stephens, *Homage to Elvis,* 1991.**
Assemblage, mixed-media, 213.5 x 109 x 53 cm.
Las Vegas, Nevada: House of Blues. Photo courtesy of the artist.

dimensional panels handcrafted from felt that depicted Kylie in a variety of poses and outfits. (Kylie has changed her image almost as often as Madonna.) Temin comes from a family with experience of the textile industry and she has made examples of 'soft sculpture'. According to curator Sue Cramer, 'being a fan is about seeing yourself reflected in the one that you adore'. However, the lack of critical distance on Temin's part towards her subject matter is disturbing – an instance of arrested development?

A lavishly illustrated book devoted to Kylie published in 1999 also included contributions from a number of fine artists; for instance, Tim Noble and Sue Webster, Pierre et Gilles, Wolfgang Tilmans and Sam Taylor-Wood.[58]

It is clear from the above that although agnostics and atheists may feel that magic, religion, superstition and witchcraft are all in decline because of rationalism, science and secularism, they have merely been displaced to the realms of art and celebrity culture.

# 3

# Simulation and Celebrities

As is well known, many fans enjoy impersonating their idols by copying their dress, body language and stage performances. Such fans are sometimes referred to as 'tribute artists'. Impersonators of a particular idol also assemble in order to hold competitions to see who is the best. Elvis Presley once secretly entered such a competition but did not win! It has been estimated that there are now circa 35,000 Elvis impersonators. Patty Carroll (b. 1946), an American artist and photographer based in Chicago who was once an Elvis fan, used her camera in the early 1990s to document Elvis impersonators and then presented the resulting colour prints in multi-image panels. An example was included in the *Elvis + Marilyn: 2 × Immortal* exhibition.[1]

In May 1999, two European photojournalists travelled across the United States for three weeks dressed in Elvis jumpsuits and capes under the name 'Elvis and Presley'. (They even visited Graceland.) Robert Huber (b. 1969, Belgium) played 'Elvis' and took colour photographs of Stephen Vanfleteren (b. 1972, Switzerland) who played 'Presley' and took black and white photographs of Huber. Their photographs have since been exhibited in art galleries and published in book form.[2] Huber confessed that he was 'the worst of all fakes' because he was imitating an impersonator who could not sing or dance. The purpose of this absurd performance and journey was to discover and document the reactions of the American public – which ranged from amusement to disapproval – to the double reappearance of Elvis.

Earlier, a number of biopics about artists were mentioned. Clearly, in these cases actors were called upon to impersonate the artists whose lives were being filmed. Compared to the number of film and rock stars impersonations, instances of members of the public impersonating artists are rare; nevertheless, they have occurred. For example, Helen Harrison, Director of the Pollock-Krasner House and Study Center on Long Island reports seeing, periodically, men dressed like Pollock in blue denim and smoking cigarettes accompanied by friends with cameras visiting Pollock's old property. Harrison was certain, from the body language simulating Pollock's and the photo-sessions, that Pollock impersonations were taking place. Her observations can be found in an anthology of texts that is itself a tribute to Pollock's art and life.[3]

Professional models, registered with the look-alike and sound-alike agencies found in major cities, also exist and earn a living by simulating the famous at private parties, corporate conventions and in advertisements. Some look-alikes maintain their own websites; for instance, Chris America (a stage name) who is a Madonna impersonator. Hiring look-alikes is normally much cheaper that hiring the stars they imitate, but it has been reported that a George W. Bush look-alike can currently earn more per hour than the actual President of the United States.

Increasingly, celebrity impersonators are becoming recognised and valued as entertainers in their own right. Janna Joos, manager of the agency International Celebrity Images, explains their popularity as follows: 'It's just that aura of celebrity, whether it's real or fake. Clients are buying into a fantasy.'[4] Bea Fogelman is the author of two books documenting leading celebrity impersonators (see Bibliography) and they have formed a professional organisation: the International Guild of Celebrity Impersonators and Tribute Artists (IGCITA).

Fine artists are not immune from the desire to imitate celebrities. In this chapter, two examples – one American and one Japanese – will be considered: Cindy Sherman and Yasumasa Morimura. The work of the British artist Alison Jackson will also be discussed because she employs celebrity look-alikes in her photographs and films.

## Cindy Sherman

Sherman (b. 1954, Glen Ridge, New Jersey) studied painting and photography at the State University of New York, Buffalo.[5] One of her tutors was the noted directorial photographer Les Krims. At Art College, she painted self-portraits and copied mass media images. In 1975, she created a set of five photographs – *Untitled A–E* – that was to prove prescient. The photographs were head-and-shoulder self-portraits but in each, Sherman assumed different facial expressions and wore different make-up, hairstyles and hats. As a student, she also enjoyed buying second-hand clothes and dressing up and going out as various characters. The characteristics that were to inform her art – metamorphoses of appearance and identity, dressing up and posing for the camera – therefore, were established very early.

Sherman, of course, later became famous in the art world for her 69 black and white photographs called *Untitled Film Stills* that she commenced in New York in 1977 and concluded in 1980. These photographs were based on publicity pictures for 1950s Hollywood B-Movie melodramas and film noir, and European art cinema but they were not exact copies of existing film stills and the parts Sherman played in different clothes and settings did not mimic particular actresses. Typically, an image evoked a mood, a sense of foreboding and mystery, and a narrative interrupted. The fictional actresses Sherman impersonated were of the following kinds: chic starlet at a seaside hideaway; domesticated sex kitten; an attractive librarian; an ice-cold sophisticate; a hot-blooded woman of the people; a blonde alone in the city at night. The women were always alone and frequently bored, pensive, passive or insecure.

The vagueness of the references and the use of the non-informative title *Untitled* indicated that Sherman wanted to harness the projective power of viewers, the knowledge of cinema they already possessed. Cinemagoers mentally and emotionally identify with the roles of characters in melodramas. Some viewers, when they leave the cinema, also imitate the stars and fashions they admired on screen. Sherman's response was to re-enact cinematic fantasies and desires and then to document them via the medium of photography. Anne Friedberg has claimed: 'In Sherman's work, the viewer recognises not the celebrity but the codes of celebrity.'[6]

However, in 1982, Sherman did impersonate a named actress – Marilyn Monroe – while kneeling on the floor and dressed informally in jeans and a shirt. The ensuing photograph served as a poster for a performance of Lorenzo Severo's opera *Marilyn* in Kassel, Germany. The image also appeared on the cover of the 'Desire' issue of the British, post-modern magazine *ZG* (short for Zeitgeist).[7]

As explained earlier, Madonna has taken a close interest in Sherman's *oeuvre* and has engaged in a comparable chameleon-like endeavour. In Sherman's colour photograph *Untitled # 131*, dated 1983, the artist appears in an outfit that may have influenced Madonna. She wears a gold-coloured, corset-like dress with ribbed breast cones similar to that worn by the pop star during the *Blond Ambition* tour of 1990. Jean-Paul Gaultier (b. 1952) was the designer of Madonna's costume.

**38. Cindy Sherman, 'Marilyn', 1982.**
Cover of *ZG* magazine No. 7, 'Desire' Issue (1982). © Cindy Sherman.

Despite the fact that her simulated film stills have been criticised
for technical faults such as careless processing, overexposure and
being out of focus, they generated much public interest and were
sought after by curators, dealers, collectors and publishers. Following
her early success, Sherman produced several substantial bodies of
work – large format colour photos – based on such themes as fairy
tales, fashion, pornography, horror and the history of art, which
prompted mixed receptions from critics. The history of art portraits
dating from 1989 to 1990 included some photographs based on
particular paintings by Caravaggio, Jean Fouquet and Raphael. In
them, Sherman dressed in the costumes and cosmetics of the individuals the three painters portrayed: Bacchus, Madonna of Melun
and La Fornarina. This particular series is cited here because of a

similar project that Morimura undertook during the 1980s (see below). In some of her later photographs, Sherman used masks and prosthetic mannequins rather than her own body. In fact, she gradually eliminated herself from her photographs. The staged scenes became increasingly elaborate, grotesque and obscene as Sherman sought to disturb and wrong-foot critics and gallery goers. In 1997, Sherman's long-term fascination with cinema reached a logical conclusion when she directed a horror movie entitled *Office Killer*. It received unfavourable reviews.

Sherman's pictorial impersonations prompted many critical commentaries, some complex verbiage and divergent opinions as to their political significance. (Did they affirm and reiterate sexist images of women, male ways of seeing women, or did they subvert them? Did they disempower or empower women?) Since they were depictions of women acting out different looks and roles, they were of special interest to feminists and those concerned with masquerade and the gaze. Sherman was admired because she was both a female creator and a female subject. Confronted by so many various images of one individual, the question 'which is the real Cindy Sherman?' was often asked. (In portraits taken by press photographers, Sherman generally appeared awkward and self-conscious, like a snail minus its shell.) Sherman herself noted that her identity did not consist of a single self but several: the self in the country, the professional self, the self in the studio, etc., and Judith Williamson argued that by offering the viewer so many characters, Sherman undermined any attempt to fix her identity. In a sceptical account of Sherman, Nadine Lemmon observed: 'while critics applaud Sherman's work for deconstructively denying the totality of a "real Cindy", the meaning of her work is dependent upon the concept of the celebrity "Cindy". Simultaneously, critics partially negate her "deconstruction", mythologizing her as the autonomous "artist-genius", harkening back to the modernist heroization of the creative individual.'[8]

Sherman's photographs did not in fact reveal her inner being or expose her private life (as Tracey Emin's art does) because what she explored were the images of women and female types that exist in the public sphere, in such media as feature films and fashion photographs. She once remarked: 'I am trying to make people recognise something of themselves rather than me.' Personal and public, of course, overlap to some degree because our lives and behaviour are conditioned by our experience of mass media representations. By raising the viewer's awareness of their influence and artifice, Sherman stimulated much reflection and provided enlightenment in addition to visual pleasure.

## Yasumasa Morimura

Morimura, a male Japanese artist – one of the best known in his native land – was born in 1951 in the city of Osaka where he has lived and worked ever since. During the first half of the 1970s, he trained at the Kyoto International Design Institute and the Design Department of the Kyoto City University of Arts. Since the mid 1980s, he has delighted in masquerading as famous individuals from the realms of fine art and entertainment, high and popular culture. Although Morimura's images purport to be 'self-portraits', his face is generally expressionless and reveals nothing personal about him except that he enjoys dressing up as historical figures and female movie stars, and altering his gender and identity. Morimura has remarked that when he wakes in the morning he is wearing his non-fictional face but when he adds make-up he becomes a fictional character. He much prefers the fictional to the non-fictional face and believes outward changes alters the inner self, so that, for instance, if one dons a priest's clothes one feels more priest-like.[9] Morimura, apparently, is so dissatisfied with his real self that he seeks to escape it by dressing up as other characters.

Information for his elaborate and meticulous reconstructions was derived from art reproductions and glamour photographs. After constructing sets, dressing up and posing as his subjects, Morimura made – with the help of assistants – a record via the medium of colour photography; however, he thinks of himself as a fine artist rather than a photographer. (He has also made videos, sculptures and images via the popular Japanese 'print-club' machines – they are like photo-booths – which enable users to superimpose their own faces on those of famous individuals.) He began in 1985 with a reprise of van Gogh's famous self-portrait with a bandaged ear. Vincent was smoking a pipe but in Morimura's version, the pipe's smoke was painted on a backdrop. The brushwork of the original was re-interpreted via thick make-up. Morimura remarked: 'I do my painting on my face.' Clearly, he enjoyed playing illusionistic games. He followed the van Gogh with the *Self-Portrait as Art History* series. For the latter, he posed as the prostitute in the well-known Edouard Manet painting *Olympia* (1863) (he also played the role of the black maid standing in the background) and the Infanta Margarita in a painting by Diego Velasquez. The latter required the making of a three-dimensional wire and plaster dummy with a hole through which the artist could poke his head. In this series, the originals were evoked but new elements were also introduced. For example, when Morimura posed as Mona Lisa, his body was nude and pregnant; when he posed as the barmaid in Manet's *Bar at the Folies Bergère*, his body was naked and his arms were crossed; however, macabre sculptures of the barmaid's arms, severed at the elbow, still rested on the bar.

During the early 1990s, Morimura found a faster and easier method of insertion: he exploited computer graphics to add his face to old master images. For instance, his visage replaced that of all nine men portrayed in Rembrandt's 1632 canvas *Anatomy Lesson of Dr Tulp* (including the corpse being dissected). Apparently, the repetition was intended to evoke the Western racist opinion about Asians, that is, 'they all look alike'. In 1991, for the *Psychoborg* series, he used the same technique to superimpose his face on images of Michael Jackson (as he appeared in the horror music video 'Thriller') and Madonna.

In the summer of 2001, the Hara Museum in Japan mounted a show of new Morimura self-portraits – over 50 large-scale photographs plus videos and mixed-media works – this time paying homage to one of Madonna's artist-heroines: Frida Kahlo. Morimura's art-historical interventions may be regarded as a witty Oriental revenge against the dominance of the Western tradition of fine art.

Since the 1980s, Morimura's photographs have been displayed around the globe in one-man shows and featured in thematic exhibitions such as *Audrey Hepburn: A Woman, The Style*, shown in Italy, Australia and Japan between 1999 and 2001. Hepburn (1929–1993), a European of upper-class origin, was one of the most charming and elegant new film stars of the 1950s and 1960s: a beautiful but delicate, waiflike actress. Morimura imitated her wearing a full-length dress with a huge hat while holding a parasol – Hepburn was playing the role of Eliza Doolittle in *My Fair Lady* (1964). This image was part of the 1990s *Actress* series in which Morimura also impersonated the female movie stars Brigitte Bardot, Marlene Dietrich, Faye Dunaway, Rita Hayworth, Catherine Deneuve and Sylvie Kristel. In addition, he imitated Elizabeth Taylor in her famous role as Cleopatra, Vivien Leigh as Scarlett O'Hara in *Gone with the Wind*, Jane Fonda as Barbarella in the 1968 film of the same name, Liza

Minnelli as Sally Bowles in *Cabaret* (1972) and Jodie Foster playing the child prostitute Iris in *Taxi Driver* (1976). Morimura has appeared on the streets of Osaka in the guise of Jodie/Iris while giving handouts to passers by.

**39. Yasumasa Morimura,**
**'Self-Portrait (Actress)/After Liza Minnelli', 1996.**
Ilfochrome photograph, edition of 10, 120 x 90 cm.
© Yasumasa Morimura, courtesy of Natsuko Odate, Tokyo.

Several images were based on Monroe, the star Morimura regarded as the most important of the American actresses of the twentieth century, an era dominated by American mass culture, particularly that of Hollywood. Since he thought the great period of the movie actress was over, his project of re-creation could be considered nostalgic. The actress, he maintained without giving a reason, could now only be played by a man. One photograph mimicked Monroe with her skirt billowing up as in *The Seven Year Itch*. Morimura has also appeared in front of an audience performing this role; as a draught of air raised the skirt, he screamed at the top of his voice. The dress he wore was white but in a more disturbing variation, he wore a black dress. This time, as the skirt billowed, viewers could see that he was wearing nothing underneath apart from a false, erect pink penis.

Another Morimura photograph – *Self-Portrait (Actress) after Red Marilyn* – reprised a calendar pin-up taken by Tom Kelley in 1949 (also featured in the first issue of *Playboy* magazine, December 1953), which showed Monroe stark naked lying on red velvet. For this image, Morimura wore a long wig and artificial breasts. (The image has also been reproduced on a paper fan so that, as the fan opened and closed, the naked body was alternately revealed and concealed.) In August 1994, the picture was published in the first issue of *Panja*, a monthly pin-up magazine intended for young adult males. In this context, the image challenged expectations and subverted the masculine gaze of any heterosexual readers. However, what was the response of women to Morimura's *Actress* photographs? At least one Japanese woman – Kaori Chino – found them beautiful and empowering. She has argued that Morimura 'receives the violent masculine gaze often aimed at women ... laughs it away, and finally nullifies it ... [he] sides with women not merely in his appearance but in his thought'.[10]

Morimura has a slim body and a lugubrious face with a long nose but in costume and make-up, he was often quite convincingly like his models. Nevertheless, as already explained, he did not seek exact copies of his appropriated images. For instance, he gave some of his images a Japanese dimension by introducing cherry blossom and pagodas into the backgrounds.

Jorge Lopez has perceptively described the character and appeal of Morimura's *Actress* images:

The double movement of surrender and appropriation is a complex one where the mimetic impulse of the former is played out to near self-obliteration through his dramatic imperson-ation of film stars, while the latter is augmented by the 'turning Japanese' of Western icons. The real catch of this series consists of the likely complicity of the viewer. The photographic character of these self-portraits (where painting is perhaps only obliquely signalled through a generous use of make-up) highlights the directness of Morimura's invitation. In Michael Tausig's terms, Morimura's self-construction communicates 'a sensuous sense of the real, mimetically at one with what it attempts to represent.' And the object (s)he incarnates is unabashedly erotic. The result is a most provocative invitation to breach the propriety of aesthetic distance and indulge in the carnality of visual involvement. Morimura's images are more than just innocent two-dimensional surfaces. 'Actress' and 'Art History' proves that rather than rejecting invasive images, it may be more profitable to occupy them. Appropriation as political praxis means regaining cultural agency. The imitation of images may allow us to share in their power. That's the magic of mimesis.[11]

Aside from the example of homosexual drag queens, there were two precedents – one Western and one Eastern – for Morimura's transsexual behaviour: first, Marcel Duchamp's invention, in 1920, of a feminine alter ego called 'Rrose Sélavy' (in New York, Man Ray took a photograph of Duchamp dressed as Sélavy and Morimura has produced a self-portrait parody of this image: *Doublenage [Marcel]*); second, the historical tradition of men playing female parts in Japan's Kabuki theatre. Morimura has performed, sung and acted female roles on stage in Japan. He has collaborated with the stage director Yukio Ninagawa and the fashion designer Issei Miyake. There is also a long tradition in Japan of male poets pretending to be women, imagining female emotions.

Morimura and Sherman once met in New York. Works by both artists have appeared in the same group exhibitions and been acquired by the same private collectors. It should be evident that there are strong similarities between their respective *oeuvres*, and that Morimura could be accused of being a mere follower of Sherman. Morimura does not deny the similarities but argues they indicate 'a family resemblance', hence his reference to Sherman as his 'little sister' in the title of a 1998 self-portrait dedicated to the American artist. For this image, Morimura impersonated Sherman as she appeared, reclining on the floor while wearing an orange top and a checked skirt, in the photo *Untitled # 96* (1981).

Morimura has declared that for him 'art is the expression of our sadness, anger, wonderment and amusement through which we share feelings'. Like Koons, he is a showman who believes art should combine beauty and humour, should entertain and be accessible to people with no previous knowledge of art. Reactions to his work vary according to the gender and sexual orientation of viewers, but the surprise and amusement many experience when they encounter his strange 'self-portraits' in galleries, cinema foyers, shop windows and during live performances indicates that he has succeeded in his aim even though there are those who think he has exploited one idea to the point of overkill.

### Alison Jackson

Jackson (b. 1960) became notorious in Britain during 1999 for producing black and white photographs that apparently showed Princess Diana and Dodi Al-Fayed with a mixed race love child. Since both adults had died before any such baby existed, the photographs were clearly impossible but they appeared convincing because Jackson had employed look-alike models to pose as Di and Dodi. The photos, part of a series entitled *Mental Images*, were technically assured, beautifully composed and lit in a manner reminiscent of old master paintings of the Holy Family.

Jackson was attracted to the subject of Diana because she was a national icon at the time of her death and by the fact that millions mourned her even though the majority only knew her through mass media images. It was also clear to Jackson that people fantasised about Diana's love life.

Jackson studied at Chelsea College of Art and the Royal College of Art (RCA) in London during the 1990s. Initially, she explored sculpture and live performance and took photographs as documentary records. These were later exhibited alongside the performances in order to highlight the difference between the image of the 'real' thing and the 'real' thing itself. From then on, she used the camera more and researched theories of images to learn how they function and seduce us. One of photography's genres interested her in particular: staged, constructed, directed or tableaux photography. This genre has appealed to numerous artists in recent decades, as the work of Calum Colvin, Les Krims, Cindy Sherman, Jo Spence and Boyd Webb testifies.

At the RCA, Jackson was taught and encouraged by the left-wing photomontagist Peter Kennard, whose political purpose was to penetrate surface appearances in order to reveal hidden truths about social reality. At least one of Jackson's photographs made a political point: it showed the leaders 'Blair', 'Clinton' and 'Milosevic' eating and drinking together in a comfortable interior while 'refugees' stood outside in the cold watching through a window. The composition was reminiscent of Victorian narrative paintings with a moral message. However, in contrast to Kennard, Jackson's general tactic seemed to be a spoiling one: she threw deceptive images into the pot in order to bemuse the public and irritate the media. However, Jackson has denied wanting to spoil and bemuse, and says her aim was to clarify by reminding viewers that supposedly documentary photographs were directed, composed and captured a fleeting moment. In other words, she wanted viewers to question the truth claims of photography.

For a long time, photography was regarded as an inherently truthful medium because cameras recorded the surface appearance of reality mechanically and so photographs were, in semiotic terminology, indexical signs; but since scenes and events can be devised specially for cameras, what they document can be fictional characters and situations. (This is especially obvious in the case of advertising photographs.) Jackson eschewed the digital generation of images from scratch or the manipulation of her images via computers – apart from retouching – precisely because she wanted to retain the 'reality effect' of traditional photography in order to make her actors and fictional scenes persuasive. Photography's objectivity is also qualified by the subjective factor that occurs when prints are viewed, that is, the feelings, desires, knowledge, memories and interpretations contributed by spectators.

Meticulous planning and preparation were required for Jackson's photo-shoots. She had to instruct wig and clothes makers and make-up artists; she had to find look-alike models by advertising in publications like *The Stage* and *Variety* or by approaching strangers or London agencies such as Susan Scott's. Hours of rehearsals in the studio were then needed to achieve the 'look' she was seeking.

While some of Jackson's photos were stylistically indebted to oil paintings by Rembrandt and Caravaggio and to formal, official portraits by photographers like Lord Snowdon, others were indebted to the 'snatched' or 'surveillance' style of photojournalists. For instance, she produced a set of images of 'David and Victoria

Beckham' that showed him wearing his wife's thong. Jackson employed a framing device to imply that one was viewing the couple through a doorway or a gap in curtains. This device, plus the visible grain of the photos, simulated a shot from distance taken with a long lens such as paparazzi use. Looking at these photos may cause disquiet because they make viewers feel like peeping toms.

Jackson, like so many of us, is fascinated by celebrities. Pop artists shared this interest and as a student, Jackson particularly admired Warhol. While millions deplore the intrusive behaviour of journalists and the paparazzi, simultaneously they are voyeurs who consume stories about and images of celebrities. As Donna Leigh-Kile has argued, today's sex symbols play the same mythological role in our lives as the Gods did in the lives of the ancient Greeks and Romans.[12]

Mass media representations of the famous are thus Jackson's starting point and therefore her work can be described as 'second order' (metaphotography or photos about photos). However, she goes further by posing 'what if?' questions – 'what if Princess Di and Dodi had lived? What if I could peek into the Beckhams' bedroom? What if I could snap Prince Charles with his lover Camilla Parker-Bowles and his son Prince William?' – and then making the desires, fantasies and speculations of the public concrete. (This explains the title *Mental Images*.) Although Jackson's photos are in one sense false (they are not genuine portraits of famous people), in another they are true, that is, when they make visible the imaginings and wishes of the public.

In addition to taking photographs, Jackson has directed a number of short films. One about Princess Di was scheduled to be screened on a huge video wall (Global Multimedia Interface) in London's Leicester Square (it was also to be connected to the Internet) but it proved too controversial and was dropped at the last minute. (However, it was screened at the Edinburgh Festival.) Controversy arose because the Di look-alike was shown crossing and uncrossing her legs Sharon Stone style – as in the notorious scene in the 1992 movie *Basic Instinct*. There was a reference to *Basic Instinct* but Jackson's film was much less explicit. Another Diana simulation using a look-alike model that provoked controversy when exhibited in Galway, Ireland in July 2001 was a computer-enhanced photograph by the Dutch photographer and filmmaker Erwin Olaf (b. 1959). Olaf's 'Diana' showed the badge of Mercedes Benz embedded in her upper arm causing blood to run. The photo was one of a series of eight entitled *Royal Blood*.

One advantage of using look-alikes and inventing scenarios is that Jackson can steal a march on the tabloids. Doubtless, the latter eagerly await the opportunity to photograph Prince William being crowned King but Jackson has already depicted this possible future event (a simulation has thus preceded reality). One of her colour photographs shows 'William' dressed in robes sitting on the throne eying the camera with that coy glance his mother favoured; his 'grandmother, Queen Elizabeth II' stands in front of him holding an old while 'Camilla' observes from the sidelines, 'Prince Charles' is absent – the mind races – did he abdicate in favour of his son?

Clearly, Jackson's project is a post-modern one that simultaneously concerns and exemplifies the phenomenon of simulation so widespread in contemporary society. Jean Baudrillard, the French theorist who has written extensively on this topic has influenced her thinking, especially his essay 'The Precession of Simulacra'.[13] In it, Baudrillard claimed that images are 'murderers of the real' and that simulations now *precede* reality. In an interview, Jackson observed:

> I recall his remarks about the difference between someone who pretends to be ill and a person who exhibits or simulates the symptoms of an illness: a doctor would not be sure if the latter was ill or not. Baudrillard argues that simulation 'threatens the difference between "true" and "false", between "real" and "imaginary"'. Similarly, my photos of look-alikes creates a confusion between what is real, what is simulated and what is imagined, which I enjoy exploring.[14]

Because Jackson's photographs playfully exploit the increasingly blurred relation between reality, imagery and mental fantasies, they can be considered intellectual conundrums but they also have a popular appeal. They straddle the divide between fine art and mass culture because they are exhibited in upmarket galleries and reproduced in tabloid newspapers and popular magazines, and have been marketed via websites such as Eyestorm.com. Indeed, Jackson became a minor media celebrity in her own right – profiled in the press, discussed by the broadsheets, interviewed on television – and was attacked by populist newspapers on the grounds that her photos and short videos were 'offensive, sick and tasteless'. As usual, the populist papers were hypocritical: they criticised Jackson because she imitated and parodied precisely what they did for reasons of sales and profits. Furthermore, even while they denigrated her, they published 'outraged' articles about her art to boost circulation. Of course, Jackson was intrigued by the cycle of events, by the fact that the mass media had taken up work based on media information.

Jackson's *Mental Images* photographs are clever, witty and aesthetically pleasurable. They are both simple and profound. The confusion they initially provoke is a productive one because, by testing our ability to decode images, they enhance visual literacy. Furthermore, they are socially useful because they stimulate reflection on the culture of celebrity and the truth or falsity of mass media representations. Given that the media and public's obsession with famous people and scandals is unlikely to fade in the near future, Jackson has struck a rich vein of subject matter.

During 2001, Jackson was commissioned by the creative London advertising agency Mother Ltd to generate provocative adverts for Schweppes drinks. The campaign strategy was to parody celebrity endorsement advertising. For instance, one amusing image showed 'Lord Jeffrey Archer' in a prison cell (the real Archer, an ex-Tory MP, popular novelist and Warhol collector, was sentenced in July 2001 to four years in prison for perjury and perverting justice) being consoled by his old friend 'Margaret Thatcher'. Two small straplines

**40. Alison Jackson, advert featuring look-alikes of Jeffrey Archer
and Margaret Thatcher in prison, 2001.**
Client: Schweppes, Agency: Mother.
Photo courtesy of Jackson and Mother.

stated: 'Sch … you know who? Sch … you know its not really them.' The campaign's aim, Robert Saville of Mother Ltd explained, was to 'juxtapose Schweppes as being authentic with the person in the shot as unauthentic'.[15]

A further instance of the mass media responding enthusiastically to Jackson's work was the 50-minute BBC2 television programme *Double Take*. It consisted of a series of short, humorous sketches videoed in a deliberately rough, surveillance manner in which Jackson used look-alikes to satirise those who had been in the public eye during the year 2001. Besides Archer and Thatcher, her targets included Prince William, Tony and Cherie Blair and Osama bin Laden.[16] Jane Root, controller of BBC2, described the programme as a 'new form of celebrity entertainment show'.

# 4

# Alternative Heroes

## Heroes and History

In May 1840, the Scottish historian and philosopher Thomas Carlyle (1795–1881) delivered six lectures entitled 'On heroes, hero-worship and the heroic in history' in which he asserted that the history of the world was, at bottom, the history of great men. He identified several kinds of hero: the hero as prophet, poet, priest, man of letters, king, and his examples included: Christ, Mohammed, Luther, Dante, Shakespeare, Rousseau, Cromwell and Napoleon. Great women were nowhere mentioned despite the fact that Carlyle was speaking shortly after the daring rescue by Grace Darling, the Northumberland daughter of a lighthouse keeper, of shipwrecked passengers using a rowing boat on 7 September 1838. Such was the attention of the press and artists, that a biographer of Darling has claimed she was 'the first media heroine'. Furthermore, Carlyle had not read (or had chosen to ignore) Giovanni Boccaccio's *Concerning Famous Women* (*De Claris Mulieribus*, 1360–74).[1]

In 1986, the American, photo-text artist Barbara Kruger reacted against the tradition of praising male heroes with a billboard image showing a girl fingering a boy's bicep with the superimposed slogan: 'We don't need another hero.' (It is surely time she updated this slogan to read 'We don't need another celebrity.') Bertolt Brecht, the left-wing playwright, also remarked, in a 1943 biography of Galileo, 'Unhappy the land that needs heroes.'

One objection to the 'great men' conception of history is that so many of the 'heroes' of the past were in reality brutal conquerors employing murder, violence and war to establish and control their empires. Carlyle also supported hero-worship:

Worship of a Hero is transcendent admiration of a Great Man ... No nobler feeling than admiration for one higher than himself dwells in the breast of man ... Society is founded on Hero-

**41. Barbara Kruger, 'We don't need another hero', 1986–87.**
Billboard poster commissioned by Artangel Trust for sites in
15 British cities, to accompany the TV Series *State of the Art*
(Channel 4, January 1987). Photo by John Carson courtesy of Artangel.

Worship. All dignities of rank, on which human association rests, are what we may call a *Hero*archy (Government of Heroes) ...[2]

Carlyle was a proto-fascist rather than a democrat. Rejecting the 'ballot-box, parliamentary eloquence, voting, constitution-building', he argued instead that the ablest men should be raised to the supreme place and loyally reverenced. (He did not explain what selection mechanism was to be used.) His grovelling faith in heroes can be viewed as an extreme version of the ideology of bourgeois individualism. Arguably, the glorification and worship of major celebrities is an updated version of this ideology.

Carlyle was convinced that the study of the lives of heroes would inspire lesser mortals and that portraits could convey their personalities even better than written biographies.[3] The Victorian politician Lord Palmeston also believed that viewing depictions of heroes would inspire 'noble actions, greater mental exertion and good conduct'. This kind of thinking led to the foundation of national portrait galleries in several countries during the nineteenth century.

One was established in London in 1856 and its collection of oil paintings, caricatures, drawings, sculptures and photographs is still being expanded. In 2001, its collection totalled more than 1 million items and the annual number of visitors too was over a million.

Carlyle influenced the foundation of England's National Portrait Gallery (NPG) and was one its first trustees. A portrait of him in the form of a stone medallion, carved by Frederick Thomas in 1894, adorns an exterior wall above the front entrance. During his lifetime, Carlyle also had his portrait painted by such leading artists of the age as Sir John Everett Millais, George Frederick Watts and James McNeil Whistler. In 1867, Julia Margaret Cameron also photographed his bearded face from several directions using dramatic lighting.[4]

At first, living people were excluded from the NPG's collection but now they are featured. Today, it includes portraits of individuals many would consider celebrities rather than heroes in Carlyle's sense. For example, in the year 2000, acquisitions included images of the footballer David Beckham, the boxer Frank Bruno, the actress Barbara Windsor, the television presenter Peter Snow and even the art dealer Leslie Waddington. In May of the same year, the NPG also mounted a show of photographs devoted to the movie star and gay icon Dame Elizabeth Taylor.

Carlyle's 'great men' conception of history was widespread and extended to disciplines such as art history: the history of art was thought to be the story of a succession of great artists and their art was explained by their biographies. In contrast, socialists and Marxists argued that social groups – classes, revolutionary mobs, political cadres, parties and trade unions – make history (although not in conditions of their own choosing). And social historians of art have pointed out that the production of art is a social process involving institutions, teams of producers, patrons, critics, curators and viewers besides artists, and that the history of art is a history of art works, technologies, genres and styles in addition to artists. This is not to say that individuals who are inventive and who have perfected particular skills, do not make significant contributions, they do, but given the importance of the artistic tradition, the originality and uniqueness of what individuals achieve tends to be exaggerated. While the work of some artists, such as David Hockney and Tracey Emin, can be considered autobiographical, other art relies on an objective response to external reality or on invention and construction. In the latter cases, biographical explanations are not that illuminating. Furthermore, social historians of art stress the influence of economic, cultural, political and scientific factors on the creative process.

Despite the Marxist emphasis on the role of classes and parties in making history, many on the Left did not abandon the habit of stressing the importance of exceptional individuals. Of course, they were no longer the royals, generals, popes and politicians admired by earlier regimes but they were great men all the same: Tom Paine, Marx, Engels, Lenin, Trotsky and Stalin, Chairman Mao, Fidel Castro, Che Guevara, Emiliano Zapata and the long-serving, left wing Labour MP Tony Benn (whose portrait was painted by the Scottish socialist artist Elizabeth Mulholland in 2001–02). A few women were also celebrated: Rosa Luxemburg being the principal example. An alternative pantheon of heroes thus came into being. Certain communist leaders who should have known better fostered the so-called 'cult of personality'. Stalin even went to the length of embalming Lenin's body and placing it on public display while at the same time erasing Trotsky from the historical record and, later, from the face of the Earth.

## Statuemania, East and West

Following the 1917 Bolshevik revolution, the question arose: what should be done with the 'monuments erected in honour of the Tsars and of their servants'? Lenin decreed that 'hideous idols' without artistic or historic merit should be dismantled and replaced by new works for a temporary period. A list of 67 proposed subjects for the new monuments, issued in August 1918, included the writers Dostoyevsky, Pushkin and Tolstoy, the painters Rublev and Vrubel, and the historic figures and revolutionaries Spartacus, Brutus, Marat, Robespierre, Garibaldi, Herzen, Bakunin, Engels and Marx. Earlier, during the nineteenth century, artists such as Courbet, Manet and Millais had painted portraits of philosophers and writers they knew and admired, such as Carlyle, Baudelaire, Proudhon, Ruskin and Zola, in preference to contemporary political leaders.

Only a few new statues were produced and erected in the Soviet Union by the deadline of 7 November 1918: Robespierre and Heinrich Heine in Moscow and Marx and Radischev in Petrograd. Later, in September 1919, a sculpture of Mikhail Bakunin by Boris Korolev was erected in Moscow. Unusually, its style was cubo-futurist. These monuments did not last long as they were made from cheap materials.

Artists who supported the Bolshevik revolution but who were avant-garde distrusted statues executed in a naturalistic, academic style and thought them regressive. Nikolai Punin, for example, criticised the first new statues saying they were 'cumbersome and awkward, uncultivated, and there is no point in talking about their artistic properties'. The critics wanted structures that were revolutionary in conception and form like Vladimir Tatlin's designs and models for the *Monument to the Third International* (1920), an experimental building made from metal and glass that was to have moving parts. It was intended to serve as an international meeting place for the proletariat and as a global communications centre.[5]

Later, after Lenin's death in 1924, Stalin's regime erected more permanent statues in bronze and stone, most of which were executed in a dull socialist realist style. An estimated 70,000 statues were erected to Lenin alone and of course, there were numerous monuments to Stalin in the USSR and Eastern Europe. One Russian official later described the proliferation of statues as 'pathological multiplication'. Western viewers regarded them as propaganda rather than art, or as examples of mediocre academic art.

However, the West also has its share of statues and monuments executed in a similar style and serving comparable ideological functions: in London, for example, there are bronze statues of political and military leaders such as Oliver Cromwell, Sir Winston Churchill, General Montgomery and Sir Arthur 'bomber' Harris standing on plinths in public places.[6] During the 1930s, Germany and Italy witnessed the cults of the fascist dictators Hitler and Mussolini who had no difficulty finding artists willing to serve them. In Italy, even members of the avant-garde movement futurism supported Mussolini for a time.[7] In 1930, the Italian painter Alfredo G. Ambrosi produced a so-called 'aero painting' glorifying Mussolini, that is, an aerial view of the city of Rome with the dictator's head superimposed.

In the United States, the National Memorial at Mount Rushmore in the Black Hills of South Dakota consists of 60-feet-tall, bas relief sculptures of the heads of four presidents: George Washington, Thomas Jefferson, Abraham Lincoln and Theodore Roosevelt. They were carved out of the face of a granite mountain with the aid of drills and dynamite. From 1927 to 1941, 400 workers assisted the sculptor Gutzon Borglum (1867–1941) and his son Lincoln to create the heads, which commemorate the first 150 years of America's history. Borglum senior, by all accounts, held racist views and was a member of the Ku Klux Klan.

**42. Alfredo G. Ambrosi,** *Portrait of Benito Mussolini*
*with View of Rome Behind,* **1930.**
Painting, oil on canvas, 124 x 124 cm. Rome: Private collection.

Naturally, some of the descandents of the Native Americans who had once roamed the Black Hills were dismayed by the appearance of the Mount Rushmore sculptures and the fact that their leaders had been ignored. Consequently, in 1939, they began searching for a sculptor to create a monument to Native American heroes. Polish-American sculptor Korczak Ziolkowski (1908–1982) accepted an offer from the Lakota Chiefs at the conclusion of World War II. His Crazy Horse Memorial, now in progress, is a three-dimensional carving of an entire mountain, located 17 miles from Mount Rushmore. It is the largest sculptural project in the world (563-feet high and 641-feet long) and is named after Chief Crazy Horse (1843?–1877) who was one of the major strategists against Lt. Colonel George A. Custer in the Battle of the Little Big Horn (1876). The sculpture depicts a mounted Native American with one arm outstretched pointing towards the horizon to illustrate Crazy Horse's remark, 'My lands are where my dead lie buried.' In addition to the mountain carving, educational and cultural programmes are an important part of the Crazy Horse Memorial. A complex for visitors includes the Indian Museum

**43. (a) Korczak Ziolkowski, '1/34th scale model for the Crazy Horse Memorial with mountain sculpture in progress in background', 1998.**
Model sculpture © Korczak Ziolkowski.
Photo Robb DeWall, courtesy of the Crazy Horse Memorial.

**(b) Close-up of face of Crazy Horse,**
© Press Association, London.

of North America and there are long-term plans for a Native American university and medical training centre. Ziolkowski died in 1982 but his wife Ruth, seven of their ten children and the Crazy Horse Memorial Foundation carried on his work. The face of Crazy Horse was dedicated in 1998 and the work proceeded immediately to the horse's head. Regarding the project's *raison d'être*, Lakota Chief Henry Standing Bear remarked: 'My fellow chiefs and I would like the white man to know that the red man has great heroes too.'[8]

When Stalin died in 1953 even Picasso made a flattering portrait drawing of him as a young man for reproduction in the communist journal *Les Lettres Françaises*. (Picasso had joined the French Communist Party in 1944 at the age of 63.) However, the party faithful strongly disliked the portrait even though it eschewed cubistic fragmentation. Three years later Stalin's spell over the Soviet Communist Party was shattered when first secretary Nikita Khruschev delivered a 'secret' speech to the party's 20th congress exposing Stalin's brutalities and denouncing the sycophantic personality cult that had surrounded him.

Following the collapse of the rule of the Communist Party in the Soviet Union during the 1980s, statues of Stalin, Dzerzhinsky, Kalinin, Lenin and Sverdlov were attacked, destroyed or consigned to monument graveyards labelled 'totalitarian art'. Leningrad became St Petersburg again and statues to Tsar Alexander II and Peter the Great were erected. More innovative than these monuments, were examples of new Russian art parodying socialist realist rhetoric and criticising the cult of Stalin. For instance, in 1989, Aleksandr Dudin (b. 1953, Moscow) painted *Demonstration*, a picture showing a procession of young comrades carrying red flags and a portrait of Stalin. Their gestures of joy are absurdly exaggerated and they are enclosed by dark blue passages featuring Stalin's victims: prisoners and people being executed.

A curious and amusing development in Russian art during the 1990s was evident in the collaborative paintings of Vladimir Dubosarsky (b. 1964, Moscow) and Alexander Vinogradov (b. 1963, Moscow). Perversely, they applied the academic skills and compulsory optimism of socialist realism to Western popular cultural icons such as Britain's Queen Elizabeth II and the Austrian-American movie star Arnold Schwarzenegger (b. 1947), who, incidentally, was one of the few actors to refuse to change his foreign name. In their 1995 canvas *En Plein Air*, the action-hero posed in a

**44. Aleksandr Dudin,** *Demonstration,* **1989.**
Painting, oil on canvas, 100 x 130 cm.
Photo courtesy of Camden Arts Centre, London.

bucolic rural setting and flexed his bicep for the benefit of admiring
children while nearby an impressionist painter toiled at his easel.[9]

Monuments to Stalin in some Eastern European states had been
demolished even earlier than those in the USSR. For instance, an
enormous stone sculpture showing Stalin leading a group of farmers,
workers and soldiers (locals sarcastically referred to it as 'the meat
queue') by Otakar Švec and Jiří and Vlasta Štursa, erected between
1949 and 1955 on a hill overlooking the city of Prague in Czechoslovakia, was destroyed in 1962. Later, in September 1996, the
economic transition from communism to capitalism, and the
cultural transition from honouring political giants to venerating
entertainment celebrities was illustrated by the appearance on the
base on which Stalin had stood of a huge inflatable (filled with
water) representing the American pop music star Michael Jackson

**45. (a) Left: Otakar Švec and Jiří and Vlasta Štursa,**
**'Monument to Stalin', 1949–55. Prague.**
**(b) Right: 'Statue of Michael Jackson', 1996.**
Photo © Tomas Turek/Associated Press, CTK.

wearing bullet belts.[10] Reporter Jeff B. Copeland sardonically commented: 'Michael Jackson and Joseph Stalin have a lot in common. Michael likes uniforms with plenty of medals; so did Stalin. They both get a lot of bad press.'[11] The statue was 9.1-metres high and had first appeared in 1995 on the Tower Records building in Hollywood as part of a promotion for Jackson's *HIStory* album. Later, in London, the statue was placed on a raft, which was then towed along the River Thames. Regarding the accompanying promo video, Cintra Wilson observed:

> Epic Records pulled out all of the promotional stops and portrayed Jackson as some kind of divine totalitarian emperor-general, unveiling statues of him in several European cities based on the three-hundred-foot-tall Monument to Victory in Volograd, Russia. The video featured people fainting and being dragged away, the power of the image overwhelming them.[12]

Only a pop star with a hugely inflated ego would have permitted such an inflatable to be manufactured and such a video to be shot.

## Mao and Warhol

Another communist leader who fostered his own cult of personality to bolster his authority was Chairman Mao Zedong (1893–1976), the supreme ruler of the People's Republic of China from 1949 to 1976. Paintings and sculptures of the socialist realist variety assisted his fame plus countless photographs and posters. Images of Mao were hung on the walls of peasant homes where they functioned simultaneously as secular icons and as a cheap form of surveillance and social control: the gaze of Big Brother replaced the all-seeing eyes of God. In the West too, during the 1970s, there were radical intellectuals and artists who were influenced by Mao's politics and his writings on art and culture. More surprising, given the virulent anticommunism of so many Americans, was the interest shown in him by one of capitalism's leading artists – Andy Warhol.

During 1972–73, Warhol produced a substantial series of paintings depicting Mao, which ranged from the quite small to the very large. Using a photo-portrait of the Chairman taken from the famous Little Red Book of quotations, he silk-screened it on to canvas over colours and brushstrokes executed in a quasi-abstract expressionist manner.[13] The effect, in many instances, was that Mao's face appeared besmirched. In addition, there were drawings, prints and purple and white wallpaper with a pattern of lithographed Maos. When this material was exhibited at the Musée Galliera, Paris in 1974, the paintings were displayed on walls decorated with the 'Mao' wallpaper.

Although on the one hand, the appropriation of Mao's image by a master of business art signalled the power of the West to appropriate, recuperate and turn into expensive commodities almost any political image – even that taken from a rival system – on the other hand, Mao's presence as an icon was still visible. If the original image of Mao commanded the worship and respect of the Chinese people, then Warhol's enlarged copy preserved enough of its charisma to awe the Western viewer even when it was displayed in 1985 in the privately owned gallery of the wealthy London collectors Charles and Doris Saatchi.

Warhol told one dealer that these paintings had been prompted by the fact that 'Mao was the most famous person in the world.' The early 1970s was also a period of rapprochement in Sino-American relations: President Nixon visited Beijing in February 1972 and the Vietnam War ended for America when a ceasefire agreement was

**46. Andy Warhol, *Mao*, 1973.**
Painting, acrylic and silk-screen on canvas, 66 x 56 cm. © Andy Warhol
Foundation for the Visual Arts/ARS, NY and DACS, London, 2002.

reached in January 1973. (Warhol himself paid a visit to Beijing and
the Great Wall of China in 1982.)

Warhol's brand of pop art had always involved the selection and
use of the most obvious, banal subjects, the most popular icons.
Inevitably, the most popular images were those in which modern
photomechanical methods of reproduction had been employed to
generate millions of copies. Most Western individualists have feared
and despised the sameness, repetition and stereotypes associated
with mass culture and with communist propaganda. One of
Warhol's great strengths as an artist was his willingness to embrace
exactly those characteristics and to make them the subject matter of
his work.

Warhol's 'Mao' portraits inadvertently revealed that Western
capitalism and Chinese communism had some common elements:
both accepted the cult of personality, the need for images of stars

and heroes with whom the masses could identify and both Western mass culture and Eastern visual propaganda relied upon industrial, mechanical forms of image-making and dissemination. Amusingly, in 1971, the surrealist painter Salvador Dalí and the photographer Philippe Halsman conflated the two star systems (and two genders) by synthesising photographs of the faces of Mao and Monroe.[14]

However, viewed in their totality, Warhol's 'Mao' series also revealed ideological differences between East and West: while the silk-screened image of Mao signified 'mechanical', 'repetition', 'sameness' and 'uniformity', the mock action painting characteristics signified 'hand made', 'change', 'difference' and 'variety'. This contrast of values conformed to the common Western opinion of the difference between Chinese and American societies at that time.

In China, even after Mao's death, his cult persists. During the 1990s, truck drivers carried images of Mao in their cabs as a protection against accidents because he had been born in the Year of the Dragon. In 1993, a six-metre-high bronze statue of Mao was erected in his birthplace Shaoshan, Hunan province. When reporter Ian Buruma visited Shaoshan some years later, he found pictures and busts for sale, plus tapes of Mao's speeches. Mao's portrait also appeared on embroideries, coins, stamps, cigarette lighters, ballpoints, pencils, CDs, T-shirts, teacups and golden amulets intended to bring good health and fortune. Buruma concluded: 'Mao Zedong has clearly entered the pantheon of Chinese folk deities ... Divine beings in every society promise salvation and good fortune, and where there are miracles, there is business to be done.' When Buruma visited a provincial museum in Changsha, he found examples of Mao relics including a lavish display of his underwear![15]

## Liebknecht and Luxemburg

Left-wingers in the West tend to revere the Spartacist revolutionaries Karl Liebknecht and Rosa Luxemburg more than Mao, because had their party's rebellion, attempted in Germany in 1919, succeeded, there would probably have been another, more democratic and humane version of a socialist society than those of the USSR and China. Unfortunately, they were brutally murdered in Berlin by paramilitary thugs in 1919. In London, in 1986, the Pentonville Gallery mounted an exhibition, which I organised, devoted to the two leaders subtitled *Revolution, Remembrance and Revolution*.[16] Works and documentation by an international range of artists, both dead and living, were displayed. The artists included Ludwig Mies van der Rohe (photos of a 1926 brick monument later destroyed by the Nazis), George Grosz, Käthe Kollwitz, R.B. Kitaj, Margaret Harrison, Giangiacomo Spadari and May Stevens plus still photographs from the Czech/German film *Rosa Luxemburg* (1986) directed by Margarethe von Trotta.

Although the exhibition consisted of memorials to two socialist martyrs, it also reflected on the character and value of such monuments. For instance, Kitaj's painting *The Murder of Rosa Luxemburg* (1960) was partly informed by a 1938 art-historical article by A. Neumeyer entitled 'Monuments to "genius" in German Classicism' published in the *Journal of the Warburg Institute* and included quoted images of monuments of different types. 'Can a memorial to a socialist martyr', the picture seemed to be asking, 'take the same form as officially approved monuments to great leaders?' The painting also indicated the conflict that exists between the goal of providing a historically accurate account of what happened to Luxemburg, and the goal of devising a monument capable of transcending the particular circumstances of her death. In fact, the problems posed by this canvas were part of a wider issue, namely, the difficulty of producing a convincing socialist mythology, one that would avoid the simplistic hagiography and retrogressive visual rhetoric of socialist realist monuments.

In the case of a late 1970s series of collages – employing photographs, photocopying and handwritten texts – by the American feminist-socialist artist May Stevens, entitled *Ordinary/Extraordinary*, the contrasting lives and fates of her working-class mother Alice and the Polish-Jewish-Marxist Rosa were compared and contrasted. Whereas Luxemburg was an articulate, politically active woman who achieved international fame, Alice Stevens was an ordinary worker, mother and homemaker who in middle age became mentally ill and retreated into silence.

Two feminist ideas informed the collages, namely, 'hidden from history' and 'the personal is political'. By treating her mother as subject matter, Stevens rescued an anonymous life from the oblivion that is the fate of the vast majority of human beings. Stevens' reflections on the unhappy experiences of her mother revealed the effects of class position and sexism: private life was inextricably linked with larger political issues. For Stevens, Luxemburg was the exemplar of that wider public realm in which she as an artist and activist was attempting to intervene. Alice and Rosa thus represented for Stevens two role models, two mothers, one natural and one ideal. Stevens' quest for self-identity and fulfilment necessarily involved them both.

Margaret Harrison (b. 1940), a British artist, is also a feminist and socialist. Her tribute to Rosa took the form of a two-part painting with both images and writing entitled *From Rosa Luxemburg to Janis Joplin*, which was produced for the exhibition *Kunstlerinen International (1877–1977)* held in Berlin in 1977. The work was also known as *Anonymous Was a Woman* because this phrase was rendered in

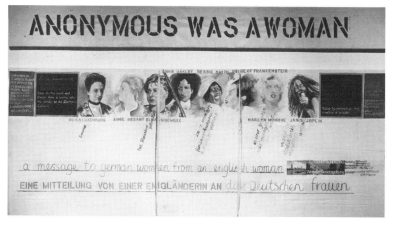

**47. Margaret Harrison,** *From Rosa Luxemburg to Janis Joplin,* **1977.**
Two-part painting, acrylic and collage on canvas,
31 x 287 cm and 114 x 287 cm. © Margaret Harrison.
Photo eeva-inkeri, courtesy of the Ronald Feldman Gallery, New York.

large letters as a kind of headline. Harrison included a frieze-like panel of eight portraits that began with Rosa and then featured Annie Besant, Eleanor Marx, Annie Oakley, Bessie Smith, the Bride of Frankenstein (Mary Shelley was the author of *Frankenstein*), Marilyn Monroe and Janis Joplin. Thus, her canvas commemorated women of achievement from different fields and periods, most of whom were eventually 'crumpled or destroyed by a society at odds with their talent or intentions'.[17] It is a painting particularly pertinent to the theme of this book because it combines images of women from the realms of politics and mass entertainment.

## Celebrating Women

Another work of art made during the 1970s that contested Carlyle's 'great men' conception of history by honouring the achievements of women was *The Dinner Party* (1974–79). Its prime mover was Judy Gerowitz (b. 1939), an American artist who changed her surname to Chicago, after her hometown, in 1970. She was from a Jewish-intellectual-Marxist family background and became a committed feminist while teaching art in California during the late 1960s. *The Dinner Party* was prompted by artistic representations of the Biblical scene The Last Supper, but reinterpreted from the viewpoint of 'those who had done the cooking throughout history'. The work was a substantial, theatrical, mixed-media installation consisting of three dining tables, each 48-feet long, arranged to form a triangle standing on a base of opalescent tiles. It took several years to design and fabricate and involved the labours of 400 women and men, most of them volunteers. Needlework and china-painting were the main crafts employed – crafts traditionally associated with women. Table-cloths and runners covered the tables, and on them were 39 place settings with cutlery, goblets and painted and sculpted ceramic dishes. The latter employed butterfly motifs and clitoral and vaginal or vulval imagery to symbolically represent historic female figures. (Chicago regarded the vagina as a positive creative symbol in a phallocentric world.) Some 999 names were inscribed in gold on the tiles making up the 'Heritage Floor'. Those honoured were selected after much research and reflection; they included women from many different spheres, nations and epochs: the goddesses Ishtar and Kali, Sappho, Boadicea, Elizabeth I, Mary Wollstonecraft, George Eliot, Virginia Woolf, Ethel Smyth and Emily Dickinson. Georgia O'Keeffe, the American artist whose 'abstract' paintings are noted for their flower/vaginal imagery, was also represented.

Germaine Greer, the feminist writer and celebrity academic, once described *The Dinner Party*, which was exhibited in a London warehouse in 1985, as 'an anti-monument monument'. Although some critics judged the work vulgar or kitsch, and others questioned its selection and theoretical bases, many women found it inspiring and there is no doubt that it was an epic and influential achievement. Since 1979, it has been exhibited 15 times in countries around the world and viewed by an estimated 1 million people. Unfortunately, it still lacks a permanent home and display space.[18]

**48. (a) Left: Judy Chicago and others,** *The Dinner Party*, **1979.**
Installation, mixed-media, 48 x 42 x 3 feet. © Judy Chicago.
Photo © Michael Alexander, courtesy of Through the Flower Corporation.
**(b) Right: Judy Chicago and others,**
**'Virginia Woolf place setting from** *The Dinner Party'*, **1979.**
Installation, mixed-media. © Judy Chicago.
Photo © Michele Maier, courtesy of Through the Flower Corporation.

Elaine Showalter is an American academic who in 2001 published
a historical text that attempted a Chicago-like project in respect of
women who could act as role models and heroines for feminists. She
documented the lives, struggles and achievements of such 'feminist
icons' as Mary Shelley, Mary Wollstonecraft, Eleanor Marx, Hilary
Clinton, Oprah Winfrey and Princess Diana.[19]

## Che Guevara

In the West, the most glamorous and popular male left-wing revolutionary of the second half of the twentieth century was Ernesto
'Che' Guevara de la Serna (1928–1967). Guevara has been dubbed
'the only sex symbol in the history of Marxism'. After Jean-Paul Sartre
met Che, he described him as 'the most complete human being of
our age'. Che came from an Argentinian, down-at-heel aristocratic

family of Spanish and Irish extraction but travels in South America as a young man made him aware of inequality, oppression, poverty and American imperialism. An idealistic, compassionate and well-read intellectual who wrote poetry, diaries and theoretical texts, he studied medicine at university before joining Fidel Castro's small revolutionary force in Mexico as it prepared to invade Cuba to overthrow a vicious dictatorship. Although Guevara suffered from asthma, he was an active and brave guerrilla fighter as well as a doctor. After Castro achieved power in Cuba in 1959, Guevara held government posts but in 1965 he decided to extend the revolution to Africa and South America. He and a band of comrades left Cuba to assist guerrilla struggles in the Congo and in Bolivia. However, both campaigns were failures. In 1967, he was captured and executed by a unit of Bolivian troops. (Of course, his violent early death, a life sacrificed in a doomed struggle for the benefit of others, added immensely to his appeal to those seeking social change.) A photograph by Freddy Alborta of his half-naked corpse lying on a stretcher viewed from below his feet, somewhat resembling a Renaissance image of the dead Christ painted by Mantegna, surrounded by soldiers and officials, was published around the world to prove he was dead. His hands were then cut off to assist identification and these are now preserved in formaldehyde in Cuba. His body was buried in secret to prevent his grave from becoming a place of pilgrimage. However, the legend and myth of Che blossomed instead of fading. After his remains were found and unearthed in 1997, they were returned to Cuba.

Alberto Diaz Gutiérrez (1928–2001), a Cuban newspaper photographer who adopted the professional name Korda, photographed Guevara in 1960 at a memorial service in Havana.[20] This photo, entitled *Guerrillero Heroico*, was a highly romantic image of a young man whose handsome face was framed by long, unruly hair. He had a wispy beard and moustache, and wore a beret adorned with a star. His eyes gazed upwards and past the viewer towards some future revolution or socialist utopia. (Korda described his expression as one of 'steely defiance'.) A print of the photo in a landscape format was displayed in the Plaza de la Revolución, Havana.

After Korda's photograph was issued as a portrait poster by the Italian publisher Giangiacomo Feltrinelli (a wealthy businessman who was also a communist) in 1967, it became world famous. (The image's dark/light contrasts lent themselves to graphic simplification.) It was also reproduced on posters published by the propaganda agency OSPAAAL (Organisation of Solidarity with Asia, Africa and Latin America, based in Havana) and countless times on placards and T-shirts during the 1960s when Che became a cult hero among young radicals and hippies. Guevara appealed to young radicals because he was an austere, principled leader who put his theories of revolution via armed struggle in the countryside and his vision of a new socialist society into practice and therefore he offered a very different model to that of cautious communist parties around the world.

Castro's regime regarded intellectual property rights as 'imperialistic bullshit' and so Korda did not try to restrict use of the image or to seek royalties from reproductions. However, in 2000 he did exercise his copyright by taking legal action in Britain after being offended by the image's commercial use in an advertisement to sell spicy, Smirnoff vodka. (Images of bottles and the hammer and sickle were superimposed on Che's face and the slogan attached was 'Hot Fiery'). Korda maintained that the advert was a slur on Che's character and trivialised his historic significance. The Cuba Solidarity Campaign, based in Britain, supported Korda's legal action and in September 2000, the advertising company Lowe Lintas and the picture agency Rex Features paid him damages in an out-of-court settlement. Korda then announced that he would donate the money to child welfare organisations in Cuba.

Che's legend and appeal continue unabated into the twenty-first century: there are now many websites devoted to his biography and writings, and others marketing a range of merchandise carrying his image. At the time of writing, two biopics are reported to be under development by Mick Jagger and Robert Redford.

1997 was a year in which the cult of Che received fresh impetus: it marked the 30th anniversary of his death; several biographies were published; the Fowler Museum of Cultural History in Los Angeles published a book, based on an exhibition, about images of Che edited by David Kunzle and another was compiled by Fernando D. García and Óscar Sola;[21] and his remains were returned to Cuba. The latter are now kept in the provincial city of Santa Clara where there is a bronze statue of Che and in the Museo Histórico de la Revolución personal relics such as his camera, jacket and pistol holster are preserved.

Writing in 1997, Jonathan Glancey opposed public monuments of the socialist realist type in Cuba because he believed Guevara would not have approved. According to Glancey, there is only one such monument to Castro in Cuba and another, a huge 'hideous' one, devoted to the Cuban patriot José Martí.[22]

Another sign of Guevara's continuing attraction was Gavin Turk's ultra realistic wax sculpture *Death of Che* in which he posed as the dead Guevara as seen in Alborta's photograph. Turk, a British artist who has made fame a theme of his work, was born in 1967, the year Guevara was killed. Like Madonna and Morimura, Turk enjoys impersonating famous people. The waxwork was first shown in *Out There*, a mixed exhibition held at the White Cube 2 gallery, London in April 2000. Turk had hoped his sculpture would also be shown in the Millennium Dome in Greenwich but the Dome's managers rejected the proposal because (according to the artist) it might offend business sponsors who were arms manufacturers.

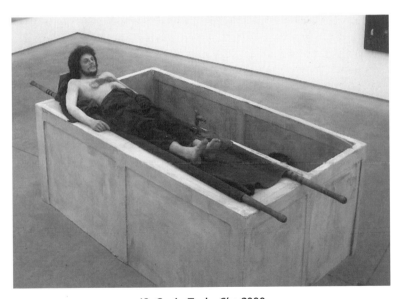

**49. Gavin Turk, *Che,* 2000.**
Sculpture, mixed-media. © Gavin Turk.
Photo Stephen White, courtesy of Jay Jopling/White Cube, London.

In January 2001, Turk was awarded £5,000 as part of the Year of the Artist celebrations, which he used to organise a two-week event or teach-in, entitled *The Che Gavara* [sic] *Story*, at The Foundry, a space in Shoreditch, London. He assembled documentation about

Che by asking members of the public to contribute (80 did so). He also organised open meetings and discussions, played music and screened films and videos, and wrote a diary recording what happened for *The Times*.

Much of Turk's work springs from the clichés of popular culture – he employs wax because of its use in tourist attractions like Madame Tussaud's – and he regarded Korda's portrait of Guevara as one such visual cliché. (In 1999, he produced a Warhol-style wall display of four, billboard-size posters of himself dressed like Che in Korda's photo.) Nevertheless, he also thought familiar images 'harboured some sort of truth' because, otherwise, they would not have such a wide appeal. Korda's photo served as 'a catalyst for looking at and thinking about Third World politics, revolution and, by inference, our own political and cultural position'.[23] Turk's event attracted considerable press attention but also some harsh reviews. Jonathan Jones, an art critic, dismissed Turk's sculpture as 'a work of transcendent stupidity' and observed acidly that 'Che is the perfect political hero for an apolitical age, because none of us is ever likely to be moved to any action by him.' He also reminded readers about the persecution of homosexuals in contemporary Cuba.[24] Other analysts believe that Che's image has become depoliticised since the 1960s, that it has 'changed from being a symbol of radical opposition and revolutionary change to a commodified expression of nostalgia'.[25] Nevertheless, Turk's event was worthwhile because it connected people in the art world to others who were politically aware and older activists who still admired Guevara and were continuing to assist Cuba by sending containers of aid. It also raised again the issue of art's pertinence to politics.

The British artist and designer Scott King, who with Matthew Worley founded the polemical creative partnership known as Crash! produced a witty pictorial response to the tendency of the fashion industry to transform Che into 'radical or terrorist chic'. (For example, supermodel Kate Moss sporting a Che T-shirt.) King replaced Che's face in the Korda photograph with that of the American singer and movie actress Cher to generate a poster with the punning title *Cher Guevara*. This image, which was reproduced on the February 2001 cover of the style magazine *Sleazenation*, succinctly conveys the idea that revolutionaries sometimes end up as part of the world of entertainment.

**50. Scott King, 'Cher Guevara', 2001.**
Poster, 59.4 x 84 cm. © Scott King and
courtesy of the Magnani Gallery, London.

## The Vacant Plinth

A curious feature of historic sculptures of supposedly famous heroes in public places is that most of the time they are ignored by local residents while foreign tourists photograph them regardless of their identity. In many instances, neither residents nor tourists know anything about the individuals represented, or hence why they have been commemorated. However, the public's attention is generally aroused when there is a change of political regime and demolitions or substitutions are proposed. In London's Trafalgar Square, there are statues of generals dating from the time of the British Empire whose names and deeds have long been forgotten. When Ken Livingstone, the first Mayor of London, suggested in 2000 replacing them with new sculptures of better-known figures arguments ensued. In accordance with the widespread view that there is no longer a consensus in our society about who counts as a hero (apart from Mandela), agreement about substitutions was hard to reach and so no change occurred.

A comparable controversy arose when the Royal Society of Arts (RSA) suggested adding a new sculpture to a fourth plinth in Trafalgar Square that had stood empty since the 1840s. As a stopgap measure, the RSA commissioned three British artists working in contemporary idioms – Mark Wallinger, Rachel Whiteread and Bill Woodrow – to provide sculptures to see which worked best. In 1999, Wallinger (b. 1959) supplied a life-size statue of Christ entitled *Ecce Homo (Behold the Man)*, which showed him as a prisoner of Pontius Pilate standing naked (apart from a loincloth and a crown of thorns) with his hands tied behind his back. Christ was also beardless and shaven-headed because the artist, an agnostic, wanted to represent him as an ordinary human rather than as a divine being. The sculpture, made from sanded polyester resin, was hyperrealist in style because it had been cast from the body of one of Wallinger's studio assistants. The subject, therefore, was traditional but Wallinger made it strange by eschewing the conventional visual rhetoric of glory and power. The figure's pale hue and vulnerable pose, its small size compared to the plinth's, and its location near the plinth's edge rather than in its centre (as if standing before a crowd or mob), made it different from most other public monuments. Furthermore, since Christ was a man of peace, he contrasted sharply with the military heroes represented nearby. Wallinger is an artist with political intentions and he has explained that Jesus, for him, was the leader of a persecuted minority, the victim of both Roman imperialism and religious intolerance.

Although *Ecce Homo* proved quite popular, especially with Christians, the RSA in partnership with Sculpture at Goodwood decided that the solution to the vacant plinth problem was to continue its programme of temporary installations. The advantage of having a changing roster of sculptures in contrasting styles by different artists was a high level of public interest. To encourage public participation, a website was established which invited users of Trafalgar Square to make their opinions known and to suggest answers to the question: 'what next?'[26]

At the time of writing, the sculptor Ian Walters is working on a bronze sculpture of Mandela for Trafalgar Square. It will be a full-length figure showing Mandela with his arms raised in the act of delivering a speech.

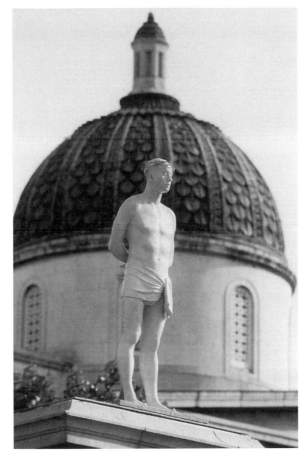

**51. Mark Wallinger, *Ecce Homo*, 1999.**
Public sculpture, life-size, white marbleised resin,
gold leaf and barbed wire, installed on plinth in Trafalgar Square, London.
© Mark Wallinger, photo courtesy of Anthony Reynolds Gallery, London.

## Depicting the People

Another development in art associated with the emergence of anarchism, democracy, socialism and trade unionism during the nineteenth century was a focus on ordinary, anonymous individuals and 'the people' in general. (This was also a century in which intellectuals became conscious of popular or folk culture and began to collect examples of such things as folk songs.) Painters such as

Gustave Courbet, Jean-François Millet, Camille Pissarro and Vincent van Gogh, for example, depicted the peasantry of Europe in a sympathetic manner. When van Gogh painted his archetypal image of a peasant sowing in the fields of Provence in 1888, he placed the orb of a huge setting sun behind the figure's head so that the man acquired a halo of natural origin and thus became a secular saint. In addition to peasants, van Gogh also drew and painted miners, doctors, postal workers and soldiers.

Courbet and the British painter Henry Wallis depicted the stonebreakers who provided material for road mending. Ford Madox Brown spent over a decade producing a highly complex painting entitled *Work* (1852–65) that showed a cross section of Victorian society and different types of labour (both manual and intellectual); at the centre of his composition he placed several male navvies engaged in water main construction in Hampstead, London. (Besides the Bible, one of Brown's literary sources for the picture was a text by Carlyle on the necessity and nobility of labour, and so Carlyle appears in the picture.) William Bell Scott produced a similar painting in 1861 entitled *Iron and Steel* for Wallington Hall, Northumberland. The three workers Bell depicted hammering were portraits of men from Robert Stephenson's works.[27] In 1891, Sir Hubert von Herkomer, a German-born artist working in England, painted a male manual labourer standing idle and grim-faced outside the open door of his dwelling because he is on strike; his anxious wife and children are behind him.

Aimé-Jules Dalou, a French sculptor, produced clay models of labourers from the fields and factories, as components for a huge *Monument to Labour* (1889–1900) that, unfortunately, was never completed. Constantin Meunier, a Belgian artist, also generated realist statues honouring agricultural and factory workers, miners and stevedores. In 1896, he was commissioned to produce a *Monument to Labour* by the Belgian Government but it too remained unfinished.

The many examples of social realism produced during the nineteenth century provided a model for the socialist realist works created in the Soviet Union and communist China in the following century.

Cities such as Paris and London expanded greatly during the nineteenth century and many artists focused on urban groups. Courbet and John Everett Millais, for instance, depicted popular heroes such as firefighters. (This subject later attracted the makers of Hollywood disaster movies and is continued today in British television soap operas set in fire stations. The firefighters who died helping others in the September 2001 terrorist attack on New York were rightly considered heroes but, of course, the Islamic terrorists who committed suicide during the attack were also regarded as heroes and martyrs by their supporters.) Gustave Caillebotte painted, in 1875, the men who planed the parquet floors of Parisian apartments while Edouard Manet painted barmaids, waiters and prostitutes. Edgar Degas depicted ballet dancers, jockeys, laundresses and streetwalkers and Toulouse-Lautrec depicted female sex workers in the brothels of Paris with humanity but without glamour. As already described in Chapter 2, he was also one of the first artists to represent popular entertainers.

In Arles, in 1888, van Gogh produced portraits of several named individuals who had different occupations: the peasant Patience Escalier, the postman Joseph Roulin, the doctor Félix Rey and the soldier Lieutenant Milliet. However, even when artists represented an individual, their intention was generally to evoke a social group, profession or occupation; in other words, the individual served as a token of a type. Henry Mayhew (1812–87), a nineteenth-century British newspaper reporter with a passion for classification, investigated during the 1840s the lives and occupations of lower-class, working and unemployed Londoners: coachmen, pedlars, pickpockets, street cleaners, vagrants and so forth. When his findings were later published in book form, illustrations – engravings based on photographs – depicted the various types of street folk whom he had researched.[28]

During the 1920s, the German photographer August Sander (1876–1964), set himself a similar task, that is, representing 'Man in twentieth-century Germany' in an objective, quasi-anthropological fashion. Sander began to take portraits of individuals belonging to different social strata, ethnic minorities, trades and professions. In 1929, 60 portraits appeared in *The Face of our Time*, volume one of a planned series. Sander documented artists, boxers, circus performers, cooks, gypsies, Jews, lawyers, peasants, students, the unemployed, and so on. Even members of the Nazi Party posed proudly in their uniforms for his camera but this did not save his endeavour from suppression by the Nazi regime in 1934.

In the Soviet Union, in addition to the cults of Lenin and Stalin, paintings and sculptures of agricultural and industrial workers were crucial to the iconography of socialist realism and state propaganda.

**52. Vincent van Gogh,** *Peasant of the Camargue (Patience Escalier),* **1888.**
Drawing, brown ink over graphite on white wove paper, 49.4 x 38 cm.
Courtesy of the Fogg Art Museum, Harvard University Art Museums,
bequest of Grenville L. Winthrop. Photo: Katya Kallsen.
© President and Fellows of Harvard College.

The sculptor Vera Mukhina and the architect Boris Iofan devised a
well-known and typical example in the late 1930s. It was a
sculptural monument, constructed from chrome-nickel steel,
standing over 100-feet high, depicting a male industrial worker
brandishing a hammer and a collective-farm woman holding a
sickle aloft. Both figures were muscular and strode forward tri-
umphantly into the future. This sculpture was first displayed on the
top of the USSR's pavilion at the 1937 International Exhibition in
Paris. After the exhibition closed, the grandiose monument to
labour was re-erected on a stone base in the permanent Exhibition
of Economic Achievement, Moscow.

Paintings showing cheerful members of a collective farm or of tractor drivers became commonplace. In the West, the idea that artists should glorify tractor drivers would normally be considered comical but during times of national crisis, such as war, workers in industry and agriculture take on a new, patriotic importance. Norman Rockwell's illustration of American war worker Rose Will Monroe or Rosie the Riveter (*Saturday Evening Post* cover, 29 May 1943) is a famous example. One of Stanley Spencer's finest achievements as an artist was his 1940s depiction of welders in Scottish shipyards. There are other British artists, such as Joseph Herman, who are not ashamed to draw and paint grape-pickers and miners.

Artistic representations of workers that show them *en masse*, as beings conscious of their class and their collective power, are rare in the history of European art but two notable examples can be cited: *The Fourth Estate* (1898–1901) and *The International* (1928–30). The former, by Giuseppe Pellizza da Volpedo (1868–1907), has been acclaimed as a masterpiece of Italian social realism and it depicts a crowd of workers marching in a calm, disciplined manner towards the viewer, from darkness into light. The latter, by Otto Griebel (1895–1972), shows workers from many nations standing shoulder-to-shoulder while singing 'The International'.[29]

**53. Otto Griebel, *Die Internationale*, 1928–30.**
Painting, oil on canvas, 126 x 180 cm.
Berlin: Deutsches Historisches Museum. Photo © the Museum.

The invention of photography in the 1840s greatly increased the possibility of generating records of people and places, and, as it gradually became a mass medium, even ordinary people could afford images of themselves and their loved ones to preserve in family albums. Some British aristocratic families possess painted portraits of their ancestors dating back centuries hanging on the walls of their country houses but most middle- and working-class families only possess photographs dating back a few generations.

Documentary photography also flourished and there were many examples of socially/politically-conscious photographers, such as Lewis W. Hine and Jacob A. Riis, who recorded the plight of the poor, squalid housing conditions, and sweatshop labour. They also honoured the heavy and frequently dangerous work performed by factory mechanics and iron or steel workers (that is, those erecting the metal frames of skyscrapers high above American cities).

During the 1930s, the Historical Section of the Farm Security Administration (a department of a liberal, reformist, 'New Deal' American government) directed by Roy Stryker commissioned a number of photographers to document conditions in the depression-hit countryside. They included: Jack Delano, Dorothea Lange, Russell Lee, Gordon Parks, Marion Post Wolcott, Arthur Rothstein and Ben Shahn. The Library of Congress in Washington DC preserves a huge archive – 270,000 photos taken between 1935 and 1942 – which includes many memorable and emotive images. One photograph, a secular Madonna and Child, that became an icon of the period was Lange's *Migrant Mother, Nipoma, California* (1936), which depicted a stoic but worried mother. She cradles a baby while two camera-shy children cling to her. The family, which had travelled west from the dustbowl of Oklahoma in search of work, was destitute; it was winter and they were living in a car's lean-to at a pea picker's camp. The mother's name, it later transpired, was Florence Neil. She had seven children and survived until she was 80. Two of the children in Lange's photograph lived to see a print of it sold at Sotheby's, New York in 1998 for over $200,000. Although bitter that they had never benefited financially from the image, they were proud that their mother had become part of American history.[30]

A well-known and admired American example of social documentary was *Let Us Now Praise Famous Men* (1941), a book written by James Agee with photographs by Walker Evans. Since their subjects were three white families, poor tenant farmers or share-croppers, living in wooden shacks in Alabama, the title of the book was ironic: none of the sharecroppers was famous before the visit of Agee and Evans in the summer of 1936, and in the book the real names of the families were not used. The title derived from a Biblical quotation, which also included the words: 'And some there be which have no memorial; who perished, as though they had never been born; and their children after them. But these were merciful men, whose righteousness hath not been forgotten.' At first, Agee and Evans' book had poor sales and seemed destined for oblivion but later it came to be regarded as a classic of its time.

A living representative of the social documentary and concerned photography traditions is the photojournalist Sebastião Salgado (b. 1944, Brazil). During the 1960s, he became a political radical and fled into exile when the military took power. He relocated in Paris where he eventually established his own agency called Amazonas. Salgado was first employed as a Third World development economist but he switched to photography in 1973 when he discovered it was better at disclosing the horrors of famine and the harsh conditions experienced by workers and migrants. Salgado became acutely aware of the inequalities associated with the North/South divide and developed a global response to global issues and conditions.

Generally, he devotes years to particular themes/projects, which involves extensive travel researching and taking black and white photographs. His images are then exhibited in touring shows, reproduced in magazine articles and information packs for schools, issued as posters and published in book form.

*Workers: An Archaeology of the Industrial Age*, a large-format and expensive volume published in 1993 after seven years of investigation, documented the manual labour of male and female workers in many, underdeveloped countries. Over 300 duotone photographs recorded such diverse activities as tuna fishing in Sicily, harvesting sulphur in an Indonesian volcano, cutting sugar cane in Cuba, fighting oil well fires in Kuwait, and assembling cars in India. However, the most astonishing pictures showed a 'human anthill' in Brazil, that is, an opencast gold mine where 50,000 male, mud-caked prospectors climbed ladders with loads on their backs. These pictures were reminiscent of scenes described in Dante's *Inferno*.

Salgado generates sequences of images – mini photo-essays – designed to tell the story of a particular industry from raw materials to finished product, and to illustrate the physical action of the labour process, but he also supplies portraits of individual workers whom he prefers not to pose. One aim is to reveal the universal characteristics

54. Sebastião Salgado, 'Transporting bags of dirt in
the Serra Pelada gold mine, Brazil', 1986.
Photograph. © S. Salgado, courtesy of Network Photographers, London.

of similar types of labour in different countries but also the cultural differences that exist. Another aim is to show how everything he depicts is interconnected via, for example, shipping, import/export, and thus constitutes a world economic and transportation system.

Naturally, Salgado hopes his photographs will prick consciences and prompt debates and improvements but even if they do not, they provide a historic document of a passing industrial age and a record of people whose existences were far removed from those of celebrities appearing in *Hello!*. Although Salgado is an atheist and humanist, some critics have detected an epic or religious quality in his depictions of workers who are often photographed *contre-jour* or enveloped in steam or smoke. (He has also been accused of 'aestheticizing tragedy'.) Salgado's justification is that, despite their privations and toil, workers are not merely victims; indeed, that they possess beauty, dignity and nobility, and many take pride in their work, and this is what he sets out to capture.

Writing in 1996, Liz Jobey claimed that photojournalism supplying images of atrocities, starvation and war had declined in the previous two decades because newspaper and magazine editors, conscious of sales figures, increasingly preferred the optimism and 'eye candy' of 'celebrity-based entertainment journalism'.[31] This is one of the reasons why Salgado has increasingly resorted to exhibitions, books and sales of prints and postcards. He has also established his own website.[32] In 1998, Salgado and his wife Lélia founded the Instituto Terra, a non-profit, environmental/reforestation project in Brazil.

A British campaigning journalist who has much in common with Salgado is John Pilger. His book *Heroes* examines the collective struggles of unsung groups around the globe who are subject to exploitation and violence from repressive governments and big business but who fight back in whatever ways they can.[33]

## Memorials to Unsung Heroes

The two examples in this section are both poignant. The first was the brainchild of the British painter George Frederick Watts (1817–1904). In 1887, to mark Queen Victoria's Golden Jubilee, Watts proposed that public memorials should be erected to those ordinary men and women – local heroes – who sacrificed their lives in order to save others. Normally, such brave deeds receive short reports in local newspapers and are then forgotten. His idea was not taken up by the authorities but 13 years later Watts himself designed plaques in the form of Doulton, glazed, ceramic tiles and placed them on a wall in Postman's Park, an open space in the City of London. Each plaque had a brief statement in simple lettering such as: 'Alice Ayres, daughter of a bricklayer's labourer, who by intrepid conduct saved three children from a burning house in Union Street, Borough at the cost of her own young life.' After Watts died, his wife continued the memorials for a time. Today, in Postman's Park, 53 plaques constitute the wall, 50-feet long, known as *The Watts Memorial of Heroic Deeds*. Every day news media report foul atrocities committed by human beings on their fellows; as a counterbalance, it is surely necessary to have some reminders that humans are also capable of supreme altruism. However, as Tim Guest has pointed out, 'it's a strange paradox that their entire lives are reduced to the spectacle of their deaths'.[34]

In 1980, the London-based artist Susan Hiller (b. 1940, Florida) discovered the plaques, which were then in a semi-derelict condition, and was inspired to make a work entitled *Monument* (1980–81). Hiller was originally trained as an anthropologist and throughout her career has taken a close interest in collections of popular culture artefacts. *Monument* took the form of a mixed-media installation, three versions of which appeared in different countries. They

consisted of 41 photographs (one for each year of her life) of the
plaques displayed in various formats on gallery walls, park benches
facing away from the photos, plus headphones so that visitors could
sit and listen to an audiotape. Hiller's sound recording reflected on
the politics of such issues as death, heroism, history, memory and
representation. In the English version of *Monument* shown at the
Ikon Gallery, Birmingham, Hiller added a photo-plaque based on
nearby graffiti which recommended: 'Strive to be your own hero.'[35]

**55. Susan Hiller, *Monument* (British version), 1980–81.**
Installation, mixed-media: 41 c-type photographs, park bench and audiotape.
Birmingham: Ikon Gallery. (Work purchased by the Tate Gallery in 1994.)
Photo courtesy of Susan Hiller.

Another memorial devoted to little-known people is the Aids Memorial Quilt, which commemorates the names and lives of those who have died from Aids. It was conceived by the gay rights activist Cleve Jones in 1985 and begun two years later when the NAMES Project Foundation of San Francisco was established. Within a few years, the quilt consisted of 13,000 colourful panels, each one created by friends and relatives of the victims. It weighed 16 tons, covered 14 acres and was described as 'the largest piece of folk art in the world'. Actually, the quilt is still being enlarged and exhibited throughout the United States. By 2000, the number of panels had reached 44,000. The Foundation has raised millions of dollars and maintains a website that provides a history of the artefact and markets merchandise about it – such as books and documentary videos – in order to raise funds for its continuation and to implement the Foundation's objectives.[36]

## 15-Minute Fame and Self-Representation

Warhol's most famous observation was that, because of the existence of the mass media and publicity, everyone would be world famous for 15 minutes. Given the size of the planet's population, this is not literally possible but it is certainly the case that thousands of ordinary citizens can enjoy brief moments of fame or notoriety by appearing in the press, on radio, television and the Internet. What people are prepared to reveal about themselves on American talk shows such as Jerry Springer's – always assuming such lurid confessions are true – indicates that the hunger for fame has reached desperate proportions.

Another possibility that new media technologies facilitate is the ability of ordinary people to represent themselves. They no longer have to rely on professional image-makers because they can acquire cameras and take photographs and video recordings of themselves. They can even establish their own websites and, via web cams placed in their homes, live their lives in real time while being watched by thousands of strangers. (For example, the American Jennifer Ringley established such a site in 1996: Jennicam.com.) Consequently, they may become famous not for any particular achievements but simply for being willing to share their everyday existences with others. In this way, their whole lives become performance, spectacle. Given the self-focused nature of their work, it is surprising that the artists Gilbert & George and Tracey Emin have not followed suit.

A final example of an initiative to honour 'real' people rather than a minority of 'predetermined celebrities' is the company/website <www.peoplecards.net> based in San Francisco, which sells and promotes collectables, specifically, trading cards. The cards have photo-portraits of ordinary people on one side and brief personal details on the other. Members of the public supply information about themselves. Potential total of the cards is 6 billion! The founders of the company guarantee that their cards are '100 per cent celebrity-free' and employ the slogan 'Fight the Glamour!' Whether or not PeopleCards will appeal to collectors and traders used to cards featuring celebrities remains to be seen.

# 5

# Art Stars

... the incremental celebritisation of the contemporary artist has been fuelled by big sales and a buoyant market ... [1]

On 20 April 2001, the British artist Tracey Emin appeared as a guest panellist on the BBC1 television comedy show *Have I got News for You*. She was the only female on the programme and wore a dress with a plunging neckline in order to show off her swelling breasts. This incident helps to clarify the difference between the majority of successful professional artists and the minority of art stars. The latter have become famous beyond their profession or the art world – which explains why Emin was invited to appear on the programme in the first place – and have shown themselves willing to play the celebrity game – which explains why Emin agreed to take part in a television show that was not a serious arts programme. Of course, Emin has also been happy to appear in specialist arts programmes; indeed, earlier that month she had featured in a new, four-part documentary series about the burgeoning art scene of the 1990s in the East End of London entitled *The New Eastenders* (BBC2). (The name of this series was itself a pun on the title of a popular British television soap opera.) Emin's career will be examined in more detail later but before then, we need to review the history of, first, the cult of the artist, and second, the history of the emergence of art stars.

## Cult of the Artist

Most art historians think the cult of individual artists dates back to the early bourgeois society known as the Italian Renaissance when artists emerged as a professional category distinct from artisans, and both patrons and historians singled out such figures as Brunelleschi, Donatello, Leonardo, Michelangelo and Raphael as geniuses. Giorgio Vasari's *Lives of the Most Excellent Painters, Sculptors and Architects*

(1550) was one of the first texts to acclaim such individuals and to supply biographies of them. Studies by a number of more recent scholars of the characters of artists and the biographical anecdotes, legends, myths and stereotypes associated with them have revealed recurring patterns.[2]

Following the Renaissance, the signature and name of the artist became vitally important to collectors and the art market: if an old canvas discovered in a junk shop can be reliably attributed to Rembrandt then it becomes highly valuable. The image of the artist, often shown in a studio holding the tools of the trade, also became significant as a promotional tool and this helps to explain the popularity among artists of the genre of self-portraiture. Rembrandt is famous for the self-portraits he made at different stages of his life. (Of course, self-promotion was not the only function they served.)

**56. Rembrandt Harmensz van Rijn,** *Portrait of the Artist,* **c. 1662.**
Painting, oil on canvas, 114.3 x 94.2 cm. London: The Iveagh Bequest,
Kenwood House. Photo © Iveagh Bequest, courtesy of English Heritage.

Most contemporary artists take steps to ensure that striking portraits of themselves – either by themselves or by others, either paintings or photographs – are produced and circulated. Some extreme twentieth-century examples exist by artists such as Robert Morris, Lynda Benglis and Sam Taylor-Wood that were designed to shock viewers. Also important was the emergence, at the time of the Romantic Movement, of the expression theory of art, that is, the view that art was a direct transcription of the artist's emotions, personality and lived experience.

Of course, during the Renaissance, a commercial gallery system and the mass media did not exist. However, by the end of the nineteenth century, these systems were in place and, after initial resistance from collectors and the public, the impressionists and post-impressionists benefited from them. Towards the end of his life, Claude Monet was acclaimed, honoured by the French state and commercially successful, and Cézanne, Gauguin and van Gogh were the subjects of posthumous cults. One sign of a cult artist is the preservation of his or her studio or house. Cézanne's purpose-built studio is preserved near Aix en Provence and is a place of pilgrimage for his admirers. Other modern artists whose studios have been preserved as museums or in museums include Constantin Brancusi, Salvador Dalí, Jackson Pollock, Henry Moore, Barbara Hepworth and Francis Bacon.

To return to van Gogh: as the twentieth century progressed, increasing numbers of people saw his work and learnt about his life. As Vincent had intended, the bright colours, simplified drawing and emphatic brushwork of his paintings had a popular appeal, but the story of his years of struggle to become an artist, accounts of his mysterious mental attacks, the mutilation of his ear and his final act of suicide captured the imagination too. Acquisitions by major museums, canvases sold at auction for huge prices, travelling exhibitions, reproductions, posters and postcards, magazine articles, illustrated books, serious art-historical monographs and fictionalised biographies, editions of his letters, Hollywood biopics, a van Gogh Museum in Amsterdam, cinema and television documentaries, cartoons, a popular song, plays, acts of homage by other artists – such as the yellow-hued, psychedelic-style poster *Vincent* designed by Martin Sharp – all combined to make van Gogh world-famous even in countries, such as Japan, far distant from Europe. A veritable van Gogh industry came into being.[3] While millions did view Vincent's drawings and paintings, there was a danger that all the

**57. Martin Sharp, 'Vincent', c. 1970.**
Poster, published by Big O Posters, London, 71 x 48 cm.
© Martin Sharp, Sydney, Australia.

secondary material with its inaccuracies, exaggerations and simpli-
fications would either distract attention away from the works or
inflect the public's interpretation of them.

## Picasso and Dalí

Pablo Picasso and Salvador Dalí, two egocentric Spaniards with
fervid, erotic imaginations, can be identified as the first art stars of
the twentieth century because millions outside the art world, even
people who detested or were indifferent to modern art, became
familiar with their names, faces and works. Both men had substantial achievements as artists but neither shunned publicity. Picasso
(1881–1973) was photographed countless times in his studios, on
holiday (bare-chested and suntanned on the beach) and at the
bullfight (sitting like a Roman emperor amidst a crowd of admirers).
Brassaï, his friend and noted photographer, made portraits of him
that were published in *Life* magazine. As biographer Arianna
Huffington has observed:

> Picasso had mastered the publicity game before the world knew
> that such a game existed. In fact, in many ways he helped to
> invent and define it. He had always recognised, and every step
> of his life had confirmed, a very basic correlation between the
> money fetched by a painting and the legend built around the
> painter. And money, for Picasso, was not so much a medium of
> exchange as the only unequivocal barometer of his success.[4]

In 1956, Henri-Georges Clouzot made the documentary film *Le
Mystère Picasso*, in which Picasso drew and painted specifically for
the camera. The film's objective was to reveal the creative process of
a genius in action. Picasso's inventiveness and productivity, his
achievement as one of the founders of cubism, his frequent changes
of media and style, his presence in Paris during the 1940s Nazi
occupation, his rivalry with Matisse, his pictorial protest against the
atrocities of war entitled *Guernica* (1937), his membership of the
French Communist Party, his appearances at events such as
bullfights, all excited the public's interest. The cubistic fragmentation and re-formation of the human body found in his art
established him as the archetypal modern artist as far as laypeople
were concerned.

**58. Brian Brake, 'Picasso at a bullfight with Jacqueline Roque [left]
and Jean Cocteau [right] with his children Paloma,
Maya and Claude behind him', c. 1955.**
© Brian Brake/Photo Researchers, New York.

Although Picasso had a small, stocky and hairy body, he was a
virile heterosexual with a magnetic personality. A succession of
young women found him attractive and he had several mistresses
who later published memoirs detailing their private lives in which
they described Picasso's seductive charm but also his cruelty towards
them. In 1996, a memoir by Françoise Gilot, an artist and mistress,
was made into a feature film – *Surviving Picasso* – a Merchant-Ivory
production for Warner Bros. Anthony Hopkins starred as Picasso and
Natascha McElhone played the part of Gilot. The Irish art historian

and playwright Brian McAvera has also written a play – *Picasso's Women: Eight Monologues* (1996) – that has been successful and featured actresses such as Susannah York and Jerry Hall.

Like contemporary celebrities, Picasso endorsed political causes such as the Republican side in the Spanish Civil War and the peace campaign (Mouvement de la Paix) for which he employed a dove symbol.

For much of his career, Picasso enjoyed a high income and lived a lavish, upper-class lifestyle – chauffeur-driven cars, country châteaux, Mediterranean vacations, servants, etc. – and after his death in 1973, his estate was estimated to be worth £650 million. (Another common characteristic of art stars is that they leave valuable estates but no wills and so legal disputes about them drag on for years.) A proportion of his art works became the property of the French state and in 1985 a museum devoted to him was added to the tourist attractions of Paris: Le Musée National Picasso. Other Picasso museums and foundations exist in Barcelona and Málaga. Currently, the British art historian John Richardson is engaged in writing a multi-volume account of Picasso that examines his life and work in exhaustive detail. In June 2001, Richardson also presented a television arts documentary series on Channel 4 entitled: *Picasso: Magic, Sex and Death*.

It may seem to outsiders that Picasso handled money, fame and success with panache but when his ex-lover Gilot was interviewed in 1998, she remarked:

> What happened in the 50s is that he [Picasso] turned into a celebrity – he lost power to be a private person ... he got into a sort of vortex, going deeper and deeper until he couldn't escape. He must have had inside him some insecurity which needed to be reassured by constant adulation. He chose to become star [and surrounded himself with 'yes men'] ... Of course, his art suffered – he lost the sense of proportion.[5]

Once established, many major celebrities acquire a court of companions who pander to their every whim, supply constant flattery and control access. If celebrities become old, ill and helpless, then they may end their days as virtual prisoners of the court or the most persistent amanuenses. Of course, celebrities do need gate-keepers and protectors, even bodyguards, because so many strangers want to reach them. Wealthy celebrities are usually inundated with business proposals, free offers, gifts and presents from those who wish to ingratiate themselves in order to gain access or an endorsement.

Some art critics believe that in his later years Picasso should have been much more self-critical, that he should have pruned his *oeuvre*, because so much of it fell short of the high standards he himself had set.

Dalí (1904–1989), who courted publicity even more than Picasso, was fortunate in having middle-class parents who encouraged his early talent for drawing and painting. After an art school training in Madrid, he became a leading figure of the surrealist movement based in Paris until he was 'excommunicated' in 1934 for his crass commercialism and reactionary politics. In his youth, Dalí was excessively timid and sexually repressed; to compensate he decided 'to play at being a genius' and then developed, as an adult, an extrovert, flamboyant personality: 'the inimitable Dalí character, the Dalí "uniform", the Dalí-ad-nauseum that dominated the media while remaining, in reality, a mask'.[6] Thus, he anticipated the strategy of artists such as Gilbert & George and pop stars like Bowie and Madonna.

Dalí became a self-obsessed exhibitionist who delighted in eccentricity and shock. He sported an absurd, upturned moustache, pulled faces for the camera and posed for celebrity photographers such as Philippe Halsman in 'surreal' settings. In 1954, Halsman (1906–1979) and Dalí collaborated to produce a small book consisting of portraits of the artist, which were all visual and verbal jokes about his moustache.[7] However, Halsman's best-known photograph of Dalí was *Dalí Atomicus* (1948), which showed the artist suspended in mid air along with flying cats, chairs, easels and a stream of water.

Dalí also wore bizarre clothes: his costume for a 1936 exhibition opening in London was a deep-sea diving suit (for descent into the depths of the unconscious) in which he nearly suffocated. He published lurid autobiographies detailing his obscene sexual fantasies and passion for masturbation. Desperate for dollars, he spent years in the United States painting flattering portraits of rich patrons, designing advertisements and window displays, a surreal installation for an amusement zone of the New York World Fair, and providing drawings for a dream sequence in a Hollywood movie (Alfred Hitchcock's 1945 *Spellbound*). During the 1930s, paintings depicting Shirley Temple and Mae West testified to Dalí's interest in American female movie stars. In a gouache dated 1934–35, West's head doubled as a surrealist apartment, so that, for instance, her ruby-red lips became a sofa (a real one was later manufactured). Today, one of the main attractions of the Theatre-Museum Dalí in Figueres is the 'Mae West Room' where Dalí's vision was realised in three dimensions by the Catalan architect Óscar Tusquets during the 1970s.

Dalí became notorious for scandals and provocations, and for dream-influenced, symbol-laden paintings featuring memorable, irrational images such as melting watches and giraffes on fire, which he rendered in a precise, illusionistic manner in order to make them seem plausible. His slick style and penchant for weird, kitsch-like imagery proved popular with millions of people with unsophisticated taste, and so his work was and is widely reproduced on posters and postcards. His brand of surrealism also influenced many advertising campaigns.

A long list of names would be required to cite all the famous people Dalí met or who visited his home in Spain but two such encounters indicate the extremes of his acquaintanceship: in London in 1938, Dalí the world's chief visualiser of the unconscious had an audience with Sigmund Freud, the world's prime expert on the unconscious. In the mid 1960s, Dalí was photographed with the American actress and beauty Raquel Welch (b. 1940), who was wearing a bikini, along with an abstract 'portrait' of her he had painted. The occasion was probably a promotional event in a New York store window for the film *Fantastic Voyage* (1966) in which Welch appeared.

In his writings and remarks to journalists, Dalí sought to confuse and intrigue the public through contradiction, paradox and perverse opinions. For example, when he was accused of supporting fascism, he declared that he was 'apolitical' but also that he was 'a monarchist and an anarchist'! To assert his identity as an exceptional individual, Dalí strove to be different from everyone else and this explains his dislike of social conventions and all forms of collectivism. His academic painting style, his willingness to embrace commerce and the mass media, to blur fact and fiction, and his opposition to the rational, socially progressive modernism represented by the architect and painter Le Corbusier, anticipated the culture of post-modernism fashionable during the 1970s and 1980s.

Dalí's final years were marred by artistic decline and physical illnesses, and it has been alleged that, during this period, he signed blanks sheets of paper and so the Dalí market became contaminated by fakes. In 1974, Dalí established his own museum – the Theatre-Museum Dalí (where his corpse is now buried) – in his home town

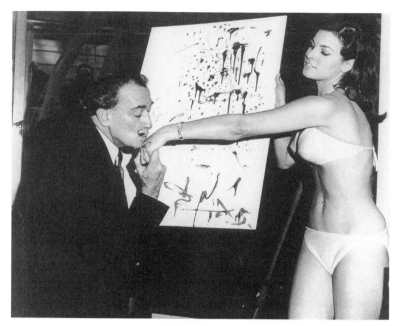

**59. Salvador Dalí with actress Raquel Welch in front of
an abstract 'portrait' of her, c. 1965.**
© Hulton/Archive, Getty Images Inc., London.

of Figueres. During the 1990s, the Gala Dalí Castle Museum House
in Púbol and the Salvador Dalí Museum House in Port Lligat were
opened. In the year 2000, these three museums attracted over
900,000 visitors. Museums and displays devoted to him also exist
in London, Paris and St Petersburg, Florida. Journalist Michael
Glover visited The Dalí Universe, London in 2000 and found it tacky
and expensive:

> Most interesting about this murkily lit spectacle is the master
> himself – photographs of him, mustachios waxed up to brilliant
> points of perfection, wild and lascivious eye blazing, as
> showman, matador, priest, jester, holiest of unholy men, master
> of all his extravagantly incongruous ceremonies; video footage
> of him beating the hell out a piano beside a raging ocean;
> slogans devised to shock the world into recognising the insur-
> passable [sic] and irrepressible genius of his cheek: 'Around Dalí
> everything is real except myself ...'[8]

Today, there are also many websites honouring Dalí and virtual galleries offering editions of his prints, other merchandise and souvenirs for sale, and supplying much needed authentication services.

While some of Dalí's early paintings and films (made with Luis Buñuel) were remarkable contributions to modern art, and one should not overlook the humour and playfulness of his art and persona, overall his career is a testimony to the dire consequences of pursuing money and notoriety instead of ethical integrity and aesthetic quality. Ian Gibson, an Irish writer who has published a substantial biography of Dalí, is one of his most severe critics. In Gibson's judgement, Dalí was a repressed homosexual who led a 'shameful' life. The title of a two-part television documentary Gibson presented in 1997 linked the words 'fame' and 'shame'.[9]

## Jackson Pollock

After World War II, New York replaced Paris as the Western world's art capital and paintings by the American abstract expressionists received national and international acclaim. Pollock (1912–1956) was the first of that generation to 'break the ice', that is, to achieve commercial success and to make a splash in the mass media. Americans were looking for a native art star to rival Europe's Picasso. In August 1949, Pollock was profiled in a *Life* magazine article that began with the question 'Is he the greatest living painter in the United States?' and was illustrated with photographs by Arnold Newman of Pollock standing in front of his drip paintings. Pollock's unconventional method of painting on canvases laid out on the floor aroused curiosity and became a talking point. The artist was photographed several times posing moodily with a cigarette in his mouth while wearing a paint-splattered denim outfit and white T-shirt or dressed in dark clothes like a beatnik poet. His once handsome face was weathered and had a furrowed brow. Such portraits suggested a rugged but emotional artisan, an outsider-rebel in the James Dean mould. (Earlier, Pollock had had a cowboy image because he was a man from Cody in the West and one photo showed him in cowboy gear with rifle and pistol.) Of course, at other times, such as when he gave interviews to the media, Pollock dressed more formally in a jacket, dark trousers, white shirt and tie.

Hans Namuth also photographed and filmed him during the early 1950s while making his action paintings in and around the wooden

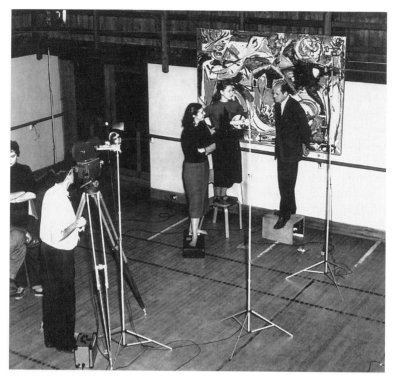

**60. Jackson Pollock being interviewed and filmed by** *The March of Time*
**for a television documentary, at Bennington College where**
**an exhibition of his work was being held, 1952.**
Photo © Pollock-Krasner Papers, Archives of American Art,
Smithsonian Institution, Washington DC.

barn that served as his studio in The Springs, near East Hampton,
Long Island. (Pollock and his wife, the painter Lee Krasner
[1902–1984], bought a house and barn there in 1945.) Namuth's
dramatic photos and films accompanied by Pollock's voice-over
commentary were highly influential in terms of increasing Pollock's
fame and revealing his unusual creative process and techniques. In
March 1951, the British photographer Cecil Beaton was commissioned by *Vogue* magazine to shoot fashion models with Pollock
paintings as a backdrop. This was an early indication that Pollock's
work might eventually lose its apocalyptic charge and end up as
mere wall decoration.

Within the New York art world, Pollock's personal problems were
well known: depression and mental instability (he was prescribed

tranquillisers and attended psychotherapy sessions), drinking binges, aggressive anti-social behaviour, assaults on women and adulteries, bar room brawls and urinating in Peggy Guggenheim's fireplace. (Mike Bidlo, the American appropriation artist, re-created Pollock's infamous urination event in a performance and photograph in the early 1980s.) Pollock might have looked macho and acted tough but he was not considered fit enough to serve in the military during World War II. His premature death in 1956 aged 44 in a self-inflicted car crash terminated his career in a dramatic, violent fashion again like James Dean. However, any sorrow at Pollock's fate should be tempered by the knowledge that he had been drinking, was in a foul mood and the crash was the result of speeding and reckless driving. He had two women passengers with him, one of whom – Ruth Kligman, his lover – was injured and the other – Edith Metzger – was killed. If he had survived, Pollock deserved to be tried and found guilty of manslaughter.

Pollock and the other abstract expressionists achieved renown and affluence after decades of poverty, struggle and public indifference, and some of them were ill equipped to cope with sudden success. Pollock's death was virtual suicide and Mark Rothko did commit suicide in 1970. While Pollock wanted attention and approval for his art, he was also tormented by self-doubt. Publicity was not positive in all respects because it also prompted jokes, ridicule and insults from conservative critics and outraged members of the public. The media's attention made him feel like a freak show, as if 'his skin had been taken off' and he feared the envy and resentment of his fellow artists: 'They only want me on top of the heap, so they can push me off.' One biography claims that, towards the end of his life, Pollock boasted drunkenly in the Cedar Bar that he was 'the greatest painter in the world', that he parodied himself and became 'trapped by his own celebrity ... playing a role; feeling week by week, more like a fraud, more like the phoney that his brothers had always accused him of being'.[10] The painter Mercedes Matter observed sorrowfully: 'The minute success entered into the art world and it became a business, everything changed. It was all ruined.'[11] Subsequent generations, particularly the pop artists, were much more at ease with living in the spotlight, with art as a business, and they developed strategies for coping with media pressure.

In the decades since his death, Pollock's artistic reputation has grown because of biographies, monographs and retrospective travelling exhibitions and the huge prices fetched by major paintings in salerooms. In 1989, a blockbuster biography (934 pages long) written by Steven Naifeh and Gregory White Smith was published and later awarded a Pulitzer Prize. Pollock's studio has been preserved and turned into a national historic landmark and research library: the Pollock-Krasner House and Study Center, which is administered by the State University of New York at Stony Brook. Visitors are required to wear padded slippers to protect the studio's paint-splattered floor. A replica of the studio appeared in the Pollock retrospective held at the Museum of Modern Art in New York in 1998. MoMA's shop also sold Pollock-related merchandise such as a jazz compact disc, a silk scarf and a poster. The complexities of Pollock's drip paintings lent themselves to jigsaw puzzles: in 1965, Springbok Editions issued a 360-piece puzzle of the 1952 canvas *Convergence*.

Somewhat belatedly, the American actor Ed Harris made a biopic – *Jackson Pollock* – in 1999. (The delay may well have been because Pollock was primarily regarded as an abstract painter.) Harris directed and played the part of Pollock while Val Kilmer played his main rival de Kooning. Harris physically resembled Pollock and spent hours rehearsing painting techniques; some scenes were shot on location on Long Island. Naturally, in this film – which received mostly favourable reviews – Pollock's private life and personal problems figured as much as his paintings.

### Francis Bacon

In London, during the 1950s, it was the homosexual painter Francis Bacon (1909–1992), who emerged as Britain's first post-war art star although his full impact took several more decades to achieve. He first became notorious for his striking and cruel imagery – crucifix-ion scenes, screaming Popes, naked grappling male figures – many of which were based on film stills, mass media photographs and repro-ductions of past art. Bacon's painterliness always ensured that horror was tempered by aesthetic pleasure. One thematic exhibition held at the Hanover Gallery in 1957 was a response and contribution to the cult of van Gogh: it consisted of expressionist-style interpreta-tions of Vincent's *The Painter on the Road to Tarascon* (1888).

Bacon's reputation as a painter gradually spread until he was regarded as one of the finest in the world. In 1971, the French honoured him with a retrospective at the Grand Palais in Paris. While Bacon attended the opening, his lover George Dyer died in their hotel room from an overdose of sleeping pills and alcohol. As time passed, media coverage increased and Bacon was interviewed by the critic David Sylvester 18 times and on television by Melvyn Bragg and profiled in the art press repeatedly. During his lifetime, such photographers as Cecil Beaton, Douglas Glass and John Deakin frequently photographed Bacon sitting amidst the carefully cultivated debris of his London studios; the mess served as a vivid emblem of chaotic creativity, and as a sign of Bacon's contempt for such bourgeois values as cleanliness and neatness. In 2001, the contents of his Kensington studio at 7 Reece Mews – even the dust – were placed on public display in Dublin, his city of birth.[12] Like so many other artists' studios, it will be a place of pilgrimage for art lovers.

61. Douglas Glass, 'Francis Bacon in his Battersea studio', late 1950s.
Photograph © J.C. Christopher Glass.

As Bacon became better known, stories about his private life and habits filtered into the public domain, namely, his childhood habits of sleeping with stable boys and dressing in his mother's clothes, the time he spent in decadent Berlin during the 1920s, the heavy drinking sessions in Soho pubs and clubs (particularly the Colony Room, a club depicted by the painter Michael Andrews in 1962), his circle of friends, his passion for violent sex with proletarian petty criminals, his table talk and his acts of cruelty and generosity. The logical culminations of this process are frank biographies and biopics. Daniel Farson wrote an example of the former in 1995 in which Bacon's life was characterised as 'gilded gutter'. An example of the latter, entitled *Love is the Devil*, was premiered in 1998; it was directed by John Maybury and starred Derek Jacobi as the painter. No genuine Bacons appeared in this film because those controlling his estate refused permission.

Even after his death, news stories about Bacon recurred because of legal disputes over his estate (worth £11 million), the emergence of previously unknown drawings, arguments about the authenticity of certain works, and the accusation that his dealers had cheated him out of millions of pounds. Few critics would want to deny the powerful impact and high aesthetic quality of Bacon's paintings dating from the 1940s and 1950s but he did repeat himself as he aged. However, it is my contention that he deserves to be counted as an art star because of his fame and the attention that has been paid to his private life and enigmatic personality.

### David Hockney

Another British homosexual artist who was to become famous after Bacon was David Hockney (b. 1937). Although most of his work was not pop, he was one of the pop art generation that emerged from the Royal College of Art in the early 1960s and he contributed to and benefited from the creative energy and social liberation associated with that remarkable decade. A skilled and witty draughts-man and illustrator, Hockney managed to sell some of his etchings while still a student. Such immediate commercial success was highly unusual at the time. He was soon having solo shows in galleries in London and New York. As already mentioned, the Kasmin Gallery in Bond Street where Hockney showed attracted celebrity collectors such as Vincent Price. Hockney's cheerful and colourful acrylic paintings were much in demand.

Extrovert and articulate, Hockney had an attractive personality besides artistic skills and was happy to participate in the social whirl and to play the celebrity game by providing quotes to journalists on any subject under the sun. Furthermore, he quickly realised the need for a distinctive public image that would appeal to photographers. He had a crew cut and dyed his hair blond (because 'blondes have more fun'), wore large spectacles and a gold lamé jacket, and carried a matching carrier bag. Lord Snowdon photographed him in this 'costume' for the *Sunday Times'* new colour supplement in May 1963 and this image later appeared in the 1965 book *Private View*. The commentary alongside the photo concluded that Hockney was 'already a hero to his generation'. This large-format volume had many colour images of artists in their studios and homes, and was a systematic documentation of the British art world. Therefore, it can be cited as one of the first examples of public interest in the contemporary art scene.

Hockney's move to California in 1964 did not diminish European interest in him because he also spent time in London and Paris. After 1960, international travel by air became much easier and artists were able to benefit in terms of making new contacts in foreign cities and having shows around the world. Numerous articles about Hockney's accessible representational works, profiles of him and his gay lifestyle, filmed documentaries about his life, biographies, serious art historical books and books he wrote himself, and television arts programmes ensured that he became known far beyond the art world and that his fame was sustained decade after decade. His support for gay rights and his criticisms of British life and institutions such as the Tate Gallery also resulted in press reports on the news pages. In 1991, he was elected to the Royal Academy and in 1999, that same institution honoured him by allocating a whole room to his work during the annual, summer exhibition. A huge colourful landscape of the Grand Canyon flanked by mirrors to make it seem even larger won the Wollaston award worth £25,000.

Contacts with other celebrities inevitably followed Hockney's art world success; he was photographed with Warhol and he frequently painted or drew portraits of those he befriended: the British art dealer John Kasmin, the American curator Henry Geldzahler, the writer Christopher Isherwood, the fashion designers Ossie Clark and Celia Birtwell, and the artists R.B. Kitaj and Patrick Procktor. Clearly, much of Hockney's output was autobiographical in inspiration and this surely provided a precedent for the confessional art of artists like Tracey Emin that came later.

Hockney's versatility has served to renew his career: he has turned his hand to stage design, photography and 'fax art' and even art history (a book and television documentary on the use of lenses and camera obscuras by painters through the centuries). There is no disputing the fact that Hockney is an accomplished and popular artist, but in terms of the history of modern art, his contribution has been a minor one. The critic Robert Hughes once rightly described him as 'the Cole Porter of contemporary art'. He is one of those artists whose fame exceeds his artistic merit.

## Yoko Ono

Ono (b. 1933), the Japanese-American artist, is an especially interesting example because she started her career in a low key way as an avant-garde, concept artist and filmmaker and then 'piggy-backed' to stardom by marrying a famous British pop star. During the early 1960s, she participated in the international Fluxus movement and was known only within art circles in New York and London. However, although she had a flair for self-publicity (witness her 1966–67 *Film No. 4 [Bottoms]* that succeeded in attracting the attention of the British press), it is unlikely that she would have become famous beyond the art world if she had not had a love affair with John Lennon. They met after she moved to London with her husband and child in the mid 1960s. (They were both married at the time.) Some accounts of their romance claim that Ono deliberately targeted Lennon. Many fans of the Fab Four blamed her when the group broke up and she had to endure years of antagonism. John and Yoko later married and throughout the 1970s, they engaged in political actions, film and musical collaborations, which catapulted Ono to world fame. She used her newfound fame and wealth to communicate political messages, such as 'no more war', to a global audience. (Much later, in 2002, she spent considerable sums hiring billboards in London, New York and Tokyo to display a peace message quoted from Lennon's song 'Imagine'.) Despite the benefits of fame that Lennon and Ono enjoyed, media intrusion clearly bothered them because in 1969 they produced a caustic condemnation of it via the film *Rape: Film No. 6*, which depicted a young woman who was relentlessly pursued by a camera crew until she became distressed.

After Lennon's murder in 1980, Ono resumed her solo artistic career and held exhibitions in prestigious galleries in Europe, Japan and the United States. She also created new sculptures and recorded new albums. In 2000, the Japan Society based in New York honoured Ono with a major retrospective exhibition, her first in America since 1971.

As Lennon's widow still resident in New York, Ono now enjoys the respect of all those who admired John. She controls the Lenono Photo Archive and has donated or lent Lennon's drawings and personal possessions – clothes, guitars, manuscripts – to the Rock 'n' Roll Hall of Fame in Cleveland, which recently hosted a special exhibition entitled *Lennon: His Life and Work* (2001), and to the John Lennon Museum, which opened in the Saitama New Urban Centre north of Tokyo in 2000. (Both institutions have websites.) The story of his life told by the museum in Japan stresses Ono's importance to Lennon's post-Beatles development and was designed to counter, finally, misogynist and racist opinions about her.[13]

In March 2002, Ono visited Liverpool's airport (renamed John Lennon International) to unveil a 7-feet bronze statue of Lennon executed in an academic manner by local sculptor Tom Murphy. Lennon is shown in his mature years, wearing round glasses and a casual suit with his hair greased back. Murphy has also made sculptures of Billy Fury and Princess Di.

## Andy Warhol

No account of art and celebrity could omit Warhol (1928–1987, aka Andy and Drella) because fame and glamour were central to his art and life. He hailed from the industrial city of Pittsburgh and came from a Czech, Catholic immigrant, working-class family. Catholics, of course, venerate icons featuring highly stylised and stereotyped images of Mary and Jesus. (Warhol's religious roots, ethnic identity and links to the folk art of the Carpatho-Rusyn region have been explored by Raymond M. Herbenick.[14]) He was Christened Andrew Warhola and so, when he moved to New York in 1949, he shortened, simplified and anglicised his name as so many movie stars do. In addition, like the stars Liz and Marilyn, Warhol became so famous people were able to use only his first name: Andy.

Warhol's 'social disease' – his daily need to attend parties and his obsession with celebrities that dated from childhood – and his many depictions of stars have already been discussed. He studied art and design at Carnegie Tech in Pittsburgh and then found employment as a commercial illustrator. One of the first articles he illustrated was about success: 'Success is a job in New York', published in *Glamour* magazine. One New York celebrity Warhol developed a crush on after seeing a book jacket portrait was Truman Capote (1924–1984), a good-looking, homosexual writer. Warhol behaved like an infatuated fan: he wrote Capote a stream of letters and lurked outside his home. Eventually, Warhol did meet the author but was told to stop pestering him by Capote's mother. In 1952, Warhol's first solo exhibition, held at the Hugo Gallery, consisted of 15 drawings inspired by Capote's short stories. The drawings were another means by which Warhol tried to attract Capote's attention.

Although Warhol was a successful graphic artist and window display designer, he wanted acclaim as a fine artist. He may also have switched to painting for economic reasons because photographs were replacing line illustration in magazines and adverts. After attracting the attention of dealers, critics and the art world public with his paintings of movie stars and death and disaster subjects in the early 1960s, Warhol diversified by adding filmmaking to his portfolio. Some 500 visitors to his studio were invited to take a three-minute screen test as if Warhol was a Hollywood mogul on the lookout for new movie stars. However, Warhol was an unusual film director because he hardly directed at all: for the screen tests he would switch on the camera and then walk away. Mary Woronov, who took one while still a university student, has recalled what an ordeal it was to be left alone with no script to face the black hole of the camera and how quickly people's public personae began to crumble:

> ... the way people's expressions changed in screen tests, making it a psychological study as their images cracked and their real personalities crept naked out of their eyeballs, the idea of conferring immortality upon unknowns – everyone's democratic little minute of fame – the deafening speechlessness of it all. Like a medieval inquisition, we proclaimed them tests of the soul ... what appealed most of all to us, the Factory devotees ... was the game, the cruelty of trapping the ego in a 15-minute cage for scrutiny.[15]

Even Dalí, it seems, found his screen test a trial.

Initially, Warhol made silent, experimental or underground 16 mm films that were the antithesis of Hollywood-type narrative films. They had no mass or popular appeal but Warhol soon decided that personality was the most important factor in movie-making and so he (and the director Paul Morrissey) began parodying the Hollywood studio system by developing his own roster of stars selected from his immediate circle of poor-little-rich girls, studs, social misfits, drug addicts and transvestites. Anyone in fact who was an exhibitionist and who liked to talk and improvise on camera. Typically, Warhol added an inflationary factor by calling them 'superstars'. (Language inflation is relentless and requires further neologisms such as 'megastar'.) René Ricard has claimed that Chuck Wein, one of Andy's circle, coined the term 'superstar' but Warhol himself credited Ingrid von Scheflin (aka Ingrid Superstar). In any case, the adjective 'super' was familiar from the comic book character Superman (a subject painted by Warhol in 1961), which in turn was derived from Friedrich Nietzsche's concept of the Übermensch.

Warhol's superstars were nothing of the kind but they did delight minority audiences such as the gay community and as Warhol's fame spread their names and faces did too: Gerard Malanga, Joe Dallesandro, the 'Pope' Ondine, Edie Sedgwick, Jackie Curtis, Ingrid Superstar, Baby Jane Holzer, Ultra Violet, Viva, Holly Woodlawn and Candy Darling. (Many of them were later to publish memoirs of their Factory years.) As Caroline A. Jones has pointed out, Warhol's superstars were, unlike stars under contract in Hollywood, 'unpaid, untrained, undirected, and eventually unemployed'.[16] They tolerated his exploitation in exchange for associating with a famous artist and the chance of personal fame. Warhol particularly admired men like Jimmy Slattery (aka Candy Darling) who imitated women because so much hard work was involved. He also valued drag queens because they were walking 'archives of ideal movie star womanhood'.

During the late 1960s, when Morrissey started to direct Warhol's films, they became more mainstream – with soundtracks, colour, storylines and editing – but the way subjects were treated was usually comic and subversive. For instance, *Lonesome Cowboys* (1968) was a camp send-up of the popular Hollywood genre of the Western shot on location in Arizona. Its gang of gay cowboys was designed to give ultra-masculine stars like John Wayne (aka Marion Morrison, Duke, 1907–1979) apoplexy. The films were screened in art house cinemas internationally and some later became widely available on videotape and via television channels.

When, in the mid 1960s, Warhol decided to organise public entertainments, that is, mixed-media happenings in which his films were projected, he needed live music to accompany them; hence, his recruitment of the Velvet Underground – one of the finest and most original rock music bands of all time – and Nico, the beautiful, German-born, blonde model, actress and chanteuse. Nico (aka

Christa Päffgen, 1938–1988) was already a minor film star and Lou Reed of the Velvets subsequently became a world-famous rock musician. (At the time of writing, Reed's partner is the artist Laurie Anderson.)

Given Warhol's experience of shoe illustration, it is no surprise that he developed a deep-seated interest in style, fashion and fashion models. In later life, he even performed as a fashion model several times (he was represented by the Ford Modelling Agency). Unlike some artists, he did not adopt a single trademark set of clothes. He wore different outfits at different times in his life and for different occasions but several of his outfits did become familiar and are now preserved in The Andy Warhol Museum, Pittsburgh. Warhol was conscious that he had a plain or even corpse-like, Dracula-like appearance – a lumpy face, albino complexion and poor skin – and took steps to improve it. (Intimates called him 'Drella', a combination of Dracula and Cinderella.) Mark Francis and Margery King have provided a summary:

> Warhol's own transformations were clearly visible in his dress, as he moved from young 1950s professional, to hip 1960s art star, to business artist in the 1970s and 1980s. Like Candy Darling, Warhol had altered photographs of himself as a young man [he made his nose thinner and added more hair]. He began to physically transform himself in the 1950s, when he had cosmetic surgery on his nose and first wore a hairpiece to cover his advancing baldness. The artist's wigs grew ever bolder, culminating in the hard-to-miss 1980s shock of white hair … Warhol was also armed with a wide array of cosmetics (to smooth his mottled skin), scents, and unguents, and had worn a corset to support his mid section ever since he was shot … In the early 1980s, the artist used heavy makeup and an array of wigs [he owned over 50] to transform himself into a variety of near-female personae, expressing in his own person the close connection between beautification, reinvention, transformation, and drag.[17]

Warhol, who had been a sickly, shy child, actively sought fame but realised he needed strategies to protect himself from the intense media pressure he knew fame would bring. He was a workaholic – always extremely active and busy – but seemed to be a passive, cool, detached, unemotional and non-judgemental voyeur rather than a participant. His acceptance of consumerism and tolerance towards weird behaviour among his coterie made him seem amoral and apolitical. (Actually, his politics were odd: he was a Democrat – he opposed Richard Nixon – but he made fun of feminism and Fidel Castro, and later celebrated such right-wing figures as Nancy Reagan and Imelda Marcos.) In the 1960s, Warhol's rejection of the humanism and spiritual values associated with abstract expressionism was disturbing. He developed a durable persona or mask that was blank, autistic even, as if there was nothing behind his outward appearance. This involved answering interviewers' questions with 'yes' or 'no' or 'don't know' or 'wow!' and hiding his eyes behind dark sunglasses. However, he was also capable of flippant, witty and outrageous remarks. (When asked what he would do if he gained political power, he replied that he would have all streets carpeted!) Warhol considered art to be a form of entertainment and he was determined to amuse the public. He evaded serious questions about his art, his past and private life or told falsehoods about them. Few in the 1960s knew that Warhol was a devout Catholic who attended church regularly and helped the homeless. He was a homosexual but the details of his sex life remained secret. (Since his death, biographers have revealed the names of his lovers and scholars have analysed the 'queer' aspects of his art in detail.)[18] He told reporters he wanted to be a machine (presumably a recording machine like a camera or tape recorder) and that he liked being instructed what to do and frequently asked others to suggest subjects to paint. He also claimed that anyone could do what he did and, on one notorious occasion, when he was invited to give talks on the college circuit, set out to prove it by sending a double (Allen Midgette) in his place. He also supported an attempt to design a robot replica of himself.

During the 1960s, silver was a favourite colour of Warhol's. His studio was lined with silver foil. It was glamorous because it glittered, had silver screen and space age associations, and reflected light like mirrors, which present viewers with a view of themselves and their environment rather than an insight into a world beyond. One of the Velvet's songs was entitled 'I'll be your Mirror'. Warhol himself remarked about mirrors: 'People are always calling me a mirror', but then asked if he, a mirror, looked into another, what would be reflected? Answer: he would see nothing, a void.

Clearly, Warhol was subverting the conventional view of artists as unique, creative, original auteurs who expressed their inner selves. He also rejected macho, angst-ridden abstraction. Using news photographs and silk-screens to reproduce them, and delegating assembly-line production to assistants, letting the film camera run while he phoned his press agent, were other ways of playing down his creativity. Warhol's work did develop a distinctive visual character but it resembled the imprimatur of a famous brand or trademark rather than the 'signature style' of a traditional painter. Eventually, this style became so familiar that it could be learnt and applied by others, a process that has been called 'Warholisation'.

At first sight, Warhol's self-portraits might be thought an exception to his refusal to admit having an inner self. It seems his dealer Ivan Karp encouraged him to make self-portraits in 1963 because, in Karp's view, the public wanted to see what the notorious pop artist looked like. Warhol followed Karp's advice but his self-portraits gave little away: in a 1967 series, his head was reduced to a two-dimensional pattern and half of it was in deep shadow. (Echoes of Jung's theories about the dark and light sides of human personality.) In so far as there was a facial expression, it was studious and composed. Variations of hue from canvas to canvas could be interpreted as signifying changing moods but more plausibly the play of coloured spotlights. A hand protected his chin and a finger poised over a closed mouth seemed to urge silence. Warhol stared directly at the camera as if to challenge the viewer to find any meaning or trace of character. (However, Warhol did believe in idealising his appearance: pimples were covered up or left out of his self-portraits.) Moreover, in the late ones, executed in the 1980s, his face was overlaid with camouflage patterns as if to say: 'you will find it hard to penetrate this disguise'.

The result of all the media attention paid to Warhol and his milieu was that he became a phenomenon, a Svengali figure, greater than any of his works of art. The formalist critic Clement Greenberg dismissed pop art as 'novelty art'; he described Warhol as 'cute' and thought the appeal of his art was 'a period thing'. It is true that Warhol's work – like that of all significant artists – was 'of its historical moment' but this has not stopped it enduring.

Warhol's protective tactics worked well for a number of years but they could not prevent him from experiencing a common fate of celebrities: an attack by a deranged fan or enemy. In 1968, the feminist writer Valerie Solanas shot Warhol and he almost died. Afterwards, his life changed: he became more fearful and security conscious. His base of operations became 'the Office' and it was less open than the Factory had been. However, it is typical of a celebrity that Warhol was willing to show the operation scars across his chest to the world by having them photographed by Richard Avedon in 1969. A year later, he also posed for the respected American portrait painter Alice Neel (1900–1984) with his torso naked apart from a surgical corset. Since Neel belonged to a social realist tradition of art, she depicted Warhol as a wounded, introspective human being rather than as an art star. According to Neel, Warhol the 'art world personality' represented 'a certain pollution of this era'.

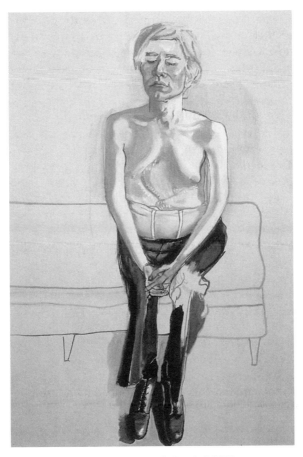

**62. Alice Neel, *Andy Warhol*, 1970.**
Painting, oil on canvas, 152.4 x 101.6 cm. New York: Whitney Museum of American Art collection. Gift of Timothy Collins. Reproduced courtesy of the Alice Neel Estate, New York.

In some respects, Warhol was a documentary artist and social archivist. He kept diaries, carried a camera everywhere, and made 4,000 tape recordings of phone calls and interviews. Periodically, he also placed fan mail, invitations, magazines, books, newspaper clippings, images and ephemera in cardboard boxes, marked them by date and then deposited them in an archive as 'time capsules'. (When he died, there were over 600 boxes and the archivists of the Andy Warhol Museum are gradually cataloguing their contents.) He must have been convinced that his life and times were worth recording for posterity and the fascination he has exerted since his death has proved him right. Many of those in his entourage, for instance Brigid Polk, Pat Hackett, Nat Finkelstein and Billy Name, felt the same way and made numerous sound recordings or took hundreds of photographs of the Factory and its passing parade. The American mass media, therefore, never ran short of sound bites, images and gossip items.

One way in which Warhol was able to get close to the celebrities he admired was to interview them for his own magazine. *Interview* was initially founded in 1969 as a monthly film journal but soon became a vehicle for glamorous publicity photographs of, and interviews with, stars in every field of entertainment. A double dose of celebrity was achieved by persuading celebrities to interview one another. (This practice is continued by *Modern Painters*: David Bowie conducts interviews with art stars.) Covers were adorned with photo-portraits modified to resemble Warhol's paintings of movie stars and inside were fashion spreads by emerging photographers. *Interview* is still being published but Brant Publications Inc. of New York now owns it. Circulation is reported to be 170,000 and Michael Wolff has described the magazine as 'the local paper of fametown ... a trade magazine for the famous or those who would like to be part of the fame profession'.[19] Michael Lassell has described *Interview* less favourably as 'a forum in which the celebrated could wallow in the fact of their celebrity, right-wing dictators ... chatting amiably with the latest vacuous supermodel or drugged out rock 'n' roll freak. "Andy Warhol", says Fran Lebowitz ... "made fame famous".'[20]

Many of the topics discussed above were explored in more detail in the 1997 travelling exhibition *The Warhol Look: Glamour, Style, Fashion*. Despite the singular 'look' of the title, as curators Mark Francis and Margery King explain, there were successive looks, a repertoire of styles associated with Warhol and his entourage and they had 'a pervasive influence on taste'.

A further characteristic of art stars already noted is their willingness to endorse merchandise and services for purely commercial
reasons. Warhol, the business artist, had no qualms on this score
and endorsed Air France, Braniff Airlines, Diet Coke, Pioneer Radios,
Puerto Rican rum, Absolut Vodka and so on.

As Warhol matured and became more adept at clinching business
deals, he expanded into more and more fields: television series, pop
music videos, magazine publishing, fashion collections and watch
designing. During the mild 1980s, when it seemed the public was
becoming bored with him, Warhol was encouraged to take up his
paintbrushes again by the rising SoHo art star Basquiat.

That there was an intelligent mind behind Warhol's idiot-savant
performance was revealed by his books (written with the help of
others because he was dyslexic) in which there are many insights
about American society, fame and celebrity. Obviously, Warhol had
first-hand experience to draw upon. His prediction that 'in the future
everybody will be world famous for 15 minutes' itself became famous
and is still in daily use. Of course, Warhol himself enjoyed fame for
far longer.

In 1981, Warhol produced a series of multiple and single image
paintings and prints entitled *Myths* for a show at Ronald Feldman's
Gallery, New York. The 'myths' in question were American icons
from the popular culture of his childhood: Dagwood, Dracula,
Howdy Doodie (a ventriloquist's dummy in a television show for
children), Mammy (Aunt Jemima), Mata Hari (Greta Garbo),
Superman, Uncle Sam, Santa Claus, The Witch and Mickey Mouse.
As Greg Metcalf has pointed out, commercial artists whose names
are not generally known created most of these icons, hence they
developed a life independent of the creators' biographies and personalities. In one painting, all these characters were repeatedly
represented in vertical strips resembling filmstrips. On the right, at
the end of the sequence was a strip featuring Warhol himself. The
self-portrait showed part of his by then battered face but most of the
image was a shadow of Warhol's profile. This was probably a
reference to the famous radio crime series of the 1930s and 1940s
called *The Shadow*, which Warhol had listened to in his youth.
Warhol was present as an observer/consumer of the icons but the
two-dimensional projection of his image also implied that he now
counted as an American myth himself. It also served as a metaphor
for his artistic procedures: transforming three-dimensional objects
into flat images.[21]

Warhol died on 22 February 1987 aged 58. On 1 April over 2,000 people, who included many artists and celebrities, attended a memorial Mass at St Patrick's Cathedral in New York. Critic Calvin Tomkins thought the event resembled 'a state funeral'. Warhol left an estate worth $600 million and since he had been a shopaholic comparable to Elton John, his 27-room Manhattan mansion was packed with Art Deco furniture, American folk art, Navajo Indian blankets, art works by Man Ray (an artist Warhol admired and was influenced by), plus junk of all kinds. An auction of his personal effects was held at Sotheby's in New York in 1988. The 10,000 lots attracted crowds desperate for souvenirs and even his collection of 134 kitsch cookie jars sold for $240,350. This was a clear instance of collectibles attaining a high value because of their celebrity association or what anthropologists call 'sympathetic magic'. Some of the money raised was used to establish a charity to help young artists: the Andy Warhol Foundation for the Visual Arts, and his legacy is also preserved and actively fostered by the staff of the Andy Warhol Museum in his home town. Warhol's art was so multifaceted the museum's curators can mount new travelling exhibitions every year that provide fresh takes on his achievements.

Since Warhol's death, his fame has continued to spread and there have been a number of feature films in which he has been portrayed by well-known actors and rock stars. For instance, in Julian Schnabel's 1996 film about Basquiat, the part of Warhol was played by Bowie; in Mary Harron's 1996 film about Solanas, Warhol was played by Jared Harris; in Oliver Stone's 1991 film about Jim Morrison and the Doors, Crispin Glover played Warhol. Several film and television documentaries about Warhol have been produced but what has not yet appeared is a full-length biopic. Surely, such a film cannot be long delayed but, of course, it would pose a challenge to its makers because its 'hero' was non-heroic and strove so hard to imitate the still centre of a hurricane.

An excellent summary of Warhol's achievement can be found in Neal Gabler's book contending that entertainment has now conquered reality:

His stardom ... was ultimately less a by-product of his art than a higher form of it. What Warhol realised and what he promoted in both his work and his life ... was that the most important art movement of the twentieth century ... was celebrity. Eventually, no matter who the artist was and what school he belonged to, the entertainment society made his fame his achievement and not his achievement his fame. The visual art, like so much else in American life, was a macguffin for the artist. It was just a means to celebrity, which was the real artwork.[22]

## Joseph Beuys

During the 1970s, the German artist Beuys (1921–1986) became Europe's rival to Warhol in terms of charisma and fame. However, Beuys exemplified a vastly different kind of artistic practice from Warhol's because he believed art was a mystical or spiritual force and a catalyst for political and social change rather than simply a lucrative business and commentary on mass culture. In 1989, Thierry de Duve summed up the differences between them as follows:

> In the art of the past twenty years, only Joseph Beuys equals Andy Warhol in legend-value – that is, media-value ... But Beuys is a hero and Warhol is a star. For Beuys, capitalism remained the cultural horizon to leave behind; for Warhol, it was simply nature. Like Marx a bourgeois German, Beuys wanted to incarnate the proletarian. Warhol, an American immigrant of working-class origins, wanted to be a machine. At the nexus of these oppositions are several related facts: that Beuys based art on will and thus on a principle of production, and Warhol on desire and thus on a principle of consumption; that Beuys believed in creativity and Warhol did not; and that for Beuys art was labor while for Warhol it was commerce.[23]

Beuys was a versatile artist who made drawings and sculptures, constructed installations and gave live performances accompanied by animals such as dead hares and live coyotes. His use of glass vitrines anticipated Damien Hirst's later fondness for them. During the 1960s, he, like Ono, participated in the international experimental art movement known as Fluxus whose name was inspired by the change and transformation conveyed by the word 'flux'. He restored the reputation of German art after the devastation of World War II and the shame of Nazi art, and to some degree, he redefined and expanded the very concept 'Art'.

Unlike most artists, Beuys did not seclude himself in a studio. He was very much a public figure willing to travel throughout Europe and the United States in order to meet people. This was because he was an idealistic political agitator and theorist who sought the reform of German art education and universities in general, indeed the entire democratic process. He advocated 'a new International School for Creativity and Interdisciplinary Research' and 'direct democracy via referenda' and helped to establish Germany's Green Party. Some of his later public sculptures were direct contributions to the environmental movement; for example, the 7,000 oak trees he planted at Documenta 7 (Kassel, 1982).

After a childhood in which his interests were botany and music, Beuys trained in art at the Düsseldorf Academy from 1947 to 1951 and, a decade later, he was appointed the institution's Professor of Monumental Sculpture. In the early 1970s, he caused a national furore in Germany because of his teaching methods and unilateral attempts to increase the number of art students. (Beuys attracted crowds of students.) He was dismissed from his teaching post in 1972 but Beuys defied the order and continued to hold classes. He declared it would take tanks to remove him, but in reality, it only took a few police.

Beuys thought all human beings had creative potential and could become artists and he held many meetings and debates in which he expounded proposals for ecological and social change. Some listeners found his ideas inspiring, while others thought them utopian fantasies.

There were autobiographical and self-mythologising aspects to his art and writings. During World War II, he flew in Nazi Stuka bombers until 1943 when he was shot down over the Crimea. Nomad Tartars found his shattered body and used felt and animal fat to restore his health. These materials thus acquired for Beuys a symbolic charge and were later key constituents of his mixed-media installations. In the 1950s, he had a nervous breakdown and spent time working on the land. He also presented himself, and was interpreted by critical supporters, as a modern day healer or shaman. His followers revered him like a saint or holy man. The British critic Caroline Tisdall was so enchanted she became his amanuensis and travelling companion; she photographed him many times.[24] Of course, there were many sceptics too who considered Beuys a 'low charlatan', 'crackpot' or reactionary because he drew inspiration from German Romanticism, alchemy, primitivism, Nordic and Celtic folklore, and Rudolf Steiner's anthroposophy.

**63. Nigel Maudsley, 'Portrait of Joseph Beuys', 1993?**
Photo © Nigel Maudsley, courtesy of Anthony d'Offay Gallery, London.

Beuys had a striking appearance: gaunt face, large eyes, thin white flesh and he generally wore a recognisable costume of felt hat and gamekeeper's vest plus, in winter, a voluminous, fur-lined overcoat. The physical presence of Beuys was essential to the impression made by his art – much of it elusive, fugitive, fragmentary and unpolished – and therefore after his death the remaining objects and multiples seemed far less potent. They took on the character of forlorn relics. Following his death, a major retrospective was held in Berlin in 1988 and forgers were soon busy because of the high prices his works were beginning to fetch in salerooms. Beuys' place in art history books is secure, but because his art did not, like Warhol's, involve the mass media he was not as popular beyond the art world as the American. However, the British critic William Feaver has claimed that 'fame was his art' and that Beuys was keen to be famous because of the power to influence society that accompanied it.[25]

## Gilbert & George

Gilbert Proesch (b. 1943, Italy) and George Passmore (b. 1942, England) met in 1967, while students at St Martin's School of Art, London. They then decided to live together and to join forces as artists. First, they dropped their surnames and used only their Christian names, which happened to alliterate. As already noted, the adoption of new names or the simplification of existing names is a common characteristic of film stars. Second, they began to sport near identical haircuts and wear traditional English suits made to order by an East End tailor. Again, the adoption of a costume that acts as a trademark and represents an invented character is typical of many entertainers (Charlie Chaplin's tramp, for example). G&G's whole *oeuvre* has been a peculiar mixture of conservative and radical elements. For instance, in the age of hippie fashion, choosing suits was at once backward-looking and outlandish. At times, they also covered their faces and hands with metallic powder and red make-up to alter their features and to make them more like objects or aliens.

Even as students they challenged the dominant conception of sculpture at St Martin's – abstract, welded metal structures – by substituting performance for constructed objects and by declaring themselves 'living sculptures'. As in the case of actors and dancers, in performance and body art, the artist's living body becomes the means and material for their art, hence it is no wonder that the two became confused in the minds of spectators. The idea of living sculptures or statues was not original: the Italian artist Piero Manzoni had already proposed it and provided a plinth for anyone to pose on. G&G wanted viewers to look at them as if they were art objects and they continued to subvert the traditional conception of sculpture by declaring that everything they subsequently produced was 'sculpture'.

The decision to collaborate, to submerge their individual identities in a joint persona, which Rosetta Brooks has characterised as 'the personification of the aesthetic attitude', itself undermined the received wisdom that art was the consequence of exceptional individuals who splurged their inner emotional turmoil on to canvas. Furthermore, the decision to be works of art 24 hours a day meant that they no longer had any separate, private lives: everything became public. (If they did preserve any private lives, they were kept very secret.) Their creative partnership thus involved considerable sacrifice, intense concentration and dedication. It has lasted far longer than many marriages.

One of their first decisions on leaving art school was to market themselves aggressively. They hired a business manager, systematically approached London galleries with proposals (none were accepted) and attended as many public events as possible. Some of the latter included rock music concerts and festivals. Therefore, in this respect, they anticipated the promotional strategies of the young British artists (YBAs) of the 1980s and 1990s. At first, G&G became noted within the British art world for their appearances at exhibition private views where they posed motionless and for lengthy performances in galleries (*The Singing Sculpture*, 1969–73) in which they moved in a stylised fashion to a recording of Flanagan and Allen's 'Underneath the Arches', a music hall song about the lives of tramps. (G&G reminded viewers of marionettes, mime artists, robots and zombies.) As the partnership of Flanagan and Allen indicates, double acts are more common in the world of entertainment than in the world of art. Dealers in Europe and the United States were intrigued and by the early 1970s, G&G had achieved international fame.

Live performance has its limitations – it is exhausting and the performers can only be in one place at a time, and unless they are paid a fee, there is no product to sell to gain a profit. It is for this reason pop stars make records and videos besides appearing live on stage. G&G quickly realised that they too had to have products to exhibit and sell and so they made charcoal drawings and paintings, and issued postcards, limited edition books and videotapes. Eventually, their main medium became photography and they devised billboard-size, multi-coloured/panelled photomurals reminiscent of sermonising, Victorian, stained glass windows. However, to preserve the idea that all these products were the output of G&G, self-portraits were nearly always included. Any signs of handwork were eliminated because they evoked individual expression. G&G demonstrated hard work, versatility and meticulous artisanship and presentation. Their performances were entertaining and their photomurals sufficiently colourful, simple and direct in terms of both form and content (some critics considered them simple minded) to be accessible to a wide audience, another characteristic shared with most YBAs.

One of their most amusing and impressive achievements was a film entitled *The World of Gilbert & George* (1981). As the expression 'the world of' makes clear, what G&G were attempting to fabricate was a new, strange realm in which they acted as tourist guides. Their eighteenth-century house in Fournier Street, Spitalfields was also transformed in terms of its furnishing and interior décor until it resembled a private museum. It regularly provided a setting for their photographs, videos and films, and so can be compared to the celebrity homes featured in magazine spreads and on television.

In later years, G&G mounted huge exhibitions of their photomurals around the globe, even in cities such as Moscow (1990) and Beijing (1993). They were the first living British artists to show in China since the advent of communism. G&G made a point of attending these shows and this is another reason why they became familiar to millions.

Another publicity stratagem G&G employed was the creation of a 'philosophy of art' which they named 'Art for All'. It consisted of short, simple statements written in an affected style mixed with offbeat opinions (often politically incorrect) that they circulated in manifestos and repeated like mantras to all interviewers. In short, it was a 'spiel' that had been carefully worked out beforehand and rehearsed. Warhol had behaved in a similar manner in interviews during the 1960s and Koons was later to develop his own brand of 'koonspeak' uttered, according to Anthony Haden-Guest, with 'breathy solemnity'. Such spiels act as a carapace protecting the celebrity from media intrusion; it precludes unguarded admissions. It also baffles because the sincerity and truthfulness of the utterances are so hard to judge.

During the 1970s, G&G became commercially successful and spent money on drunken binges, one of which led to an arrest. Their alcoholic antics were all documented in their art works. Despite their apparent narcissism, G&G decided that art should be about the urban life around them and so they began to record in photographs and films young skinheads, tramps and members of ethnic minorities. (G&G have generally preferred to depict anonymous people rather than celebrities.) The fact that they always represented boys or men led to speculation about G&G's sexual preferences – were they homosexuals? This they refused to admit but they did assert that they never made 'gay art'. (However, they have supported Aids charities.) Their representations of 'Pakis' with themselves looking on voyeuristically also prompted accusations of racism, which they have denied. Over the years they have admitted admiring the British royal family and the Conservative politicians

Edward Heath (a personal friend), Margaret Thatcher and William Hague, and detesting left-wing critics.

Whatever the truth about their sex lives and politics, the controversies in the press increased their notoriety. Headlines also followed their use of dirty words, obscene graffiti, swastikas and photographs of their own blood, faeces, urine and naked bodies. In 2000, their shift of allegiance from the dealer Anthony d'Offay to Jay Jopling, a YBA specialist, prompted news stories as did their first show at Jopling's White Cube 2 gallery in 2001, which was called *The New Horny Pictures* and consisted of images of adverts by male prostitutes extracted from the press. It seems G&G were trying to update themselves by association with a younger generation of artists and art entrepreneurs.

It is evident from the above summary that G&G have tried to maintain a high public profile by shock tactics but, paradoxically, they became establishment figures in terms of the art market, arts councils and public museums. (G&G have upset some religious bigots but shocking art world habitués has become a thankless task because the latter have become so blasé – they are now virtually shock proof.) Art book publishers loved them too because their emblematic images reproduced so well.

Reviewing the G&G video *A Portrait of the Artists as Young Men*, critic Jonathan Jones wondered if this was a portrait in the traditional sense or a 'superlit image, a mask concealing nothing'. (Wolf Jahn, a G&G scholar, has claimed that their invented identity epitomised 'the total hollowness and abstractness of life'.) Jones added:

> Gilbert & George have become celebrities on such a scale that it is sometimes hard to see their work at all. They are jokers, storytellers and the patron saints of contemporary British art. Like Andy Warhol before them, Gilbert & George present a flat, unemphatic image to the world and somehow, because of this emptiness, they become charged with meanings from the wider culture. Their art is porous to social history. Indeed, the best way to understand this artwork may be in relation to pop music. The year in which this video was made, 1972, was the peak of Glam in pop culture and this is a Glam work of art. The ultra-stylised poses of Gilbert & George are those of self-conscious decadents, infinitely refined aesthetes, just like the image created by Roxy Music or David Bowie.[26]

It has also been claimed that G&G themselves influenced pop music during the 1980s, specifically, the duo known as the Pet Shop Boys (Chris Lowe and Neil Tennant). British advertising agencies have also plundered G&G's imagery.

In November 2001, G&G-designed merchandise was featured in the British media when it was bizarrely associated with the murder of a South Korean female student: her body had been tied up with G&G gift-wrap tape only sold via Tate art galleries.

## Julian Schnabel

The 1980s was a decade in which greed was declared good because it fuelled capitalism. Trading on Wall Street created many new multimillionaires some of whom spent their surpluses on contemporary art. In New York, a boom in, and expansion of, the art market led to a situation in which artists such as Basquiat, Haring and Schnabel came to be regarded as the new movie or rock stars. Schnabel was not convinced by this opinion and asked: 'What artist is famous, compared to Burt Reynolds?' Nevertheless, the work and personalities of these artists did become extremely widely known, in Europe, Japan and Australia as well as North America.

Schnabel (b. 1951), a larger-than-life character with tremendous self-belief, came from a middle-class Jewish family and spent the first 14 years of his life in Brooklyn. His father Jack, an immigrant from Czechoslovakia, was successful in the meat trade and real estate businesses, while his mother Esther, who took Julian to museums, led a Jewish voluntary organisation. Schnabel studied fine art at the University of Houston in Texas and moved back to New York in 1973 to join the Whitney Museum's Independent Study Programme. While working as a cook in a restaurant frequented by artists, critics and dealers, he invited customers to visit his studio to see his art. Eventually, the young, thrusting dealer Mary Boone – who herself became a media celebrity – spotted his potential. By dint of preselling, she ensured that his first one-man New York show held in 1979 was sold out even before it opened. The British collectors Charles and Doris Saatchi were among the first to buy his work and later, in 1982, they were instrumental in Schnabel exhibiting at the Tate Gallery in London while many established British artists still pined for such a privilege.[27]

Economically speaking, Schnabel benefited greatly from the art boom of the 1980s and the vogue for neo-expressionism that was a

**64. Timothy Greenfield-Sanders, 'Portrait of Julian Schnabel wearing a cape', 1989.**
Conversion from an original colour photograph, 50 x 60 cm, taken with a Polaroid 20 x 24 Studio camera. Appeared on the cover of *L'Uomo Vogue*.
Photo © Timothy Greenfield-Sanders, New York.

reaction against the conceptual, feminist and political art of the 1970s. To the relief of dealers and collectors, Schnabel and his European counterparts such as Francesco Clemente and Georg Baselitz, supplied unique, portable, saleable commodities that bore the marks of an individual auteur. The American art world, journalists considered, was 'ripe for a hero', one comparable in stature to Pollock.

To stand out in the overcrowded and competitive New York art world, Schnabel needed an artistic gimmick or trademark and this took the form of brash, crudely-rendered figurative images painted over grounds of broken crockery. Antonio Gaudí's tile mosaics seen on a trip to Barcelona inspired them. Naturally, Schnabel was compared to a bull (in the proverbial china shop) while his chief rival in New York, David Salle, was compared to a fox. Schnabel also painted on unusual surfaces such as black and crimson velvet and his reliefs included such bizarre additions as antlers. His 'bad', bombastic paintings had plenty of content: pseudo-religious symbols, implied narratives and scrambled iconography pillaged from the history of art and the mass media. For instance, self-portrait drawings by the French writer Antonin Artaud (one of Schnabel's heroes) were appropriated and transferred to canvas much enlarged. As mentioned earlier, Schnabel painted a memorial to the British rock musician Ian Curtis. David Bowie has interviewed Schnabel and Elton John has collected his sculptures.

The highly prolific and garrulous Schnabel was the subject of immense promotional hype and so became a 'boy wonder'. Catalogues devoted to him were published with pretentious introductions, quotes from poems and photographs of the artist out of doors wearing Brando-style vests. A tough, macho but romantic image was fostered. In 1981, René Ricard claimed in *Artforum* that Julian had 'reinvented the art world'. Robert Hughes thought the artist was the art world equivalent of the movie star Stallone playing Rambo or Rocky Balboa. Schnabel reminded the British artist Jake Chapman of 'The Boss', that is, the American rock star Bruce Springsteen.

Later, the epic scale of paintings executed on sailcloth and tarpaulins signified Schnabel's vaunting ambition. He occupied enormous studios in old factories, employed assistants, gave numerous interviews and became a minor media star. He purchased a ten-bedroom country mansion in Bridgehampton, Long Island with a swimming pool and a tennis court converted into an open-air studio. (Schnabel was fond of painting in the rain while wearing silk pyjamas.) Profiles and photo spreads of him, his wife and their sumptuous New York apartments appeared in such non-art magazines as *American Vogue, House & Garden* and *Vanity Fair*.

At the age of 36, Schnabel was vain enough to write a self-mythologising autobiography entitled *C.V.J. – Nicknames of Maitre D's and Other Excerpts from Life* (New York: Random House, 1987); it was an expensive book and is now a collector's item. The initial manuscript described a fistfight with the abstract painter Brice Marden and angry encounters with the critics Clement Greenberg and Robert Hughes. (Hughes had the reference to him removed because he had never in fact met Schnabel.) In a review, Hughes characterised the book as 'flatulent self-congratulation mingled with affectless chit chat'. Hughes also sought to puncture Schnabel's overblown reputation with a satirical poem published in 1984. It read in part:

> And now the hybrid child of *Hubris* comes –
> Julian Snorkel, with his ten fat thumbs!
>     Ad Nauseum, he babbles, honks and prates
> Of Death and Life, Careers and Broken Plates
> (The larger subjects for the smaller brain)
> And as his victims doze, he rants again
> Poor SoHo's cynosure, the dealer's dream,
> Much wind, slight talent, and vast self-esteem.[28]

Hughes' attack had no effect on the feeding frenzy of collectors eager for profit. Regrettably, criticism proved impotent in the face of greed and hype. Schnabel's commercial success meant that he could disregard the harsh opinions of art critics and enjoy the rewards of fame: good tables in gourmet restaurants, staying at the best hotels when travelling abroad.

In 1996, Schnabel diversified into filmmaking by making an impressionistic account of his fellow painter Basquiat whom Schnabel had known. (Basquiat had ridiculed Schnabel.) For a first-time effort, the film *Basquiat* was competently made and had some vivid sequences. As one reviewer remarked, the film presented 'the sad spectacle of Basquiat being cynically used, consumed by success and celebrity, and seduced into the drug addiction that took his life'. Schnabel's own high profile and friendships with other celebrities meant that he was able to persuade other stars to play roles in the film: David Bowie as Warhol, Dennis Hopper as an art dealer, Courtney Love as a groupie, Christopher Walken as a journalist, and Willem Dafoe as an artist-electrician. John Cale supplied the music and the British actor Gary Oldman played the part of Milo, a character based on Schnabel himself. Jeffrey Wright, the little-known actor who played Basquiat, thought that Schnabel 'aggrandised himself through Basquiat's memory'. Basquiat's estate would not permit any genuine pictures to be filmed and so Schnabel and his assistants had to create simulations.

A second biographical feature film Schnabel directed (and funded) was *Before Night Falls* (2000), which is about the Cuban poet and novelist Reinaldo Arenas (1943–1990), who was persecuted in Cuba for being gay. Arenas became an exile in New York and committed suicide rather than die from Aids. (Thus, both of Schnabel's films have been about creative individuals who died prematurely.) Schnabel's movie star friends Sean Penn and Johnny Depp agreed to play minor roles in the film. As mentioned earlier, Schnabel is also friendly with Hopper – who refers to the artist as 'big opera' – and has painted his portrait. The film was more accomplished than *Basquiat* and so deserved the favourable reviews it received. It also caused controversy because of its negative picture of Castro's regime. While Schnabel continues to paint and sculpt, at the end of his career he may be respected more as a film director than as a fine artist.

### Jean-Michel Basquiat

Basquiat was born in Brooklyn in 1960 and came from a mixed race, middle-class background: his father was a Haitian accountant and his mother was a Puerto Rican who had been a dress designer; she used to take her son to visit art galleries when he was a child. He liked Picasso's paintings and it was through them that he first encountered 'primitivism' (the use of African art) that he too was later to exploit ironically. Basquiat enjoyed drawing and painting, and during a spell in hospital, he was given a copy of *Gray's Anatomy*. He was educated in a private school that was all white apart from him. After falling out with his father, Basquiat left home at the age of 15 and lived rough for a time. During the late 1970s, with a friend Al Diaz, he sprayed cryptic statements and drawings on walls in the art gallery districts of SoHo and the East Village; their graffiti tag was SAMO (short for 'same old shit') plus the copyright sign ©. Later, when Basquiat became accepted as a fine artist, he disliked being categorised as a graffiti artist even though it continued to influence his work.

During 1980–81, Basquiat starred in a quasi-documentary film to be called *New York Beat* about a day in the life of a young, poverty-stricken artist who is trying to sell a painting while searching for a beautiful woman in nightclubs. The photographer Edo Bertoglio directed it and Glenn O'Brien wrote the script. The cast included Debbie Harry and several Hip Hop bands and Basquiat's own band Gray; rap music was also featured. Unfortunately, Basquiat did not benefit from this film because it was not completed until 2000 when it was released with the title *Downtown 81*.

Basquiat had no formal art training but, as explained earlier in reference to his painting of his jazz heroes Parker and Gillespie, he developed a fast, appropriational (or sampling) and improvisational method that suited him. He also knew – via museum exhibits and art books – about the history of art and drew upon the work of such twentieth-century artists as Picasso, Pollock, Franz Kline, Jean Dubuffet and Cy Twombly, and referenced masters of the past such as Manet and Leonardo. Language was as important to Basquiat as imagery and the complex iconography of his paintings also featured material taken from African rock art, hobo signs and American commercial and popular culture. His celebration of black heroes has already been described.[29]

Basquiat was the first American black/Hispanic artist to gain an international reputation and he enjoyed a short but meteoric career, which involved the sale of paintings to important collectors but also to celebrities such as Debbie Harry, Richard Gere and Paul Simon. Other ethnic minority artists associated with the graffiti craze did receive some attention from the gallery system in the early 1980s, but Basquiat was the one who proved most acceptable to the white-dominated art world. As his biographer Phoebe Hoban has pointed out, Basquiat's celebrity owed 'more than a little to an almost insti-tutionalised reverse-racism that set him apart from his peers as an art-world novelty … [he was treated as] a multicultural hero during his lifetime and a sacrificial lamb after his death'.[30] Although Basquiat was aware of how rarely blacks had been depicted in art and often portrayed black faces and himself in order to correct this, he did not want to be categorised as a black artist making black art for a black audience. His art synthesised many cultures and he made it for himself, his friends and intellectual equals as well as affluent white collectors whose motives were probably mercenary rather than cultural. In terms of his art's content, there was much about the history of slavery, racism and black politics, which was surely intended to unsettle white viewers. Such was the demand for his canvases that collectors who visited his studio would buy and carry away paintings that were half finished.

Basquiat had a cavalier attitude to art dealers – he had as many short-term relationships with them as he had with women. In 1981, Basquiat was taken up by the dealer Annina Nosei and allocated the basement of her SoHo gallery in Prince Street to use as a studio. This was highly convenient for visiting collectors who could view the artist at work and buy canvases while the paint was still wet; however, some thought the arrangement smacked of slavery or a zoo for exotic animals or a freak show. The time he spent there was dubbed his 'dungeon period'. Among the stream of visitors was Mick

Jagger. Basquiat was paid in cash, which he immediately spent on designer clothes, drugs, books, records and video cassettes, expensive food and wine, limousines and nightclubbing; he also used it to employ assistants and gave much of it away. The Italian, 'trans-avant-garde' painter Francesco Clemente lived and worked in New York at this time and appeared in fashion magazines modelling Armani suits. Basquiat went one better by painting in Armani suits with his feet bare. Another distinctive characteristic of his appearance was a spiky hairstyle that resembled a crown. Crowns frequently appeared in his paintings as a motif. Once, when asked about his subject matter, he replied: 'Royalty, heroism and the streets'.

Later, when Basquiat travelled to Europe to meet the demands of European collectors and dealers, such as Bruno Bischofberger and Robert Fraser, spaces and materials were supplied so that he could generate enough paintings for a show in a short time. In effect, Basquiat became a travelling artisan or performer. The collaboration with Warhol during 1984–85, a commercial ploy proposed by Bischofberger, was mentioned earlier. Both artists painted on the same canvases which, when exhibited, brought them both fresh waves of publicity but not critical acclaim. The collaboration was friendly but the fact that it also involved competition was made visible when the two artists appeared in a humorous poster – advertising a joint art exhibition held in 1985 – dressed like boxers as if squaring up for a violent contest. Both artists also produced portraits of one another.[31]

Basquiat's fame was confirmed in February 1985 when he was profiled by the *New York Times Magazine* and featured on its cover. According to his friend Arden Scott, celebrity was more important to Basquiat than the quality of his art. He wanted to become famous and rich first and then learn to draw.[32] The artist once remarked that he desired to be 'a star' rather than merely a 'gallery mascot'. Klaus Kertess has argued that Basquiat sought fame by invoking it via titles like *Famous Negro Athletes* and that 'fame bristled sardonically on Basquiat's surfaces and fame surrounded his life … fame turned to infamy, occasionally with racist fangs, as Basquiat's short life began its downturn; infamy continued after he died'.[33] Richard Marshall has also observed: 'Basquiat first became famous for his art, then he became famous for being famous, then he became famous for being infamous …'[34]

**65. 'Warhol ∗ Basquiat, Paintings', 1985.**
Poster for an exhibition of collaborative paintings at the Tony Shafrazi Gallery,
New York. Photographer Michael Halsband. Pittsburgh: the Andy Warhol
Museum collection. © 2002 Andy Warhol Foundation/ADAGP,
Paris/Artists Rights Society (ARS), New York. All rights reserved.

Basquiat was addicted to both soft and hard drugs, and financial
success enabled him to increase his consumption until he died of a
heroin overdose in 1988 a year after his mentor Warhol. (If, as Artaud
claimed, van Gogh had been 'suicided by society', then Basquiat was
suicided by the art market.) In his final years, as his mental state and
body deteriorated, so did his painting; it ceased to evolve, became
repetitious and degenerated into self-parody. Hoban comments:

success had an untenable price … even drugs could not blind him to the fact that in the harsh reality of the marketplace, all that mattered was profit. And that the more successful he became, the less the quality of his art actually mattered … Basquiat tried to anaesthetise himself with drugs, but he couldn't escape the fact that the very success he had always sought was destroying him.[35]

Perhaps Basquiat realised that a self-destructive death at an early age was the ultimate career move, the one that would guarantee mythic status.

Afterwards there were the usual debates about the importance of his art (Robert Hughes concluded Basquiat was 'a featherweight') and the usual disputes about the disposition of his estate (worth several million dollars) – which is now controlled by his father Gerard. Fakes appeared on the art market while prices fetched at auction for Basquiats rose steeply and most museums of modern art ensured that they had at least one example in their collections. In 1990, Geoff Dunlop made an arts television programme for Channel 4 about Basquiat's career ('Shooting Star', *Without Walls*, November 1990) and in 1992 the Whitney Museum of American Art mounted a Basquiat retrospective curated by Richard Marshall. Since over 2,000 attended the opening, it was evident that Basquiat still had many fans. Four years later Schnabel's cinematic tribute was released. Hoban's detailed and compelling biography was published in 1998. She concluded it by saying that art students were writing dissertations about Basquiat because in their eyes he was 'an art hero'.

As explained earlier in the section on Madonna, artists such as Basquiat and Haring were associated with the graffiti, rock music and club scenes; thus, they had street credibility as well as art world credibility. Furthermore, as Deyan Sudjic has remarked: 'Artists were now being photographed for society magazines. They also began to be paid handsomely for their art. They gave up starving and were to be found instead lunching at the smarter restaurants. Suddenly they could join the gravy train.'[36]

## Jeff Koons

Koons was born in 1955 and raised in the town of York, Pennsylvania. Because of his business acumen and enthusiasm for popular culture, Koons is widely regarded as Warhol's heir. He knows all about selling himself because he was the son of a businessman who owned a furniture store and designed interiors, and a mother who sold wedding dresses. Before he became a full-time artist, Koons worked as a membership salesman for New York's Museum of Modern Art and as a commodities broker on Wall Street. As a boy, Koons enjoying drawing and painting; his father even exhibited and sold examples of his work in the furniture store. Koons liked Dalí's work and learning the Spaniard was in New York, Koons telephoned him and amazingly, Dalí agreed to a meeting. His art school training took place during the early 1970s at the Maryland Institute College of Art, Baltimore and at the School of Art Institute in Chicago. At the latter, the Chicago imagist artist Ed Paschke influenced him and encouraged an interest in readymades and pop culture. Koons moved to New York in 1977 and adopted an objective manner of working rather than a subjective one.

During the 1980s, Koons was part of a movement called neo-geo. In his case, it meant the presentation of new consumer goods such as Spalding basketballs and Hoover vacuum cleaners in glass cases, and the casting of inflatable bunny toys and model trains in stainless steel. Koons, 'the ideas man', used readymades or delegated the making of his sculptures to others such as Italian craftsmen who carved enlarged wooden figures of pink panthers, bears with policemen and a couple holding a string of puppies from photographs and postcards supplied by the artist. (By 2000, he occupied a huge studio in New York where many assistants laboured under his direction making sculptures and billboard-size paintings with the aid of computers.) The porcelain statue of Michael Jackson and his chimp made in Italy has already been described, as has 'koonspeak', the salesman's patter or 'New Age waffle' Koons developed for publication and interviews; for example: 'By some I am viewed as a sinner but I am really a saint, God has always been on my side ... I have my finger on the eternal.'[37]

To market himself via the art press, Koons appeared in staged, full-colour photo/adverts for his own exhibitions along with pigs and nubile young women wearing bikinis (*Art Magazine Ads*, 1988–89, photos taken by Greg Gorman). Koons has expressed admiration for advertising because it is generally positive and optimistic. He seeks to communicate the same values via his art. The optimism of his art is as compulsory as that of socialist realism in the USSR during the 1930s. Appropriating the trademarked products and copyrighted photographs of others led to well-publicised legal proceedings for plagiarism. Perhaps Koons thought the risk and the fines were worth it for the free publicity it generated. Damien Hirst subsequently employed similar tactics.

Koons has dressed in a succession of different outfits and so he did not adopt a uniform comparable to those of Beuys and Gilbert & George. Nevertheless, D.S. Baker found his appearance significant: 'he is a devilishly handsome white stockbroker-playboy ... a confident bourgeois entrepreneur ... well-spoken, good looking sex symbol media superstar'.[38] Bowie, who interviewed him for *Modern Painters* in 1998, considered Koons 'a great American artist' but also found him 'goofy' and his work 'disturbingly dysfunctional'.[39]

The commercial gallery and public museum system eagerly embraced Koons' cute, Disney-style art but his use of popular icons and kitsch objects enabled it to appeal to an audience beyond the art world. His most popular work thus far is probably *Puppy* (1992), a gigantic West Highland terrier made from earth and thousands of flowers attached to a wood and steel frame, that has been exhibited in public places in Australia, Europe and the United States. It attracted crowds wherever it was displayed.

What differentiates Koons' work from that of most pop artists of the 1960s is that Koons' enthusiasm for kitsch and banality was sincere; there was no trace of distance, irony or critique. Like Gilbert & George, Koons wanted an 'Art for All' and realised he needed to harness the communicative power of the mass media and, if possible, be as entertaining as Madonna and Michael Jackson. Pop music stars normally provide a succession of albums and concerts based on different themes. Koons followed suit by creating bodies of work for his various exhibitions that had a certain degree of shock value and were easily digested by journalists. Initially, he funded his work from his earnings from selling. Later, he relied on financial backing from dealers and collectors but so high were the fabrication costs of some of his most ambitious projects that he faced bankruptcy several times.

A notorious body of work entitled *Made in Heaven* (1989–91) consisted of a series of photographs, a billboard poster, lithographs and wood and glass sculptures showing Koons having sexual relations with Ilona Staller. During the late 1980s, Koons had developed a crush on Staller, a Hungarian-born, hard-core porn actress known in Italy as 'La Cicciolina' (variously translated as 'cuddles', 'little dumpling', 'little tasty morsel' and 'little pinchable one'). Besides porn, she was famous in Europe for being elected to the Italian Parliament for the period 1987 to 1992 as a member of the Radical Party. Koons courted Staller and the marriage 'made in heaven' – because it joined stars from two different fields – took place in Budapest in 1991. A year later, the couple had a son they named Ludwig Maximillian. However, the marriage did not last and they are now divorced. A bitter and expensive legal struggle over the custody of their son followed in which Koons hypocritically used the porn profession he had exploited in his art as an argument for Staller being an unfit mother. At the time of writing, Staller lives in Rome with Ludwig while Koons resides mainly in the United States. To earn money she makes celebrity appearances and sells erotica via her own porn website: <www.cicciolina.com>. She is also reported to be writing an autobiography. Meanwhile Koons acquired a new partner: Justine Wheeler, a South-African artist who was one of his studio assistants; they have a son named Sean.

*Made in Heaven* exhibitions were held in Cologne, London, New York and Venice. Since such explicit depictions of sex had not been visible in art galleries before, they generated immense publicity. Koons denied the works were pornographic because he and Ilona were lovers not porn actors. He also claimed that they 'promoted narcissism, showing the public what it feels like to be star'.

Many pundits regard Koons as an art world superstar if not its leader but doubts have also been expressed about the quality of his 'lowest-common-denominator-mass-franchise art'. He has been accused of dumbing down serious culture, of selling out to commercialism, and of encouraging adults to regress to an infantile state. Certainly, he shares with Jackson a delight in children's cloying, sugary pleasures. Abstract expressionism was limited because it ignored the commercial mass culture of the United States; Koons' late-capitalist pop art is similarly limited because it ignores the suffering and tragedy in the world and because its celebration of consumerism takes no account of the dire ecological consequences.

## Damien Hirst

Between 1988 and 1996, Hirst (b. 1965) became Britain's most notorious artist, a figure comparable to the Americans Schnabel and Koons. Articles about him appeared in tabloid newspapers and lifestyle magazines as well as the art press. In fact, his dealer Jay Jopling encouraged tabloid reporters to visit Hirst's exhibitions thinking that any ridicule would be worth the publicity, which in

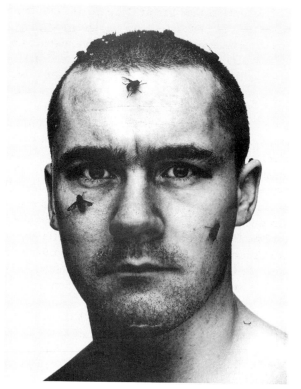

**66. Fergus Greer, 'Portrait of Damien Hirst with flies', 1994.**
Photo © Fergus Greer, Los Angeles.

turn would be more valuable than reviews by serious critics. Hirst was regarded as the leader of a new generation of British artists called 'the YBAs' (young British artists) due to a series of shows mounted by Charles Saatchi in his own North London gallery. (Julian Stallabrass prefers the more sarcastic label 'High Art Lite'.) Saatchi was Hirst's main patron and ensured that his favourite received plenty of press coverage. Hirst also had a flair for self-promotion and marketing. Like his patron, he was an entrepreneur who curated mixed exhibitions with absurd titles and undertook a variety of business ventures.

Hirst was born in Bristol into a poor, proletarian, Catholic family. He was illegitimate and never knew his real father. His mother used to draw and encouraged her son to follow suit. School friends associated his first name with the son of Satan in the horror film *The*

*Omen* (1976) rather than with Saint Damien. An ebullient child and wild teenager, he enjoyed practical jokes. He grew up in the northern industrial city of Leeds where he studied at the Joseph Kramer School of Art and took a foundation course at Leeds School of Art (1985). A taste for the macabre was manifested early when, at the age of 16, he gained access to a hospital mortuary to draw corpses and had his portrait taken laughing next to a severed head. Like Francis Bacon, an artist he admired, he was fascinated by the images in the pathology textbooks he stole because they combined horror and beauty. Medicines in the form of pills were later to preoccupy him and he constructed a number of cabinets in which bottles of pills, laboratory specimens and surgical instruments were displayed.

Hirst was one of the art stars to emerge from the fine art course at Goldsmiths College in South London, which he attended between 1986 and 1989. Conceptual art was a pervasive influence and so it was the artist's ideas that counted most: any medium could be used and the task of making the art works was a secondary matter that could be delegated to assistants once finances permitted. It was due to tutors such as Richard Wentworth, Jon Thompson and Michael Craig-Martin that students came to regard themselves as professional artists and to focus on cracking the commercial gallery system. To promote himself and his friends, Hirst organised a now legendary student show called *Freeze* (1988) in an old building in Docklands and made sure it was seen by influential curators and collectors. He raised sponsorship money and published a good quality catalogue, which he circulated to London's art dealers.

What really made Hirst famous far beyond the art world were shock-horror sculptural installations using dead animals – cows, lambs, fish and sharks – presented whole or sliced into parts, preserved in formaldehyde in large vitrines. (The animals were presented not represented; hence, no modelling skills were required. Hirst's aim was to introduce reality into art directly, not to depict it.) As Hirst pointed out, humans have often killed animals in order to look at them (but was this any reason to continue the practice?). These works resembled exhibits found in natural history museums and were easy to understand and so became popular but they also attracted vandals, cartoonists, and parodic advertisements and angry protests by animal rights activists. Some of the latter were arrested and fined by the courts.[40] Hirst's obsession with animals and death was certainly appropriate to Britain in the late twentieth century given that fox hunting was a contentious issue and the nation's livestock experienced serious diseases, such as foot and mouth, which necessitated wholesale slaughter.

Hirst's supporters claim that his art deals with the serious issues of life and death: like Koons, he uses physical things in a metaphorical way to symbolise feelings and ideas (for example, a shark = death), and as in photomontage and surrealism he combines images and objects to generate new meanings. There are those who think he adds few fresh insights; however, *A Thousand Years* (1990) was a genuinely gruesome achievement. Inside a glass enclosure, a life/death cycle took place via a rotting cow's head, maggots, flies and an 'insect-o-cutor'. Many of Hirst's ideas for art works derive from the 1960s and this one's antecedent was the ecological art of that decade. (In 2002, Hirst turned his attention to green issues when he made a work about carbon dioxide emissions to promote a campaign by the environmental organisation Future Forests.)

Hirst's steel and glass vitrines had the rational structure and polished finish of minimal art but inside was dead flesh. The vitrines that protected viewers from the smells of corpses and chemicals were paradoxical because they enabled viewers to see inside but not to enter, smell or touch. Gordon Burn discerned a connection with celebrity:

> Celebrity is about control and distance; it is about adding space to the space that inevitably exists between human beings and remaining apart from the flock. It is about degrees of separation and personal insulation and choosing, as Jeff Koons apparently did, to place the flesh cell of your person inside a second, more unbreachable container tank.[41]

One of Hirst's most popular product lines consisted of deliberately dumb abstract paintings designed to eliminate the last vestige of angst and spirituality from the genre. These 'trademark' works were of two kinds: 'spot' or 'dot' paintings, executed with household gloss paints, consisting of variously coloured discs arranged in horizontal rows across the canvas and 'spin' or 'swirl' paintings executed by pouring cans of liquid paint on circular supports while they were revolving. Like Warhol before him, Hirst was happy for his 'decorator's colour charts' to be printed on dress fabrics by the fashion designer Rifat Ozbek. The Acid-house 'spin' paintings repeated a child's activity and were popular with children. They were produced by assistants and generated at a fast pace to cater for a queue of collectors seeking an 'original' Hirst. A third series of paintings consisted of monochrome canvases with dead butterflies attached.

Stallabrass has argued that such infinitely extendable painting series function like 'a logo for the artist's personality' and that Hirst was able to market them successfully because of his celebrity status.[42] Hirst's own thoughts on celebrity are as follows:

> You've got to become a celebrity before you can undermine it, take it apart, show people that there's no difference between celebrities and real life. Celebrity is a fucking lie. It's like: I'll do a magic trick, and I want it to be *amazing*. But if anyone asks me how to do it, I'll show them exactly how to do it. I want you to be amazed twice. Once you're amazed because it seems impossible, and then, you're amazed because it's fucking easy. That's what it's like.[43]

An art work that sums up Hirst's experience of celebrity will be described shortly.

In 1994, Hirst was profiled on BBC1 television's *Omnibus* strand and the following year he won the Turner Prize. Television exposure made him known nationally to millions. Hirst has always had a populist agenda – he thinks art can appeal to the people if only they can see it at first hand in public galleries. The huge prices his works fetch mean that they are out of reach of the majority of the populace but he does sell prints and posters at cheaper prices via virtual galleries on the Internet.

Once Hirst's income increased, he stepped up production and diversified. Like his patron Saatchi, he became a businessperson by investing in London restaurants and bars, such as *Quo Vadis* in Soho and *The Pharmacy* in Notting Hill Gate, which he then 'branded' or 'themed' by decorating them with examples of his art. In 1999, stories appeared in the press about a tiff between the artist and chef Marco Pierre White, his partner in *Quo Vadis*. White replaced Hirst's works with his own humorous Hirst imitations after claiming that business had fallen off and that many visitors had been disappointed with Hirst's pieces. *The Pharmacy* was also in the news because of complaints that its name would mislead people into thinking it was a real drugstore. Inside there were medicine cabinets full of pills but they were art works by Hirst.

Again, like Warhol, Hirst was willing to endorse products, such as Absolut Vodka, and to make advertisements for billboards and television, to direct pop music videos (*Country House* for Blur) and to design record cover albums (for the Eurythmics and Joe Strummer). Like Schnabel, he tried his hand at feature film directing: *Hanging Around* (1996). Film critics were not impressed by this gloomy effort screened at the Hayward Gallery in 1996. An expensive autobiography/monograph by Hirst and the designer Jonathan Barnbrook with paper pop-up sections entitled *I Want to Spend the Rest of My Life Everywhere, with Everyone, One to One, Always, Forever, Now* was published by Booth-Clibborn Editions in 1998. (The inspiration for it was probably Warhol's famous *Index Book* of 1967 because it too had pop-ups.) If there are any Martians on Mars then they will be able to view a Hirst via the contents of a British spacecraft launched in 1999.

Hirst, a short, stocky individual, has an extrovert personality and seems to revel in all the media attention he receives. His grit and self-belief meant that he seemed not to need protective strategies of the kind Warhol devised or new, artificial identities such as the one Gilbert & George adopted. However, Burn thinks he did develop an 'art yobbo' persona. Like the punk rockers of the 1970s, Hirst glared, grimaced and grinned at the camera and cultivated a puckish image by not shaving, wearing long or very short hair and a weird assortment of clothes along with oversize boots. His fashion statements have generally been anti-fashion but he has also been willing to don a green, pinstripe suit when the occasion called for it; witness Lorenzo Agius' photo in the 'London Swings Again!' issue of *Vanity Fair* (March 1997). When attending exhibition openings, Hirst alternated between dressing like a tramp and like an executive in order to bewilder observers. In one photographic portrait used to illustrate a gallery show in an art magazine, Hirst put something in his mouth to distort his features. Photographed by Lord Snowdon in 1991, he appeared naked as if in a vitrine along with fish and crabs. Hirst proved photogenic not because he was handsome but because he was an entertaining, laddish, almost cartoon 'character' (no doubt one taken from *Viz*, a publication he reads).

When giving interviews Hirst tends to make contradictory statements and admits his opinions may be different the next day so any quotes must be read with caution. About art, fame and celebrity, Hirst has remarked:

> Art's about life and the art world's about money, and money and celebrity are just tiny aspects of life. So if you keep your

perspective on that, it's fine. I think art should be able to deal
with celebrity. I don't think you should ever let celebrity
become more important than art but I think it's part of it. I
think a desire to be famous is a desire to live forever which is
very fundamental to art.[44]

These observations appeared in a magazine sold in the streets by the
homeless to which Hirst had donated one of his spin paintings
worth £40,000 for a readers' competition. Like most celebrities, Hirst
is willing to support some good causes.

Keith Allen, the Welsh actor and comedian, is a close friend of
Hirst's. They formed a pop group or 'prank art collective' called Fat
Les which recorded, with Alex James of Blur, raucous football
anthems such as *Vindaloo* (1998) and *Jerusalem* (2000). Hirst designed
a record cover for *Vindaloo* and music videos were shot to promote
both records. In January 1998, Hirst and Jan Kennedy started a
record label called Turtleneck. For a time, Hirst and his mates
enjoyed carousing in pubs and clubs, smoking heavily and getting
drunk, and exposing their genitals and bottoms. Hirst also took
drugs (cocaine). He has been described as a 'hooligan genius', 'over-
wrought degenerate' and 'art yobbo' and he himself has admitted:
'I'm basically getting more yobbish. Yobbish is visceral.' Like the
tennis star John McEnroe, Hirst realised that outrageous behaviour
attracted attention and media coverage.

After Hirst began to experience blackouts, he changed his lifestyle.
He bought land and a farmhouse in Devon, far from the fleshpots of
London, where he now lives with his partner Maia Norman (an
American jewellery designer who used to go out with Hirst's dealer
Jay Jopling) and their two sons Connor and Cassius. Journalists
delight in visiting Hirst to report on his rural lifestyle and even the
conversion of a farm building into a summerhouse provided the
subject for a television programme. (Nevertheless, Hirst remained a
country member of the Groucho Club in London until he resigned
in May 2002. This club was highly fashionable during the 1990s as
a hang-out for arts and media folk. Tracey Emin held receptions there
and entertained her guests by screening her films.) He also obtained
a huge, windowless studio near Stroud in Gloucestershire in order to
gain the peace and quiet to make a new body of work for a show in
America, his first solo exhibition for four years. So ambitious and
complex were the new works that ten months of preparation were
needed plus the help of numerous assistants and technical experts.

The works were also very costly to produce and so Hirst, like Koons, had to rely on advance funding from dealers and collectors.

In April 2000, Hirst unveiled a 20-feet high, ten-ton, painted bronze sculpture entitled *Hymn* that was an enlargement of a young scientist's anatomy set, an educational toy designed by Norman Emms and sold by Humbrol Ltd. (A number of exhibitions of sculptures exposing the innards of the human body had taken place in the late 1990s.) As Koons had previously demonstrated with *Puppy*, gigantism is one way of grabbing the public's attention. Like Koons, Hirst was accused of plagiarism (by Humbrol) and had to pay damages to charity to reach an out-of-court settlement. Perhaps like Koons he thought the extra publicity the legal action brought was worth the expense. (Hirst's agents have also resorted to law whenever commercial companies have used his copyright images without permission.) By paying the memorable sum of £1 million for *Hymn*, Saatchi assured a further round of headlines.

Hirst is one of the few living British artists who have made a significant impact in the American art world and mass media. A solo show he held in 1996 in New York worried local health inspectors who thought his animal remains were a danger to Americans. In September 2000, he mounted another one-man exhibition at the Gagosian Gallery in New York entitled *Damien Hirst: Theories, Models, Methods, Approaches, Assumptions, Results and Findings*. (Much of Hirst's creative effort is expended devising portentous titles, which even he admits are clumsy and designed to confuse.) The opening was packed and during its run 100,000 attended. Some visitors found it 'amusing, witty and poignant' and many American critics were impressed. Jerry Saltz described Hirst as 'the one true pop-star artist'. All the exhibits were sold before the public arrived.

Perhaps Hirst's impact in the United States was because he evinced certain American characteristics and values: big, expensive, vulgar art works with high production values; ambition, brashness, energy and self-confidence; the hard sell, being media friendly and good at show business. In other words, there is no vestige of the traditional English reserve and refined taste that American critics such as Clement Greenberg used to complain bedevilled British art. Naturally, the New York show was the subject of an hour-long arts television documentary – *Life and Death and Damien Hirst* – transmitted on 28 December 2000 by London Weekend Television.

Hirst has many fans and supporters but detractors too. The latter have complained his art is obscene, tasteless, a con trick, and they deplore the role model he represents for younger artists. They also regard him as a frivolous clown whose showmanship robs art of its dignity. His habit of exposing his genitals in public has also caused offence to some women. Several critics think his work has contributed to the dumbing down, coarsening and vulgarisation of British culture associated with the right-wing regime of Margaret Thatcher.

Saturation media coverage of a star almost invariably results in the public becoming bored and then irritated. Journalists began to predict a backlash against the YBAs and a 1998 article indicated a reaction against Hirst: it claimed he was passé and quoted younger artists who now asserted 'the art star is a bore'. Even other YBA artists such as Rachel Whiteread – whose art has generated several controversies and extensive media coverage – made a point of telling interviewers that they had no interest in being celebrities.

Since 1988, Hirst has played the celebrity game as effectively as forebears such as Dalí and Warhol but as he ages it becomes more difficult to repeat *enfant terrible* outrages because the public is becoming increasingly inured to shock. He faces the challenge that confronts all major celebrities: how to reinvent himself and think of fresh ideas to avoid regurgitating earlier achievements. That Hirst himself eventually began to feel the pressure associated with fame and success was indicated by remarks made to Burn in 2000:

> The art world's very shallow and small and it's very easy to get to the top of it. And then you burst through the top of it and you've got no idea where the fuck to go. You know, they've all been waiting for me to die. Now they're all phoning up. I've got so many people on my back trying to get me to make things, pushing me in the wrong direction. It's a constant effort telling people to just go away.[45]

Burn described Hirst as 'a man imprisoned by the monster he created' and reported that the artist felt the knives were out for him. A sculpture exhibited in New York consisting of a white beach ball hovering on air currents above a base in which sharp Sabatier knives had been vertically embedded summed up Hirst's precarious condition. This work was entitled *The History of Pain* (1999) but a friend significantly misheard it as *The History of Fame*.

Compared to a watercolour landscape painter such as Prince Charles, Hirst is an avant-garde artist but he is no social outsider or political radical. The art market and the modern arts establishment adore him and so it may turn out that in a hundred years he will be judged to have been the Bouguereau of his era rather than its Cézanne.

## Tracey Emin

During the 1990s, Emin became as famous in Britain as Hirst when interviews, gossip items, satires, caricatures and photographs proliferated in the press, in fashion and art magazines and on the Internet. She also appeared on television several times and, like Hirst, was honoured by television arts editor Melvyn Bragg when, in 2001, he devoted a *South Bank Show* to her. Like Hirst, Emin paid no heed to the traditional stereotype of the English: being modest, polite, liking privacy and suffering adversity with a stiff upper lip.

Her life story is known in some detail, mainly because she herself has made it the subject of so much of her art, which has therefore been called 'confessional', 'angry vagina' and 'victim art'. (It could also be called 'me, me, me art' and 'misery art'.) She is an artist who has taken the commodification of the self to a new extreme. Emin has used art galleries to confess her sins the way Catholics use confession booths. As many television programmes and autobiographies testify, the willingness of people to confess all in public – especially experiences of childhood abuse – has become very widespread in recent years. (There is one subject celebrities are generally reticent about: their personal finances.) However, one of Emin's photographs comments ironically on the relation between money and her body. It shows her sitting on the floor naked pushing banknotes between her thighs with coins in front of her. Its title is: *I've Got it All* (2000).

Unlike Madonna or Sherman, Emin does not adopt fictional personae or masks. In her case, it seems there is no artifice, only authenticity. She concluded a Radio 4 interview in July 2001 by insisting: 'I am genuine.' Sincerity by itself, however, is no guarantee of high quality art.

Emin was born in London in 1963 but grew up in the downmarket seaside resort of Margate. Its only previous claim to fame in terms of visual art was that J.M.W. Turner (1775–1851) lived and worked there at various times. (Margate plans to open a Turner Centre in 2004 to attract more visitors.) One of Emin's nicknames is 'Mad Tracey from Margate' and she once remarked angrily: 'I grew up in Margate and somebody's going to FUCKING PAY FOR IT.' By birth, she was only half English: her father, Enver Emin, was a Turkish-

Cypriot chef and hotel manager with black African ancestors. Pamela Cashin, her mother, was an English chambermaid. Both were married to other people when they met; they lived together for seven years. Enver, a lothario, is proud of his many sexual conquests and lovechildren. Emin's stepmother currently assists her by sewing her quilts. Emin has a twin brother Paul who complains about the publicity that she has attracted to the family and he has dismissed her art as 'a load of bollocks'.

Emin, according to her own accounts, has experienced much pain and unhappiness during her life: a rape at the age of 13, a series of underage sexual encounters, two abortions and a miscarriage, anorexia, severe depression, an attempted suicide, bouts of excessive drinking, ill health and heavy cigarette consumption. As in the case of Dennis Hopper, many of her troubles were due to self-destructive behaviour. Her education ceased early when she left school at the age of 13 and so she never learned to spell accurately. However, the numerous grammatical and spelling errors and reversed letters in her embroidered designs are now part of their charm and artistic effect. She gives her exhibitions melodramatic titles such as *Every Part of Me is Bleeding* and one of her neon signs stated: 'My Cunt is Wet with Fear.' One of Emin's few works about someone else was about her Uncle Colin but he, poor fellow, was decapitated in a car crash.

Despite having no educational qualifications, Emin managed to escape her miserable background during the 1980s by attending several art schools. She studied fashion at Medway College, Chatham, then switched to the Sir John Cass School of Art, London (1982–83), and studied fine art at Maidstone School of Art (1983–89), and painting and drawing at the Royal College of Art (1991–93). She also learnt printmaking, was a youth tutor for Southwark Council and took a part-time course in philosophy at Birkbeck College, London University. In 1992, in a fit of despair, she destroyed all the art she had created up to that time.

An important influence on Emin's development during the 1980s was an older man with anti-establishment attitudes – Billy Childish (b. 1959, aka Steven Hamper). An artist, punk musician, dyslexic poet and small press publisher, he was the victim of an abusive, traumatic childhood. They met in Chatham in 1982 and had an intense affair for four years. Articles on Childish argue that Emin's art derives from his because it was expressionist and autobiographical.[46] The two have feuded because Childish, a defender of traditional craft skills and art forms such as painting, despises conceptual art, while Emin accused Childish of being 'stuck, stuck, stuck!' (in the past). He embraced this criticism by founding, with others, 'Stuckism, the first Remodernist art group', which regularly issues denunciations of the Turner Prize from which the Stuckists are excluded. (He has since left the group.) Childish favours amateurishness, independence and self-organisation; he rejects the official art world and the culture of celebrity to which Emin now belongs. However, he maintains his own website to assist sales and the mass media are increasingly taking an interest in him.[47]

Childish was later to exploit his past relationship with Emin by displaying photographs taken by Eugene Doyen in the early 1980s of her posing naked and semi-naked alongside Childish's works in the exhibition *Billy Childish and Tracey Emin: Alive and Well and Dying in Chatham* (London: Pure Gallery, November 2000). One unflattering image showed that Emin had no front teeth.[48] Others make it clear that Emin was happy to play the role of a glamour model.

Emin's looks have been characterised as 'feral' and 'wanton gypsy' and some think she resembles Frida Kahlo. When David Bowie met her, he noted her 'elastic lips, broken teeth and half-closed eyes' but at the same time found her 'sexy and exhilarating'. There is no doubt that part of her appeal has been her sexually alluring body that she has been as willing to flaunt as any model working for erotic magazines. Yet, Emin was offended when a picture of her in the nude was reproduced on page three of the *Star*. She has also had no qualms about revealing details of her sex life: boasting about how many men she has slept with, but then complaining when accused of being 'a slag'. She has also been dubbed 'Racy Tracey' and characterised herself in one appliquéd blanket as a 'psyco [sic] slut'. There are many echoes of the body and feminist art of the 1970s in her *oeuvre*.

Emin has employed a variety of art forms. In addition to drawings, paintings and sculptures, she has produced books/diaries, photographs, prints, videos, Super 8 films, neon signs, appliquéd chairs, tents and wall hangings, mixed-media installations and live performances.

Two noted instances of self-publicity and marketing were The Shop, an exhibiting and selling space she and her 'Bad Girl' friend and fellow artist Sarah Lucas opened in London's East End during 1993 and the Tracey Emin Museum in Waterloo Road (1995–98). During the mid 1990s, Carl Freedman was one of Emin's lovers and the fact that he curated exhibitions assisted her career.

**67. Eugene Doyen, 'Billy Childish and Tracey Emin,
photograph for poetry book, Chatham', 1981.**
Photo © Eugene Doyen.

Like Hirst, Emin benefited immensely from the collecting passion
and publicity skills of Charles Saatchi even though he was slow to
appreciate her work and she was at first reluctant to sell to him
because of his agency's advertisements supporting the Conservative
Party. (She favours the Labour Party.) His *Sensation* show at the Royal
Academy in 1997 included a small camping tent by Emin embroidered on the inside with 102 names entitled *Everyone I Have Ever Slept
with 1963–1995*. Only a minority of the names were sexual partners
and Emin has remarked that the tent – which viewers had to crawl
into to see properly – was more about 'intimacy' than sex.

In 1997, Emin appeared on a television arts programme discussing the question 'Is painting dead?' She had a broken finger and was blind drunk. Contemptuous of the intellectual debate being conducted by a number of male critics, she uttered some dismissive remarks, swore and then staggered from the studio saying she was going home to phone her mum. Such boorish behaviour, which served to reinforce the view that many visual artists are anti-intellectual, made her instantly notorious.

During 1998, Emin collaborated with the pop music star Boy George to make a sound recording entitled *Burning Up*. George provided the music while Emin supplied the lyrics, which she also spoke on record.[49] In 1999, Emin was nominated for the Turner Prize and exhibited several works at Tate Britain. The principal piece was entitled *My Bed* and consisted of a mattress, stained sheets and pillows, plus the debris of indulgence: dirty knickers, used condoms, empty vodka bottles, cigarette butts, slippers, etc. (The assemblage was a memorial to several days Emin had spent in bed drunk and miserable.) In other words, this was not a sculpture that had been made by the artist's hands; it was more like a Duchampian readymade: objects the artist had selected; again, like Hirst, it was a *presentation* rather than a *representation* but nonetheless the objects functioned symbolically, that is, they evoked such themes as 'loss, sickness, fertility, copulation, conception and death'. (The American artist Robert Rauschenberg had presented a bed earlier, in 1955, but in his case it was transformed to some degree: he slapped paint on it and hung it on a wall.) Although Emin did not win the Turner Prize, her bed attracted the most publicity and visitors. (Arguably, the Tate Gallery used her as a loss leader.) Two Chinese artists – Jian Jun Xi and Yuan Chai – then jumped on the bed and had a pillow fight; this satiric action prompted further press reports. When Saatchi noticed how much attention *My Bed* was receiving, he bought it for £150,000.

A year later Saatchi paid Emin £75,000 for a dilapidated, blue-painted wooden beach hut (in which she had once lived with a male lover) that she had rescued from the seafront at Whitstable, Kent. It was entitled *The Last Thing I Said to You is Don't Leave Me Here* and was exhibited in the Saatchi Gallery along with photos of Emin crouching naked inside the hut taken by her current male partner and artist Mat Collishaw. During September 2001, one of these photos appeared several times in the *Guardian* advertising a competition sponsored by British Telecom and the Tate Modern gallery. The photograph was one of the prizes.

In 2001, Christie's of London auctioned an Emin installation – *Exorcism of the Last Painting I ever Made* (aka *The Swedish Room*) – which had previously appeared in a Swedish gallery (Galerri Andreas Brandström, Stockholm, 1996). It fetched £108,250. When Emin inspected it, she complained about how badly it had been treated by the owner and stated that the knickers that were part of it were not the original pair she had supplied. Emin had lived inside the installation for a fortnight while naked. Holes with fish-eye lenses punched in the enclosing walls enabled visitors to watch her try to overcome a six-year painting block. It would seem, therefore, that this work appealed to voyeurs and was not that different from sex industry peep shows. Some of the time Emin used her body as a living paintbrush to make marks on canvas. This piece was clearly derivative – reprising Yves Klein's *Anthropometry* performances of 1960 and it was, therefore, incestuous – art about art. Since the Stockholm exhibition had combined live performance and installation, the new purchaser – Charles Saatchi – surely acquired only half a work of art.

Another puerile and derivative piece executed in Scandinavia referred to Munch's famous image of angst: *The Scream*. Emin was filmed in a field near Oslo standing naked while screaming her head off.

When Emin was invited on the comedy programme/news quiz *Have I Got News for You* in 2001, it was a clear sign of her newfound celebrity status. However, reviews of her performance were very rude. Philip Hensher described her as 'thick' and 'gormless', and went on to argue that she was too stupid to be a good conceptual artist.[50] He also deplored her 'insatiable enthusiasm for publicity'. A woman wrote to Emin accusing her of being 'a media whore'; however, Emin remarked that the letter writer had no idea how many invitations she was turning down. As media pressure increased, she also started to moan about 'lack of privacy' even though she was by now employing a PA to filter calls. Once an artist reaches a certain level of fame, it seems, there is no need to pursue publicity because offers come pouring in unbidden as others seek to exploit the artist's high news value.

Two examples of such offers can be cited: first, after meeting the controversial British fashion designer Vivienne Westwood, Emin was invited to model her clothes on a catwalk in Paris (she also appeared in Westwood's adverts and made friends with the professional supermodel Kate Moss); second, an invitation from the British Museum asking Emin – who had recently taken a cruise on the Nile and visited Cairo to make a film and to exhibit at the Cairo Biennale – to host an event accompanying an exhibition about Cleopatra (2001), arguably a major celebrity of the ancient world. (Represen-tations of Cleopatra range from Egyptian and Roman statues to movie portrayals by Theda Bara and Elizabeth Taylor.) It was a sign of the times that a key British cultural institution should have felt it necessary to rely on the notoriety of two celebrities, one old and one contemporary, in order to attract publicity and visitors. One reviewer described the show as 'an oppressive and cynical exercise, an unholy alliance of marketing and scholarship'. Another mark of Emin's celebrityhood was her willingness to accept sponsorship from such companies as Beck's beer and to appear in advertisements endorsing commercial products such as Bombay Sapphire Gin. Thus, Emin promoted the very drinks that had contributed to her drunkenness and ill health.

Although Emin has created art works such as drawings with her own hands, the metonymic presentation in galleries of her personal possessions or objects associated with her past inevitably reminds sceptical viewers of the relics of saints and martyrs that Catholics venerate. (The objects themselves are of little intrinsic interest; what counts is their association with holy beings. Eugene Doyen has remarked that Emin 'consecrates' her objects.) Emin is certainly no saint but her sufferings perhaps place her in the martyr category. The sufferings of van Gogh and Kahlo aroused sympathy and contributed to their posthumous cults. Princess Diana's willingness to confess all and to expose her wounded feelings also struck a chord with the public. Therefore, Emin somewhat resembles Diana and her confes-sions have certainly encouraged a following among young female art students who admire her honesty and vulnerability. (When Emin gave readings from her books, such as *Exploration of the Soul* [1994], in London art schools, the events were packed out.) Other young women, who post notes on the Internet, claim to find her art liberating, inspiring and empowering. Many neurotic, dysfunctional young women end up in prison where they mutilate their bodies. The art world has at least provided Emin with a means to turn her misery into cash and a career.

How much longer, one wonders, can Emin continue to mine her own life story? Since her commercial and media success, her life has become significantly different and it may be that the subject of success will not prove as fecund as her years of struggle. Probably, the history of art will be increasingly exploited. Emin has also announced her intention to make a feature film about Margate, to be entitled *Top Spot*, showing the resort in a glamorous light.

Recently, Emin has become concerned by the prevailing opinion that her art is simply an unmediated expression of her personal experiences, as if no thought, control or craft skills were involved, because in 2001 she insisted. 'It's all edited, it's all calculated, it's all decided. I decide to show this or that part of the truth, which isn't necessarily the whole story.'[51]

Critical opinion about the quality of Emin's art is divided. She has her admirers but, according to Julian Stallabrass, her critic-fans, in the face of revelatory displays of adolescent sex and angst,

> forget all they ever knew about 'theory' and, more particularly, about the critique of expressionism and authenticity, the death of the author, the fracture of the self and the gendered politics of representation. Indeed, in wittering on about religion and the soul, they have produced some of the most craven nonsense ever written about a 'young British artist'.[52]

Negative opinions have included: 'thin gruel', 'household junk', 'drawings a terrible cliché', 'drama queen', 'she has become a bore', 'tortured nonsense'. Jonathan Jones, in contrast, praised Emin's solo show, *You Forgot to Kiss My Soul*, at White Cube 2 gallery in April 2001 for being gentle, passionate and poetic. One exhibit was a tall wooden reconstruction of a Helter Skelter ride reminiscent of Tatlin's *Monument to the Third International*. In this instance, the reference was not to Russian constructivism but to Emin's seaside childhood. The structure was a rather obvious metaphor: a downward spiral. Her life, as one of her statements put it, had been 'Hellter Fucking Skelter'.

Since certain collectors queue up to pay high prices for her art and some dealers and curators are keen to exhibit it around the world, and publishers are happy to pay her large advances (she has a contract to write a novel), it is obvious they value her work despite the negative critical opinions. When such criticisms were repeated on a television arts review programme, a female panellist remarked: 'She's not a terribly good artist, but I think she's a fantastic phenomenon', thereby implying that conventional aesthetic criteria did not apply in her case. David Lee observed in similar vein: 'Tracey is not an artist but she is an amazing force of nature.' Critic Richard Dorment thought she was 'the Queen of No-brow – that indeterminate middle ground between highbrow culture and lowbrow entertainment where questions such as "Is she any good?" simply don't apply'. Again, as in the case of Hockney, there is a discrepancy between the degree of fame Emin enjoys and the merit of her art. However, since life and art are so closely intertwined in Emin's case, perhaps critic Laura Cumming was right when she remarked: 'performance is what she does best: dramatising, and now sending herself up ...'[53]

Emin and Hirst were the most prominent artists of the YBA or BritArt generation and so they deserve to be the central characters of any future feature film about that generation. In January 2001, the celebrity website Peoplenews.com reported that a biopic of the YBAs was in development and named John Maybury as a possible director. The movie would 'reveal their lives before they became famous, the incestuous relationships within the group and their excessive drink and drug consumption ... the corrupting influence of fame ...' Will Hirst and Emin be invited, one wonders, to play themselves?

### Appropriating Fame

Certain contemporary artists have made fame the subject of their work. In 1965–67, for instance, Richard Hamilton created a screen print with a painted self-portrait showing him wearing a cap and smoking a cigar on the cover of *Time* magazine. (*Time* is noted for commissioning artists to create portraits for its front cover; an exhibition and book – *Faces of TIME* [1998] – have been produced about them.) Hamilton is quite well known but he is not famous enough to rate a *Time* cover. In 1975, Hamilton also produced a vitreous enamel sign on steel that featured his first name RICHARD in bold yellow lettering on a blue ground. The name later appeared on a carafe (1978) and on an ashtray (1979). Hamilton was pretending that his Christian name was as famous as the French trademark RICARD associated with the popular anis-flavoured drinks of southern France.

Tim Noble (b. 1966) and Sue Webster (b. 1967), a British artist-duo who met at Nottingham Polytechnic, are notorious for their rudeness and aggressive self-promotion. Their work is also self-reflexive: one of their sculptures is entitled *The New Barbarians* (1997–99) and depicts them as small, low-browed, naked Neanderthals. Assemblages and heaps of rubbish that yielded self-portraits in terms of shadow silhouettes when lit from below established their artistic reputation in the late 1990s. Matthew Collings has commented:

> They're a typical modern art success story, but also atypical, since success seems to be their theme in an open and frank way, rather than a hidden way. Their installation in 'Apocalypse' [exhibition, Royal Academy, 2000] was a shadow-image of themselves, apparently on a rubbish heap, with a neon sunset opposite. It was as if they'd made it to the top of the pile and now they were looking out over an urban romantic trash landscape. They cleverly express a success and celebrity theme, but also distance themselves from success, as if they're saying 'It's only rubbish!'[54]

Noble and Webster have also employed photomontage to substitute images of their own faces for those of Patsy Kensit and Liam Gallagher as they appeared in a Union Jack bed on the front cover of *Vanity Fair*'s 'London Swings Again!' issue (March 1997).

Gavin Turk has also depicted himself, wife and new baby on the cover of a mass circulation magazine – the celebrity magazine *Hello!* – via a photograph, screen print and light box entitled *Identity Crisis* (1995). It is a bucolic representation of a white, nuclear family. Turk has addressed the issue of fame throughout his career and critiqued the notion of the artist as auteur and the role of the artist's signature. His sculptural 'impersonations' of Sid Vicious and Che Guevara have already been discussed. Other 'impersonations' have included the dead Marat and a modern tramp.

Turk's MA degree show, entitled *Cave*, held at the Royal College of Art, created a stir in 1991. It consisted of a white-painted room that was empty apart from a blue, English Heritage wall plaque of the kind that commemorate the London addresses of famous historical figures. It declared: 'Borough of Kensington, Gavin Turk, sculptor, worked here, 1989–1991.' The circular ceramic plaque treated him as if he was already a celebrated artist, as if he was already dead. What should have been a show that marked the commencement of a career paradoxically represented its end. The RCA's examiners were not amused and refused him a post-graduate qualification. However, their decision did not hinder Turk's progress and the plaque was later issued in a limited edition.

Mark Wallinger (b. 1959) is another British artist who has played with the idea of personal fame and with British identity, and the British passions for horse racing and soccer. In 1994, he had his name emblazoned across a huge Union Jack, which was then held aloft among a crowd of football supporters who, in all likelihood, had no idea who 'Mark Wallinger' was. (British football fans often add the names of their local clubs to Union Jacks.) Wallinger was reclaiming the national flag – which has often been the preserve of far right groups – for himself and for art. The final art work was a large colour photograph of the scene laminated on to MDF board. Its lengthy title – *Mark Wallinger, 31 Hayes Court, Camberwell New Road, Camberwell, London, England, Great Britain, Europe, The World, The Solar System, The Galaxy, The Universe* – spelled out his precise location in the scheme of things in the way that children enjoy doing.

Finally, there was Jessica Voorsanger's work *Art Stars* temporarily displayed in London in 1998. It consisted of 122 variously coloured concrete slabs, arranged like a pavement, which were inscribed with the names and palm prints of living artists, critics and curators, some well known, others little known. Among the British 'Artocracy' were: Glenn Brown, the group BANK, Matthew Collings, Martin Creed, Dexter Dalwood, Matthew Higgs, Cornelia Parker,

**68. Jessica Voorsanger, *Art Stars* (detail), 1998.**
Installation, 122 concrete slabs, each 46 x 56 cm, at 7 Vyner Street, London.
Photo courtesy of the artist.

Gavin Turk and Richard Wilson. Clearly, this work imitated the forecourt of Grauman's Chinese Theatre in Hollywood with its hand and footprints, and autographs of movie stars, which attracts 2 million visitors per year. A later Voorsanger project involved casting the boot prints of leading footballers such as Michael Owen of Liverpool and England.

Although the art works cited above were tongue in cheek, they surely revealed a desire on the part of many artists to attain the status of major celebrities.

# Conclusion

It is time to summarise the pros and cons of celebrity art and artists. The advantages of celebrityhood for professional artists are clear:

- International fame, which leads to international travel and spells of residence in foreign lands. Great fame today makes it likely (but does not guarantee) that the artist will be remembered by posterity.
- Flattery, praise and admiration from critics and gallery goers.
- Demand for their work from dealers, collectors, museum curators, fellow artists and celebrities.
- Commissions, business and commercial endorsement opportunities, honours, prizes and awards, plus sales of any merchandise (T-Shirts, ties, multiples, etc.) the artists decide to produce.
- Demands for interviews and photo-sessions from the media – the opinions of artists on virtually any subject become important – illustrated articles, books and television programmes about them are inevitable.
- Attention – being recognised in restaurants and the street; social invitations and the chance to meet and mix with other celebrities – fame guarantees access to other VIPs, even government ministers and heads of state, and enables the artists to assist charities and political causes of their choice.
- Free publicity – when fine artists depict major celebrities, the mass media carry reports and images. In April 2002, for example, Peter Howson achieved massive international publicity by unveiling two unauthorised, unflattering paintings of Madonna (shown naked with a muscular body) plus various drawings and prints when his one-man show opened at the McLaurin Gallery, Ayr, Scotland. Some Madonna supporters thought the representations were 'disgusting', 'ugly' and derived from photographs. Howson was accused of 'voyeurism', 'self-promotion' and 'piggy-backing on Madonna's superstardom'.
- Wealth.

**69. Peter Howson, *Madonna*, 2002.**
Painting, oil on canvas 214 x 153 cm.
Photo Gareth Winters, reproduced courtesy of the artist.

The last enables artists to enjoy a more secure and luxurious standard
of living, to dress and eat well, to acquire land and houses, and to
afford larger and better-equipped studios. They can then buy more
materials; increase their output and tackle projects that are more
ambitious. They can employ studio assistants and secretaries, and
hire specialist technicians. They can also diversify into other fields
as Schnabel and Sherman did with their feature film directing and as
Hirst did with restaurants. If a fortune remains when the artist dies,
then charitable foundations can be established – like the Andy
Warhol Foundation – to assist other, needy artists. Even after death,
an artist's estate and name may continue to generate income for
heirs and charities.

Celebrities who produce art in their spare time already enjoy the benefits of celebrityhood; however, their fame and wealth will ensure that they can exhibit internationally and sell work. Alternatively, they can donate work to charity auctions. If their art has merit in terms of form and content – as in the cases of Don van Vliet and Dennis Hopper – then respect for them will extend beyond their usual fan base.

The benefits for the public of celebrity art and artists are harder to specify but there is no doubt they are a source of amusement and entertainment, and topics for gossip. It has also been argued, by Tyler Cowen, that the public benefits because fame increases in quantity with economic growth, and because the competitive character of the commercial forces behind fame production results in a wide diversity of celebrities in different spheres. Competition between artists may benefit audiences because they strive harder for dominance. One thinks of the rivalries between Matisse and Picasso, Pollock and de Kooning, Basquiat and Warhol, Schnabel and Salle.

Let us turn now to the disadvantages:

- Art that is made by celebrities, such as movie and rock stars, tends to be traditional and conventional in medium, content, form and technique; it takes few risks and is often amateurish, mediocre and derivative (indebted to past styles such as impressionism, fauvism and expressionism). Furthermore, the public usually value it for who is depicted or who made it rather than for its aesthetic merits.

- Paintings and sculptures depicting celebrities tend to be naturalistic or photo-realistic in style and poor in artistic quality; either they are kitsch or they simulate kitsch.

- Art stars tend to hog most of the art world and media's attention and so many serious and worthy artists receive less attention and support than they deserve.[1]

- The stress on the personalities and lifestyles of art stars means that their works of art take second place or are considered as expressions or relics of the artist. After such artists die, their works are unlikely to sustain the same level of interest. This surely applies to the objects Beuys left behind and is likely to apply to Emin's relics. In a critique of the vogue for 'concept art', Ivan Massow, Chairman of London's Institute of Contemporary Art, argued: 'current trends seem to have replaced the art with the artists. As for the artists themselves, they must be "glossy" – or risk being replaced by those who understand the celebrity game better.'[2] The *reductio ad absurdum* of the tendency to prioritise artists over their art are The Three, a trio of anonymous fashion models/conceptualists who make no work at all but simply exhibit everything that has appeared about them in the media.[3]

- Art that is made by art stars often lacks genuine aesthetic qualities and intellectual complexity because of the influence of money, publicity and the desire to attract the media's attention and to shock or entertain gallery goers. The commercialisation of art and the cult of art stars results in the separation of fame from artistic achievement.

- Living the life of a celebrity and mixing only with other celebrities removes artists from their roots and contact with ordinary humans and this may adversely influence the character of their work. Warhol's shallow celebrity portraits of the 1970s are an example. Surrounded by a retinue of sycophants, art stars may develop a huge ego, become extremely selfish and arrogant, and lose the faculty of self-criticism with the result that they can no longer recognise when their work is bad.

- The media pressures associated with celebrity can result in the artist's alienation or self-estrangement, in artists adopting masks, behaving in machine-like ways, in order to protect their inner selves. Warhol's zombie-like mask is an example. Art stars come under tremendous pressure to reinvent themselves periodically in order to surpass their earlier achievements and this results in a succession of new, fictional identities, which may cause a feeling of inauthenticity.

- Even artists able to cope with the pressures of being celebrities, will find it difficult to obtain the peace and quiet to make new work. This is surely one reason why artists like Hirst buy farms and obtain studios far from the urban centres of the art trade.

- Some artists cannot cope with the pressures of being celebrities and indulge in exhibitionist, anti-social behaviour and resort to excessive consumption of alcohol and drugs, which sometimes results in suicide, as was virtually the case in the deaths of Pollock and Basquiat.

- To meet the sudden increase in demand for work that occurs when professional artists become celebrities, some will be tempted to work too fast, to overproduce, to allow mediocre and poor work to be exhibited and sold. Basquiat's late work can be cited as an example. Inflated egos and wallets can result in overblown art – enormous canvases full of empty rhetoric, as in the case of Schnabel, or gigantic sculptures, as in the cases of Koons and Hirst. They may also resort to shock tactics in order to retain the media and public's interest. Surely, this is what has occurred in the careers of Koons and Hirst. However, as shock follows shock, their emotional impact diminishes and artists are compelled to become increasingly extreme.

- Art stars need to develop thick skins because they are likely to become the targets of caricatures, jokes, harsh criticism, contempt, envy and hate mail. A few can expect stalkers and physical attacks, as in the cases of Warhol and Scholte.

- Some art stars will have to adjust to a sudden loss of interest as overexposure results in the media and public becoming bored with them.

- The appearance of fine artists in advertisements and on television quiz shows, and their endorsement of commercial products elides the difference between high and low culture, compromises the artist's independence and lessens the respect in which art and artists are held (unless such acts are part of a deliberate strategy of business art, as in Warhol's case). Some celebrities cynically endorse products they do not like and never use, and some endorse products that are irrelevant to their professions. One would be more likely to trust an artist's endorsement of a product if it was one they had professional knowledge of – such as a brand of crayons – and if one knew that they were not being paid to praise it. Since dead artists cannot give permission for the use of their names and reputations to sell goods, it is surely an unethical practice.

    Artist-endorsement of charities and political parties seems more meritorious but can reflect a lack of critical analysis and judgement – are private charities the solution to social problems? Instead of simply donating an art work for sale to benefit, say, a charity assisting the homeless, should not the artist make this issue part of the content of their art? (Hirst did the former while Wallinger did the latter.)

Art of aesthetic quality, intellectual integrity and political commitment continues to be made in 'an age crazed by celebrity' (Mark Lawson's phrase), an era dominated by entertainment and market forces – witness the view of Philip Dodd, Director of London's Institute of Contemporary Arts: 'I believe in entertainment before Art. Art is mediated through entertainment ...'[4] – but it becomes harder for it to gain respect and public recognition. It is surely significant that artists who have international reputations but who are not celebrities, for example, Conrad and Terry Atkinson, Victor Burgin, Hans Haacke, Margaret Harrison, Mary Kelly, Peter Kennard, John Stezaker and Jamie Wagg, have had to rely on salaries from teaching in art schools rather than from sales via commercial galleries. The values that their art represents are increasingly threatened by those associated with celebrity art. One can only hope that education in the arts will result in more discrimination on the part of curators, collectors, dealers and the viewing public. Over-exposure to superficial and bad art, like over-consumption of junk food, may eventually cause revulsion and prompt a demand for higher quality, more profound visual culture. Already there are voices calling for such a change.

Meanwhile, one has only to open a listings magazine at the exhibitions and galleries pages to see that the fine arts currently exist as a minor category of entertainment and leisure activities. However, within that category there are artists, galleries and organisations (many publicly funded) that still present work that offers an alternative to celebrity art. Moreover, as we have seen, there are some painters and sculptors, like Elizabeth Mulholland and Ian Walters, who continue to believe in heroes, such as Tony Benn and Nelson Mandela, and to commemorate them in traditional styles.

Many graphic artists have also satirised celebrities via caricatures and cartoons, and the smiles and laughter their images arouse seem to have a therapeutic effect as far as viewers are concerned. However, the very fact that celebrities are caricatured confirms their fame and often the images are affectionate rather than coruscating. Some politicians – the British Tory Kenneth Baker and the Labour MP Tony Banks, for instance – appreciate caricatures and cartoons and so collect them. For almost a decade, the London-based group of artists called BANK mounted a frontal attack on the art stars and pretensions of the British art world via crude exhibitions and a scurrilous newspaper but then ceased when their parasitic critique had exhausted every strategy. One member, John Russell, concluded: 'If someone is famous their work is worth a lot and they get talked about. It is a magical effect. And it is impossible to compete against.'[5]

**70. Elizabeth Mulholland,** *Portrait of Tony Benn,* **2002.**
Painting, oil on gore-tex fabric, 124.5 × 129.5 cm.
Artist's collection. Photo supplied by artist.

While it is possible to rail against celebrity culture, and some writers have done so, it is now so pervasive it resembles a widespread disease – critic Matthew Collings has remarked: 'Celebrity is a kind of sickness in Britain now.'[6] The icons of popular culture fascinate virtually everyone; even left-wing academics and critics share that fascination, albeit at one remove. To end it, as journalist Suzanne Moore has remarked, 'one would have to destroy the entire media industry' and this would surely mean destroying capitalism itself, but, as we have seen, the 'communist' societies of the twentieth century were not free from the cult of personality either.[7] We need, therefore, to reflect upon our psychological need for glamorous beings and consider whether we would be better off without them. Perhaps admitting our addiction and seeking to understand the seduction of the celebrity phenomenon are the first steps to moderating its spell. Art that addresses the subjects of fame and celebrity critically, such as Gavin Turk's and Alison Jackson's, is of value in this respect. Turk has remarked: 'Hype and PR exercises intrigue and revolt me.'[8] Jackson, I maintain, has been especially effective in subverting the media's cult of celebrity via her visual simulations.

## Coda

The terrorist attacks on New York and Washington DC on 11 September 2001 and the ensuing war against the Taliban regime in Afghanistan ushered in a new era of seriousness, which prompted columnist Barbara Ellen of the *Observer* to declare it marked 'the end of celebrity as we know it'. Certainly, the attacks put celebrity culture in a new perspective, one that made it seem even more superficial than before. However, predictions of its demise were premature because it soon reasserted itself. It was only a short time after the attack that Hollywood stars appeared on television to raise funds for the families of the victims, and pop music stars (including Bowie and McCartney) performed in a charity concert in New York. Economic effects, such as a decline in advertising revenue, caused some magazines to fail but celebrity vehicles such as *Hello!* and *OK!* continue to appear and there are as many items about celebrities in the West's media as before. A new image of infamy has been added: the face of Osama bin Laden. In addition, Americans rediscovered heroes: New York's police and firefighters and its Mayor Rudy Giuliani. Tributes to rescue workers in the form of life-size Polaroid photo-portraits taken by Joe McNally were soon exhibited in a show entitled *Faces of Ground Zero* (New York: Vanderbilt Hall, Grand Central Terminal, 2002).

The destruction of life, architecture and even art works (for example, sculptures by Rodin) on 11 September, and the reasons behind it, also presented fine artists with a tremendous challenge: how to memorialise the event, how to make art about this subject that would surpass the spectacular images already provided by photography, film and television.

# Notes

## Introduction

1. Ziauddin Sardar, 'Trapped in the human zoo', *New Statesman*, Vol. 14, No. 648 (19 March 2001), pp. 27–30.
2. Janis Bergman-Carton, 'Media: like an artist', *Art in America*, Vol. 81, No. 1 (January 1993), pp. 35–9.
3. Rosie Millard, *The Tastemakers: U.K. Art Now* (London: Thames and Hudson, 2001), p. 74.
4. Chris Rojek, *Celebrity* (London: Reaktion Books, 2001), p. 102.
5. For an excellent recent account, see Rojek, *Celebrity*.
6. On the psychology of teenage fans, see: Andrew Evans and Glenn D. Wilson, *Fame: The Psychology of Stardom* (London: Vision Publishing, 1999), pp. 101–3.
7. Daniel J. Boorstin, *The Image or What Happened to the American Dream* (London: Weidenfeld and Nicolson, 1962), p. 67.
8. Neal Gabler, *Life the Movie: How Entertainment Conquered Reality* (New York: Alfred A. Knopf, 1998), p. 146.
9. Irving Rein, Philip Kotler and Martin Stoller, *High Visibility: The Making and Marketing of Professionals into Celebrities* (Chicago, IL: NTC Business Books, 1997), pp. 14–15.
10. Joseph Campbell, *The Hero with a Thousand Faces* (Princeton, NJ: Bollingen Foundation/Princeton University Press, 1949).
11. Boorstin, *The Image*, p. 70.
12. Boorstin, *The Image*, p. 55.
13. Camille Paglia, *Sex, Art and American Culture: Essays* (New York: Vintage Books/Random House, 1992), p. 264. A recent book re-examining the subject of beauty is: *Beauty Matters*, ed. P.Z. Brand (Indianapolis, IN: Indiana University Press, 2000); it includes an essay on the artist Yasumasa Morimura.
14. See, for instance, Dennis Loy Johnson, 'Authorial beauty contest', *Mobylives* (16 July 2001), <www.mobylives.com/Authorial_Beauty_Contest.html> and Joe Moran, *Star Authors: Literary Celebrity in America* (London and Stirling, VA: Pluto Press, 2000).
15. See: <www.forbes.com>.
16. Joey Berlin and others, *Toxic Fame: Celebrities Speak on Stardom* (Detroit, MI: Visible Ink Press, 1996), p. xi.
17. Paglia, *Sex, Art and American Culture*, p. 105.
18. For examples of the latter, see: Paul Trent and Richard Lawson, *The Image Makers: Sixty Years of Hollywood Glamour* (New York: Harmony Books/Crown, 1982).
19. Rojek, *Celebrity*, pp. 147–8.

20. See: Robert Katz, *Naked by the Window: The Fatal Marriage of Carl Andre and Ana Mendieta* (New York: The Atlantic Monthly Press, 1990).

21. Arianna Stassinopoulos Huffington, *Picasso: Creator and Destroyer* (London: Weidenfeld and Nicolson, 1988), p. 12.

22. Richard Schickel, *Intimate Strangers: The Culture of Celebrity in America* (Garden City, NY: Doubleday, 1985).

23. Sharon Krum, 'Stars in their eyes: what do the new celebrity mags say about American women?' *Guardian* (*G2*) (26 April 2001), p. 11.

24. Ed Helmore, 'Meet the enforcer', *Observer* (3 June 2001), p. 23.

25. Maria Malone, *Popstars: The Making of Hear'Say* (London: Granada Media, 2001).

26. See Chapter 5, 'Fame', in his book *From A to B and Back Again: The Philosophy of Andy Warhol* (London: Michael Dempsey/Cassell and Co. Ltd, 1975).

27. See: Gerald Scarfe, *Scarfe on Scarfe* (London: Hamish Hamilton, 1986). Sebastian Krüger and Michael Lang, *Stars* (Beverly Hills, CA: Morpheus International, 1997) and <www.krugerstars.com>. Wendy Wick Reeves and Pie Friendly, *Celebrity Caricature in America* (New Haven, CT and Washington, DC: Yale University Press/National Portrait Gallery, Smithsonian Institution, 1998).

28. See: John Lloyd and others, *The Spitting Image Book (The Appallingly Disrespectful Spitting Image Book)* (London: Faber and Faber, 1985). L. Chester, *Tooth and Claw: The Inside Story of Spitting Image* (London: Faber and Faber, 1986).

29. Michael Joseph Gross, 'Signs of the times', *Sunday Telegraph Magazine* (12 August 2001), pp. 20–2.

30. For examples, see: Jeffrey Deller, *The Uses of Literacy* (London: Book Works, 1999) – with poems and images by fans of the Manic Street Preachers.

31. Gary Lee Boas and others, *Starstruck: Photographs from a Fan* (Los Angeles, CA: Dilettante Press, 1999).

32. The video was shown in New York at the Whitney Museum's 1993 Biennial Exhibition.

33. Paglia, *Sex, Art and American Culture*, pp. 102–3.

34. McCartney quoted in *Paul McCartney: Many Years from Now*, by Barry Miles (London: Vintage, 1998), p. 303.

35. David Buckley, *Strange Fascination: David Bowie: The Definitive Story* (London: Virgin Books, 1999), p. 15.

36. For an account of one such false persona, see: Maud Lavin, 'Confessions from *The Couch*: issues of persona on the Web', in *Clean New World: Culture, Politics, and Graphic Design* (Cambridge, MA and London: MIT Press, 2001), pp. 168–81.

37. Cleveland Amory, *Who Killed Society?* (New York: Harper and Brothers, 1960), Chapter 3, 'Celebrity', pp. 107–88.

38. James Monaco and others, *Celebrity: The Media as Image Makers* (New York: Dell Publishing Co., 1978), p. 4.

39. Deyan Sudjic, *Cult Heroes: How to be Famous for more than Fifteen Minutes* (London: André Deutsch, 1989), p. 43.

40. For an analysis of celebrity endorsement of charities, see: Polly Vernon, 'The price is right', *Evening Standard* (10 August 2001), pp. 25–7 and Andrew Smith, 'All in a good cause?' *Life: The Observer Magazine* (27 January 2002), pp. 45–7.

41. Cintra Wilson, *A Massive Swelling: Celebrity Re-Examined as a Grotesque, Crippling Disease and Other Cultural Revelations* (New York: Viking Penguin, 2000), p. xix.

42. Tyler Cowen, *What Price Fame?* (Cambridge, MA and London: Harvard University Press, 2000), p. 169.

## 1 Celebrities as Art Collectors and Artists

1. For more information on most of these films, see my book *Art and Artists on Screen* (Manchester and New York: Manchester University Press, 1993).

2. See: Paige Rense (ed.), *Celebrity Homes: Architectural Digest Presents the Private Worlds of Thirty International Personalities* (Los Angeles, CA: Knapp Press, 1977) and Charles Jencks, *Daydream Houses of Los Angeles* (New York: Rizzoli, 1978).

3. For a biography, see: Edward G. Robinson (with Leonard Spigelgass), *All My Yesterdays: An Autobiography* (London and New York: W.H. Allen, 1974).

4. Wendy Baron and Richard Shone (eds), *Sickert: Paintings* (New Haven, CT and London: Royal Academy/Yale University Press, 1992), pp. 344–5.

5. Quote from a speech given in 1971, printed in: Jane Robinson and Leonard Spigelgass, *Edward G. Robinson's World of Art* (New York: Harper and Row, 1971), p. 113.

6. For a biography of Price, see: Victoria Price, *Vincent Price: A Daughter's Biography* (New York: St Martin's Press, 1999; London: Sidgwick and Jackson, 2000).

7. Quoted in, Victoria Price, *Vincent Price*, p. 186.

8. Vincent Price, *I Like What I Know: A Visual Autobiography* (Garden City, NY: Doubleday and Co., 1959).

9. <http://members.aol.com/vpgallery/Collection.html>.

10. Judith Thurman, 'Sylvester Stallone: life on the grand scale for the actor in Miami', *Architectural Digest*, Vol. 54, No. 11 (November 1997), pp. 212–21, 280–2, plus front cover.

11. Frank Sanello, *Stallone: A Rocky Life* (Edinburgh and London: Mainstream Publishing, 1998), pp. 121–2.

12. See Danielle Rice, 'Rocky too: the saga of an outdoor sculpture', <[pdf] tps.cr.nps.gov/crm/archive/18–1/18–1–4.pdf> and articles in the *Philadelphia Inquirer*.

13. Henry J. Seldis, *Hollywood Collects* (Los Angeles, CA: Otis Art Institute of Los Angeles County, 1970).

14. Tod Volpe and Peter Israel, 'Going, going, gone!' *Life: Observer Magazine* (21 January 2001), pp. 22–8.

15. For a collection of reproductions of drawings of flowers by celebrities, see: Victoria Leacock and Justin Bond, *Signature Flowers: A Revealing*

*Collection of Celebrity Drawings* (New York: Broadway Books/Melcher Media, 1998).

16. There two books by Jim McMullan and Dick Gautier documenting this genre: *Actors as Artists* (Boston, MA: Charles E. Tuttle, 1992) and *Musicians as Artists* (Boston, MA: Journey Editions/Charles E. Tuttle, 1994).
17. Mariella Frostrup, 'It's like ...', *Life: Observer Magazine* (2 December 2001), pp. 8–13.
18. Ronnie Wood and others, *Wood on Canvas: Every Picture Tells a Story* (Guildford: Genesis Publications, 1998). See also: Ron Wood and Bill German, *The Works* (London: Fontana/Collins, 1987).
19. Anthony Quinn, *The Original Sin: A Self-Portrait* (London: W.H. Allen, 1973), p. 138.
20. For a tragic-comic memoir of Barrymore, Decker and their circle, see: Gene Fowler, *Minutes of the Last Meeting* (New York: The Viking Press, 1954).
21. See, Wendy Wick Reaves and Pie Friendly, *Celebrity Caricature in America* (New Haven, CT and London: Yale University Press; Washington, DC: National Portrait Gallery, Smithsonian Institution, 1998), pp. 260–1.
22. Quinn, *The Original Sin*, p. 287.
23. Anthony Quinn (with Daniel Paisner), *One Man Tango: An Autobiography* (London: Headline Book Publishing, 1995), pp. 337–8.
24. Stallone quoted during an interview: <eonline.com/Celebs/Qa/Stallone/intrview4.html>.
25. *LA Weekly*, <www.laweekly.com/ink/00/03/art-harvey.shtml>. See also: Baird Jones, 'Celebrity art', <www.artnet.com/magazine/news/jones/jones1-12-99.asp>.
26. Hopper quoted in, *Dennis Hopper: A Madness to His Method*, by Elena Rodriguez (New York: St Martin's Press, 1988), p. 95.
27. Hopper quoted in, *Groovy Bob: The Life and Times of Robert Fraser*, by Harriet Vyner (London: Faber and Faber, 1999), p. 115.
28. Jim Hoberman, *Dennis Hopper: From Method to Madness* (Minneapolis, MN: Walker Art Center, 1998), 40-page booklet.
29. Rudi Fuchs and Jan Hein Sassen, *Dennis Hopper (A Keen Eye): Artist, Photographer, Filmmaker* (Amsterdam: Stedelijk Museum; Rotterdam: NAi Publishers, 2001). The exhibition in Vienna (MAK, May–October 2001) was accompanied by a different publication: Peter Noever (ed.), *Dennis Hopper: A System of Moments* (Ostfildern-Ruit: Hatje Cantz Verlag, 2001).
30. Sarah Schrank, 'Picturing the Watts Towers: the art and politics of an urban landmark', in *Reading California: Art, Image, and Identity, 1900–2000*, eds Stephanie Barron, Sheri Bernstein and Ilene Susan Fort (Los Angeles, CA: Los Angeles County Museum of Art/University of California Press, 2001), pp. 372–86.
31. Fuchs and Sassen, *Dennis Hopper*, p. 83.
32. Lynn Barber, 'American Psycho', *Life: Observer Magazine* (14 January 2001), pp. 10–14.
33. Shirley Dent, 'Turning art into a peepshow', <www.spiked-online.com> (11 December 2001).

34. Vince Aletti, 'Ray of Light' (1998 interview with Madonna), *Life: Observer Magazine* (12 December 1999), pp. 12–19. A longer version was published in *Male Female: 105 Photographs* (New York: Aperture Books, 1999), pp. 44–51.
35. Quoted in 'Keith Haring' by John Gruen, <www.haring.com>.
36. See: Phoebe Hoban, Chapter 15, 'Who's that Girl?' *Basquiat: A Quick Killing in Art* (London: Quartet Books, 1998), pp. 164–74.
37. Andrew Morton, *Madonna* (London: Michael O'Mara Books Ltd, 2001), p. 115.
38. Madonna, 'Me, Jean-Michel, love and money', *Guardian* (5 March 1996).
39. One was to be directed by Julie Taymor and star Salma Hayek as Kahlo and the other was to be directed by Luis Valdez and star Jennifer Lopez as the painter. In the event, only the former was actually made, during 2002. An earlier film – *Frida, Naturaleza Viva* (1984) – was directed by Paul Leduc and starred Ofelia Medina as Kahlo.
40. See Margaret A. Lindauer's book about Frida or Kahlomania: *Devouring Frida: The Art History and Popular Celebrity of Frida Kahlo* (Hanover, NH and London: Wesleyan University Press/University Press of New England, 1999).
41. Janis Bergman-Carton, 'Like an artist', *Art in America*, Vol. 81, No. 1 (January 1993), pp. 35–9.
42. <http ://daswww.harvard.edu/users/students/Zheng_Wang/Madonna/ Mnws9705.html>.
43. Camille Paglia, 'Madonna 1: Animality and artifice' (1990), *Sex, Art and American Culture: Essays* (New York: Vintage Books/Random House, 1992), pp. 3–5.
44. Paglia, *Sex, Art and American Culture*, pp. 103, 193.
45. P. David Marshall, *Celebrity and Power: Fame in Contemporary Culture* (Minneapolis, MN and London: University of Minnesota Press, 1997), p. 194.
46. Richard Corliss, 'Madonna goes to camp', *Time* (25 October 1993).
47. Stephen Holden, 'Madonna: the new revamped vamp', *International Herald Tribune* (21 March 1989), p. 20.
48. <www.salon.com/ent/music/feature/2000/10/10/madonna/>.
49. Dylan Jones, 'Madonna: the most famous woman in the world interviewed', *Independent* (10 February 2001).
50. George Tremlett, *The David Bowie Story* (London: Futura Publications Ltd, 1974), p. 152.
51. Tremlett, *The David Bowie Story*, p. 120.
52. David Buckley, *Strange Fascination: David Bowie: The Definitive Story* (London: Virgin Books, 1999), p. 9.
53. Bowie quoted in Tremlett, *The David Bowie Story*, p. 102.
54. An illustrated, 16-page brochure of 'proto-types and Polaroids' was published to accompany the show: *Davie Bowie: Paintings and Sculpture, New Afro-Pagan and Work 1975–1995* (London: Chertavian Fine Art, 1995).
55. Holly Johnson, 'Real people in Cork Street', *Modern Painters*, Vol. 8, No. 2 (summer 1995), pp. 48–9.

56. Damien Hirst and Gordon Burn, *On the Way to Work* (London: Faber and Faber, 2001), p. 221.

57. David Bowie talking to Emma Brockes, 'Tomorrow's rock 'n' roll,' *Guardian Unlimited* (15 January 1999), <www.guardian.co.uk>.

58. Information about McCartney's interest in art derives from two principal sources: Paul McCartney & Barry Miles, *Paul McCartney: Many Years from Now* (London: Secker and Warburg, 1997) and Karen Wright's interview with him, 'Luigi's alcove', *Modern Painters*, Vol. 13, No. 3 (autumn 2000), pp. 102–5.

59. For an account of the interaction between pop music and the visual arts, see my book *Cross-Overs: Art into Pop/Pop into Art* (London and New York: Comedia/Methuen, 1987).

60. Brian Clarke and others, *Paul McCartney: Paintings* (Boston, MA, New York and London: Little, Brown and Co., 2000), p. 43.

61. Clarke and others, *Paul McCartney: Paintings*.

## 2 Artists Depict Celebrities

1. For a biography of Madame Tussaud, see: Pauline Chapman, *Madame Tussaud: Career Woman Extraordinaire* (London: Quiller Press, 1992).

2. See: Clive James, 'Prince Philip as James Cagney (and other horrors)', *Observer Magazine* (31 August 1980), pp. 16–17, and front cover.

3. See also the book: Tracey Bashkoff and others, *Sugimoto Portraits* (New York: Guggenheim Museum Publications/Harry N. Abrams, 2000).

4. An exhibition *Toulouse Lautrec and the Spirit of Montmartre: Cabarets, Humor and the Avant-Garde 1875–1905*, was held at the Legion of Honor de Young Museum, San Francisco in March 2001. See also the book: Phillip Cate and Mary Shaw (eds), *Toulouse Lautrec and the Spirit of Montmartre: Cabarets, Humor and the Avant-Garde 1875–1905* (New Brunswick, NJ: Jane Voorhees Zimmerli Art Museum/Rutgers University Press, 1996).

5. See: Robin Gibson, *Max Wall: Pictures by Maggi Hambling* (London: National Portrait Gallery, 1983), 36-page catalogue.

6. George Melly and Maggi Hambling, 'Life support', *Observer* (13 August 2000).

7. Xan Brooks, 'Cary Grant country', *Guardian (Friday Review)* (17 August 2001), pp. 1–5. See also: <www.carygrant.co.uk>.

8. <www.morecambe.co.uk/Ibbeson/grahamibbeson/website.html>.

9. For more on Green, see: David Mellor, Jane England and Dennis Bowen, *William Green: The Susan Hayward Exhibition* (London: England and Co., 1993), 24-page catalogue. John A. Walker, 'The strange case of William Green', *Art and Outrage: Provocation, Controversy and the Visual Arts* (London and Sterling, VA: Pluto Press, 1999), pp. 37–42.

10. David Mellor, *The Sixties Art Scene in London* (London: Barbican Art Gallery/Phaidon, 1993), p. 139. A younger British artist who abstracts the appearances of celebrities, as recorded in photographs, using a dot technique similar to that of Laing, is Francis John Poole. In 2000 and

2001 Poole depicted Jarvis Cocker, Tommy Hilfiger, Charles Saatchi, Janet Street Porter and others.

11. Information supplied by Laing in a letter to the author dated 27 August 2001.

12. See: Donald H. Wolfe, *The Assassination of Marilyn Monroe* (London: Little, Brown and Co., 1998).

13. William V. Ganis, 'Andy Warhol's iconophilia', *In[ ]visible Culture: An Electronic Journal for Visual Studies*, No. 3 (2000), <www.rochester.edu/in_visible_culture/issue3/ganis.htm>.

14. For a perceptive account of Warhol's celebrity images, see: Cécile Whiting, 'Andy Warhol, the public star and the private self', *Oxford Art Journal*, Vol. 10, No. 2 (1987), pp. 58–75. This article also reproduces images of Monroe by the artists James Gill and Derek Marlowe.

15. See Robert Rosenblum, 'Andy Warhol: court painter to the 70s', in *Andy Warhol: Portrait of the 1970s*, ed. David Whitney (New York: Whitney Museum of American Art, 1970), pp. 18–20; David Bourdon, 'Andy Warhol and the society icon', *Art in America*, Vol. 63, Nos 1 and 2 (January–February 1975), pp. 42–5; and Andy Grundberg, 'Andy Warhol's Polaroid pantheon', in *Reframing Andy Warhol: Constructing American Myths, Heroes and Cultural Icons*, ed. Wendy Grossman (College Park, MD: The Art Gallery at the University of Maryland, 1998), pp. 15–17.

16. David Kirby, 'Marilynmania', *Art News*, Vol. 99, No. 9 (October 2000), pp. 158–61.

17. See: Sharon Krum, 'Happy birthday, Marilyn', *Guardian* (*G2*) (29 May 2001), pp. 8–9.

18. For more on Kitaj and cinema, see: Alan Woods, 'Shootism, or, whitehair movie maniac Kitaj and Hollywood kulchur', in *Critical Kitaj: Essays on the Work of R.B. Kitaj*, eds James Aulich and John Lynch (Manchester: Manchester University Press, 2000), pp. 169–80.

19. Christine Keeler (with Douglas Thompson), *The Truth at Last: My Story* (London: Sidgwick and Jackson, 2001).

20. For more on Boty, see: Sue Watling and David Alan Mellor, *Pauline Boty: The Only Blonde in the World* (London: Whitford Fine Art and Mayor Gallery, 1998) and John A. Walker, *Cultural Offensive: America's Impact on British Art* (London and Sterling, VA: Pluto Press, 1998), pp. 93–5.

21. John A. Walker, *Cross-Overs: Art into Pop, Pop into Art* (London and New York: Comedia/Methuen, 1987). See also: David S. Rubin, *It's Only Rock and Roll: Rock and Roll Currents in Contemporary Art* (Munich and New York: Prestel-Verlag, 1995).

22. For a critical biography, see: Christopher Anderson, *Michael Jackson Unauthorized* (New York: Simon and Schuster, 1994).

23. Doreet Levitte Harten (ed.), *Heaven: An Exhibition that will Break your Heart* (Ostfildern-Ruit: Hatje Cantz Publishers, 1999), p. 92.

24. Anderson, *Michael Jackson Unauthorized*, p. 14.

25. Letter from Birk to the author, June 2001.

26. Julian Stallabrass, *High Art Lite: British Art in the 1990s* (London and New York: Verso, 1999), p. 44.

27. Cedar Lewisohn, 'An interview with Gavin Turk', n.d., <www.boilermag.it/english/arts/gavin.htm>.
28. Brian Sewell, 'Young guns fire blanks', *Evening Standard* (20 April 1995).
29. Richard Dorment, 'Could this be the real thing?' *Daily Telegraph* (5 April 1995).
30. Christopher Miles, 'Elizabeth Peyton', *Artforum*, Vol. 38, No. 5 (January 2000), p. 119.
31. Gean Moreno, 'High noon in desire country: the lingering presence of extended adolescence in contemporary art', *Art Papers*, Vol. 24, No. 3 (June 2000), <www.artpapers.org/24 3/adolescence.htm>.
32. Jon Savage, 'True Brits', *Guardian* (*Friday Review*) (20 December 1996), pp. 1–3, 19.
33. Jacqueline Cooper, 'Controlling the uncontrollable: heavy emotion invades contemporary painting', *New Art Examiner*, Vol. 28, No. 10 (September 1999).
34. Linda Pilgrim, 'An interview with a painter', *Parkett*, No. 53 (1998).
35. See, for instance: Miranda Sawyer, 'Self-portrait in a single breasted suit with hare', *Life: Observer Magazine* (11 November 2001), pp. 10–15, plus front cover.
36. Andrew Billen, 'There is more to me than cancer and celebrities', *Evening Standard* (21 November 2001), pp. 27–8.
37. For a history, see Walker, *Cross-Overs: Art into Pop/Pop into Art*.
38. Jonathan Jones, 'A Gainsborough for the 21st Century', *Guardian* (28 February 2001).
39. For an analysis of the 1981 Organ portrait and its vandalization, see: John A. Walker, *Art and Outrage: Provocation, Controversy and the Visual Arts* (London and Sterling, VA: Pluto Press, 1999), pp. 113–18.
40. David Hearst, 'Small thanks Moscow monumentalist scales down for Diana', *Guardian* (5 July 2001), p. 16.
41. For further information on Durand and neomodernism see: <www.arachne-art.net/web/news/html>.
42. *Hello!* No. 422 (31 August 1996).
43. Richard Cork, 'Heavenly bodies in earthly poses', *The Times* (15 December 1999), p. 34.
44. For reproductions of some of these subjects, see: *Karen Kilimnik Paintings* (Zürich: Edition Patrick Frey, 2001) and *Drawings by Karen Kilimnik* (Zürich: Edition Patrick Frey/Kunsthalle Zürich, 1997).
45. Jonathan Jones, 'Portrait of the Week No. 12: Karen Kilimnik's Hugh Grant (1997)', *Guardian* (1 July 2000).
46. Adrian Searle, 'Heaven isn't all it's cracked up to be', *Guardian* (*G2*) (14 December 1999), pp. 12–13.
47. Jonathan Jones, 'Art: Queen of hurts draws adulation', *Guardian* (22 July 1999), p. 18.
48. Gallery press release.
49. For illustrations, see the catalogue: *John Keane: Making a Killing (Rupert, Charles and Diana), Paintings and Prints* (London: Flowers East, 2000).
50. John Davison, 'Leading artist stages voodoo protest at "destabilising" influence of Saatchi', *Independent* (23 November 1999).

51. For a history of the interior décor of Graceland, see: Karal Ann Marling, 'Elvis Presley's Graceland, or the aesthetic of rock 'n' roll heaven', *American Art*, Vol. 7, No. 4 (fall 1993).

52. See: Jan Koenot, *Hungry for Heaven: Rockmusik, Kultur und Religion* (Düsseldorf: Patmos Verlag, 1997); Rogan P. Taylor, *The Death and Resurrection Show: From Shaman to Superstar* (London: Blond, 1985). See also: Gary Vikan, 'Graceland as Locus Sanctus', in *Elvis + Marilyn: 2 × Immortal*, ed. Geri DePaoli (New York: Rizzoli, 1994), pp. 150–67; Chris Rojek, *Celebrity* (London: Reaktion Books, 2001), pp. 51–99; and John Maltby and others, 'Thou shalt worship no other gods – unless they are celebrities ...', *Personality and Individual Differences*, Vol. 32, No. 7 (2002), pp. 1173–84.

53. Robin Gibson, *Painting the Century: 101 Portrait Masterpieces 1900–2000* (London: National Portrait Gallery Publications, 2000; New York: Watson-Guptill Publications, 2001), pp. 262–3.

54. I am grateful to the staff of Manchester City Art Gallery for supplying press cuttings. Bryan Appleyard, 'Painted into a corner by history', *Sunday Times* (20 April 1997).

55. <www.rednews.co.uk/features/featoe06.htm>.

56. Tim Cumming, 'Hopelessly devoted', *Guardian* (7 March 2001), pp. 16–17.

57. Letter from the artist to the author, June 2001.

58. Kylie Minogue and others, *Kylie* (London: Booth-Clibborn Editions, 1999).

## 3 Simulation and Celebrities

1. See, Geri DePaoli (ed.), *Elvis + Marilyn: 2 × Immortal* (New York: Rizzoli, 1994), p. 72.

2. A show was held at the Open Eye Gallery, Liverpool in December 2001–January 2002; book: *Elvis and Presley* (Hamburg: Kruse Verlag, 2001).

3. Helen Harrison (ed.), *Such Desperate Joy: Imagining Jackson Pollock* (New York: Thunder's Mouth Press, 2000), p. 1.

4. Joos quoted in David Greenberg, 'Familiar faces', *Los Angeles Business Journal* (23 April 2001), <www.findarticles.com>.

5. For an account of Sherman's work, see: Amada Cruz and others, *Cindy Sherman: Retrospective* (Los Angeles, CA: Museum of Contemporary Art; London and New York: Thames and Hudson, 1997), book/catalogue of a touring exhibition.

6. Anne Friedberg, 'Fame and the frame', in Fred Fehlau and others, *Hollywood, Hollywood: Identity under the Guise of Celebrity* (Pasadena, CA: Pasadena Art Alliance/Alyce de Roulet Williamson Gallery, Art Center College of Design, 1992), p. 22.

7. *ZG*, No. 7 (1982).

8. Nadine Lemmon, 'The Sherman phenomena: the image of theory or a foreclosure of dialectical reasoning?' *Part 2*, n.d., <www.brickahus.com/amoore/magazine/Sherman.html>.

9. Statements made in the documentary film/video: *Go on Stage Morimura*, directed by Yasuhi Kishimoto (Kyoto: Ufer! Art Documentary, 1996).

10. See Kaori Chino, 'A man pretending to be a woman: on Morimura's "Actresses"', in *Beauty Matters*, ed. Peg Zeglin Brand (Bloomington, IN: Indiana University Press, 2000), pp. 252–65.

11. Jorge Lopez, <www.arts.monash.edu.au/visarts/globe/issue4/morimtxt.html>.

12. Donna Leigh-Kile, *Sex Symbols* (London: Vision Paperbacks, 1999), p. 2.

13. Jean Baudrillard, 'The Precession of Simulacra', *Art and Text*, No. 11 (spring 1983), pp. 2–46. First published in French in 1978.

14. John A. Walker, 'Keeping up appearances' (Interview with Alison Jackson), *ArtReview*, Vol. LIII (February 2001), pp. 36–9.

15. Saville quoted by Meg Carter, 'Looks the part', <http://Media.Guardian.co.uk> (22 October 2001).

16. Jemma Rodgers of Tiger Aspect Productions was the programme's producer and it was transmitted on 27 and 30 December 2001.

## 4 Alternative Heroes

1. For a recent translation, see: Giovanni Boccaccio, *Famous Women*, ed. Virginia Brown (Cambridge, MA: Harvard University Press, 2001).

2. Thomas Carlyle, *On Heroes, Hero-Worship and the Heroic in History* (London: J.M. Dent, 1902), p. 14.

3. In 1967, the art critic John Berger wrote an essay entitled 'No more portraits' that was sceptical about the claims made for portraits. In his view, most painted portraits of the past had not provided any deep psychological insights and in the modern age they had lost further power because of the invention of photography and a loss of faith in the social value of the social roles offered by capitalist society. See: *Arts in Society*, ed. Paul Barker (Glasgow: Fontana/Collins, 1977), pp. 45–51.

4. Richard Ormond and John Cooper, *Thomas Carlyle 1795–1881* (London: National Portrait Gallery, 1981), booklet to accompany an exhibition. Another exhibition, entitled *Thomas Carlyle: A Hero of His Time*, was held at the Scottish National Portrait Gallery, Edinburgh in 2001.

5. See John Bowlt's translation and introduction to V. Tatlin and S. Dymshits-Tolstaia's document 'Memorandum ... 1918', *Design Issues*, Vol. 1, No. 2 (fall 1984), pp. 70–4.

6. For a history of 'statuomania', see: Sergiusz Michalski, *Public Monuments: Art in Political Bondage 1870–1997* (London: Reaktion Books, 1998).

7. The relationship between the futurists and the fascists is a complex one. For histories, see: Richard Jensen, 'Futurism and fascism', *History Today*, Vol. 45, No. 11 (November 1995), pp. 35–41; Emily Braun (ed.), *Italian Art in the 20th Century: Painting and Sculpture 1900–1988* (London and Munich: Royal Academy of Arts/Prestel-Verlag, 1989); Dawn Ades and others, *Art and Power: Europe under the Dictators 1930–45* (London: Hayward Gallery, South Bank Centre/Thames and Hudson, 1995).

8. I am grateful to Michael Marek, public relations officer of the Crazy Horse Memorial organisation, for information supplied.

9.  See: Gemma de Cruz, 'Two Russians, one result', *ArtReview*, Vol. LIII (September 2001), pp. 64–5, plus front cover.
10. Pavel Büchler, 'Stalin's shoes (smashed to pieces)', *Decadent Public Art: Contentious Term and Contested Practice*, eds David Harding and Pavel Büchler (Glasgow: Foulis Press, 1997), pp. 26–39.
11. <www.eonline.com/News/Items/Pf/0,1527,111,00.html>.
12. Cintra Wilson, *A Massive Swelling …* (New York: Viking Penguin, 2000), pp. 45–6.
13. For a more detailed account, see: John A. Walker, 'Unholy alliance: Chairman Mao, Andy Warhol and the Saatchis', *Real Life*, No. 15 (winter 1985/86), pp. 15–19.
14. The image was reproduced on the cover of the French edition of *Vogue* magazine (December 1971–January 1972).
15. Ian Buruma, 'Cult of the Chairman', *Guardian* (G2) (7 March 2001), pp. 1–3.
16. John A. Walker, *Rosa Luxemburg and Karl Liebknecht: Revolution, Remembrance and Revolution* (London: Pentonville Gallery, 1986), catalogue.
17. Margaret Harrison quoted in, *Margaret Harrison: Moving Pictures*, by Lucy R. Lippard and others (Manchester: Faculty of Art and Design/Manchester Metropolitan University, 1998), p. 11.
18. For more information, see: <www.judychicago.com>.
19. Elaine Showalter, *Inventing Herself: Claiming a Feminist Intellectual Heritage* (New York: Scribner, 2001).
20. Stuart Jeffries and Vanessa Thorpe, 'Now fight begins to save Che legacy', *Observer* (27 May 2001), p. 3.
21. David Kunzle (ed.), *Che Guevara: Icon, Myth, and Message* (Los Angeles, CA: UCLA/Fowler Museum of Cultural History, 1997); Fernando D. García and Óscar Sola (eds), *Che: Images of a Revolutionary* (London and Sterling, VA: Pluto Press, 2000), first published in Spanish in 1997.
22. Jonathan Glancey, 'Don't put Che on a pedestal', *Guardian* (G2) (14 July 1997), pp. 10–11.
23. Gavin Turk and others, 'You ask the questions', *Independent* (31 January 2001), <www.independent.co.uk>.
24. Jonathan Jones, 'Glad to be Che', *Guardian* (22 January 2001), <www.guardian.co.uk>. *Before Night Falls* (2000), Julian Schnabel's film about one such persecuted Cuban homosexual, the writer Reinaldo Arenas, deserves the high praise it has received from reviewers.
25. See: Hanno Hardt, Luis Rivera-Perez and Jorge A. Calles-Santillana, 'Death and resurrection of Ernesto Che Guevara: U.S. Media and the deconstruction of a revolutionary life', <www.che-lives.com>. This substantial essay examines differential responses to Che by the American media in 1967 and 1997. Obviously, the meanings associated with Che's image and legacy varies over time and according to the nationality and politics of commentators and viewers.
26. See Lynn Barber, 'For Christ's sake', *Observer Review* (9 January 2000), p. 5 and <www.fourthplinth.com>. See also: Lynn Barber, 'Someday, my plinth will come', *Life: The Observer Magazine* (27 May 2001), pp. 30–5.
27. Linda Nochlin's book *Realism* (Harmondsworth: Penguin Books, 1971) provides a more detailed survey of the kind of art summarised here.

28. Henry Mayhew, *London Labour and the London Poor* ... 4 Vols (London: 1861–62).
29. The Pellizza da Volpedo painting is in the Civic Gallery of Modern Art, Milan and the Griebel is in the German Historical Museum, Berlin.
30. Peter Lennon, 'Whatever happened to all these heroes?' *Guardian (G2)* (30 December 1998), pp. 2–4.
31. Liz Jobey, 'In the age of celebrity journalism ...', *New Statesman*, Vol. 10, No. 455 (30 May 1997).
32. <www.terra.com.br/sebastiaosalgado/>.
33. John Pilger, *Heroes* (London: Vintage, 2nd edn 2001).
34. Tim Guest and Susan Hiller, *Susan Hiller 'Monument'* (Birmingham: Ikon Gallery; Toronto: A Space, 1981), p. 5.
35. See: Fiona Bradley and others, *Susan Hiller* (Liverpool: Tate Gallery, 1996), pp. 77–80.
36. <www.aidsquilt.org>.

## 5 Art Stars

1. Rosie Millard, 'The Tastemakers', *The Times Magazine* (6 October 2001), p. 24.
2. See: Ernst Kris and Otto Kurz, *Legend, Myth and Magic in the Image of the Artist: A Historical Experiment* (New Haven, CT: Yale University Press, 1979), and Catherine M. Soussloff, *The Absolute Artist: The Historiography of a Concept* (Minneapolis, MN and London: University of Minnesota Press, 1997).
3. See: John A. Walker, 'The van Gogh industry', *Art and Artists*, Vol. 11, No. 5 (August 1976), pp. 4–7, reprinted in *Van Gogh Studies: Five Critical Essays* (London: JAW Publications, 1981), pp. 41–6; Kōdera Tsukasa (ed.), *The Mythology of Vincent van Gogh* (Tokyo and Amsterdam: TV Asahi and John Benjamins, 1993); Nathalie Heinich, *The Glory of van Gogh: An Anthropology of Admiration* (Princeton, NJ: Princeton University Press, 1996).
4. Arianna Stassinopoulos Huffington, 'Picasso: creator and destroyer', *The Atlantic Monthly*, Vol. 262, No. 6 (June 1988), pp. 37–78.
5. John Whitley and Françoise Gilot, 'Life with Picasso was a bullfight', *Sunday Times Lifestyle* (27 September 1998).
6. Robert Descharnes, 'Introduction', in *Salvador Dalí* (Montreal: Montreal Museum of Fine Arts, 1990), p. 13.
7. Salvador Dalí and Philippe Halsman, *Dalí's Mustache: A Photographic Interview* (Paris: Flammarion, 1954).
8. Michael Glover, 'Dalí in County Hall? It doesn't get any more surreal', *Independent* (27 June 2000), <www.independent.co.uk>.
9. Ian Gibson, *The Shameful Life of Salvador Dalí* (London: Faber and Faber, 1997; new edn 1998); 'The Fame and Shame of Salvador Dalí', *Omnibus* (BBC1, October 1997).
10. Steven Naifeh and Gregory White Smith, *Jackson Pollock: An American Saga* (New York: C.N. Potter, 1989; London: Barrie and Jenkins, 1990), p. 759.

11. Matter quoted in Naifeh and Smith, *Jackson Pollock*, p. 763.
12. See: John Edwards and Perry Ogden, *7 Reece Mews: Francis Bacon's Studio* (London: Thames and Hudson, 2001).
13. Jonathan Watts, 'Japanese see Yoko's take on life of Lennon', *Guardian* (10 October 2000), p. 17.
14. Raymond M. Herbenick, *Andy Warhol's Religious and Ethical Roots: The Carpatho-Rusyn Influence on his Art* (Lewiston, NY: Edwin Mellen Press, 1997).
15. Mary Woronov, 'My 15 minutes with Andy', *Guardian* (*Saturday Review*) (21 July 2001), p. 4. See also her memoir *Swimming Underground: My Years in the Warhol Factory* (Boston, MA: Journey Editions, 1995). Several *Screen Tests* were screened in the *Andy Warhol and Sound and Vision* season at the ICA, London (July–September 2001).
16. Caroline A. Jones, *Machine in the Studio: Constructing the Postwar American Artist* (Chicago, IL and London: University of Chicago Press, 1996), p. 236.
17. Mark Francis and Margery Kind (eds), *The Warhol Look: Glamour, Style, Fashion* (Boston, MA, New York, London, Toronto: Bullfinch Press/Little, Brown and Co.; Pittsburgh, PA: the Andy Warhol Museum, 1997), p. 190.
18. See: Jennifer Doyle, Jonathan Flatley and José Muñoz (eds), *Pop Out: Queer Warhol* (Durham, NC: Duke University Press, 1995).
19. Michael Wolff, 'Fametown', *New York Magazine* (23 October 2000), <www.newyorkmag.com/page.cfm?page_id=3955>.
20. Michael Lassell, 'Saving face(s) or: I con, you con, we all con those icons', in *Hollywood, Hollywood: Identity under the Guise of Celebrity*, eds Fred Fehlau and others (Pasadena, CA: Pasadena Art Alliance/Alyce de Roulet Williamson Gallery, Art Center College of Design, 1992), p. 28.
21. For a more detailed analysis of *Myths* and his self-portrait, see the essays in the catalogue: Wendy Grossman (ed.), *Reframing Andy Warhol: Constructing American Myths, Heroes and Cultural Icons* (College Park, MD: The Art Gallery at the University of Maryland, 1998).
22. Neil Gabler, *Life the Movie: How Entertainment Conquered Reality* (New York: Alfred A. Knopf, Inc., 1998), p. 135.
23. Thierry de Duve, 'Andy Warhol, or The machine perfected', *October*, No. 48 (spring, 1989), pp. 3–14.
24. Jonathan Jones, 'The man who fell to earth', *Guardian* (19 July 1999), pp. 14–15. See also: Caroline Tisdall, *Joseph Beuys: We Go this Way* (London: Violette Editions, 1998).
25. William Feaver, 'The absent friend', *Observer* (28 February 1988).
26. Jonathan Jones, 'Portrait of the Week No 15: Gilbert & George: *A Portrait of the Artists as Young Men* (1972)', *Guardian* (*Saturday Review*) (22 July 2000), p. 4.
27. For a critique of this show, see: John A. Walker, 'Julian Schnabel at the Tate', *Aspects*, No. 20 (autumn 1982), unpaginated.
28. Junius Secundus, 'The SoHoiad: or, the Masque of Art, a Satire in Heroic Couplets Drawn from Life', *New York Review of Books* (29 March 1984), p. 17.

29. For several essays discussing Basquiat's iconography and his cultural identity, see the exhibition catalogue: Richard Marshall and others, *Jean-Michel Basquiat* (New York: Whitney Museum of American Art, 1992).
30. Phoebe Hoban, *Basquiat: A Quick Killing in Art* (London: Quartet Books, 1998), pp. 16, 351.
31. For an insightful account of the Basquiat/Warhol relationship and their portraits, see: Jonathan Weinberg, *Ambition and Love in Modern American Art* (New Haven, CT and London: Yale University Press, 2001), pp. 211–41.
32. Reported by Hoban, *Basquiat*, p. 350.
33. Klaus Kertess, 'Brushes with beatitude', in Marshall and others, *Jean-Michel Basquiat*, p. 55.
34. Richard Marshall, 'Repelling ghosts', in Marshall and others, *Jean-Michel Basquiat*, p. 15.
35. Hoban, *Basquiat*, p. 309.
36. Deyan Sudjic, 'Art for Art's Sake', in *Cult Heroes: How to be Famous for more than Fifteen Minutes* (London: André Deutsch, 1989), pp. 115–27.
37. Robert Rosenblum and Jeff Koons, *The Jeff Koons Handbook* (London: Thames and Hudson/Anthony d'Offay Gallery, 1992), pp. 39, 36.
38. D.S. Baker, 'Jeff Koons and the paradox of a superstar's phenomenon', *Bad Subjects*, No. 4 (February 1993), <http.//eserver.org/bs/04/Baker.html>.
39. David Bowie, 'Super-Banalism and the innocent salesman', *Modern Painters*, Vol. 11, No. 1 (spring 1998), pp. 27–34, plus front cover.
40. For a case study, see: John A. Walker, '1994: Hirst's Lamb vandalised', in *Art and Outrage: Provocation, Controversy and the Visual Arts* (London and Stirling, VA: Pluto Press, 1999), pp. 181–7.
41. Gordon Burn, 'Hirst World', *Guardian* (*Weekend*) (31 August 1996), pp. 10–14, plus front cover.
42. Julian Stallabrass, *High Art Lite: British Art in the 1990s* (London and New York: Verso, 1999), pp. 29–30.
43. Hirst quoted by Gordon Burn, 'The height of the morbid manner', *Guardian* (*Weekend*) (6 September 1997), pp. 14–21, plus front cover.
44. Steve Beard, 'Nobody's Fool' (interview with Hirst), *Big Issue* (1–7 September 1977), pp. 12–14.
45. In Gordon Burn, 'The knives are out', *Guardian* (*G2*) (10 April 2000), pp. 1–4. See also: Damien Hirst and Gordon Burn, *On the Way to Work* (London: Faber and Faber, 2001), p. 49.
46. See: Graham Bendel, 'Being Childish', *New Statesman* (3 July 2000).
47. Witness Ted Kessler's profile of Childish: 'My Hero is Vincent van Gogh ...', *Life: Observer Magazine* (24 March 2002), pp. 10–14.
48. Several of these photographs appear on the Internet: Mick Brown, 'The growing pains of Billy Childish', <www.southlife.net/childish/bc.htm> and <www.support.synergy-interactive.co.uk/stuckism/eugene/65.jpg>.
49. It can be found on an audio CD that accompanied the book *We Love You* (London: Booth-Clibborn Editions/Candy Records, 1998).
50. Philip Hensher, 'Bad news Tracey you need brains to be a conceptual artist', *Independent* (27 April 2001).

51. Emin quoted by Lynn Barber, 'Show and tell', *Life: Observer Magazine* (22 April 2001), pp. 8–12.
52. Stallabrass, *High Art Lite*, p. 42.
53. Laura Cumming, 'What a sew and sew', *Observer Review* (29 April 2001), p. 11.
54. Matthew Collings, *Art Crazy Nation: The Post-Blimey! Art World* (London: 21 Publishing Ltd, 2001), p. 175.

## Conclusion

1. This is a complaint the American critic Jed Perl has made in his book *Eyewitness: Reports from an Art World in Crisis* (New York: Basic Books, 2000). He even believes: 'the art stars are destroying the visual arts', p. 5.
2. Ivan Massow, 'Why I hate official art', *New Statesman* (18 January 2002).
3. The Three are promoted by the British art critic and theorist Adrian Dannatt and held a show at London's Percy Miller Gallery (December 2001–January 2002). See also: Simon Mills, 'This page is a work of art', *Evening Standard* (10 December 2001), p. 32. <www.art-online.org/percymiller/current.html>. A. Dannatt, 'The Three', <www.lacan.com/lacinkVII5.htm>.
4. Dodd quoted by Rosie Millard, *The Tastemakers: U.K. Art Now* (London: Thames and Hudson, 2001), p. 112.
5. Russell quoted by Millard, *The Tastemakers*, p. 146.
6. Matthew Collings, *Art Crazy Nation: The Post-Blimey! Art World* (London: 21 Publishing Ltd, 2001), p. 196.
7. Suzanne Moore, 'Worshippers at the shrine of St Tara of Klosters', *New Statesman*, Vol. 12, No. 582 (22 November 1999), pp. 36–7.
8. Turk quoted by Millard, *The Tastemakers*, p. 86.

# Bibliography

Limited to general studies. Arranged in date of publication order.

Carlyle, Thomas, *On Heroes, Hero-Worship and the Heroic in History* (London: Chapman and Hall, 1840).

Campbell, Joseph, *The Hero with a Thousand Faces* (Princeton, NJ: Bollingen Foundation/Princeton University Press, 1949).

Amory, Cleveland, *Who Killed Society?* (New York: Harper and Brothers, 1960).

Morin, Edgar, *The Stars: An Account of the Star-System in Motion Pictures* (New York: Grove Press, 1960). First published in France in 1957.

Boorstin, Daniel J., *The Image or What Happened to the American Dream* (New York: Atheneum, 1962).

Klapp, Orrin E., *Heroes, Villains, and Fools: The Changing American Character* (Englewood Cliffs, NJ: Prentice-Hall, 1962).

Lubin, Harold, *Heroes and Anti-Heroes: A Reader in Depth* (San Francisco, CA: Chandler, 1968).

Walker, Alexander, *Stardom: The Hollywood Phenomenon* (London: Michael Joseph, 1970).

Barthes, Roland, 'The face of Garbo', in *Mythologies* (New York: Hill and Wang, 1972).

Schickel, Richard, *His Picture in the Papers: A Speculation on Celebrity in America based on the Life of Douglas Fairbanks, Sr* (New York: Charterhouse, 1973).

Thomson, David, *A Biographical Dictionary of Film* (New York: William Morrow and Co., 1976).

Margolis, Susan, *Fame* (San Francisco, CA: San Francisco Book Co., 1977).

Goode, William J., *The Celebration of Heroes: Prestige as a Social Control System* (Berkeley, CA: University of California Press, 1978).

Monaco, James, and others, *Celebrity: The Media as Image Makers* (New York: Dell Publishing Co., 1978).

Dyer, Richard, *Stars* (London: BFI, 1979; 2nd edn 1997).

Sinclair, Marianne, *Those who Died Young: Cult Heroes of the Twentieth Century* (London: Plexus, 1979).

Trent, Paul, and Lawson, Richard, *The Image Makers: Sixty Years of Hollywood Glamour* (New York: Harmony Books/Crown, 1982).

Brooks, Rosetta (ed.), 'Heroes Issue', *ZG*, No. 8 (1983).

Nash, Jay Robert, *Murder Among the Rich and Famous: Celebrity Slayings that Shocked America* (New York: Arlington House, 1983).

Schickel, Richard, *Common Fame: The Culture of Celebrity* (London: Pavilion/Michael Joseph, 1985).

Schickel, Richard, *Intimate Strangers: The Culture of Celebrity in America* (Garden City, NY: Doubleday, 1985; with a new Afterword, Chicago: Ivan R. Dee, 2000).

Taylor, Rogan P., *The Death and Resurrection Show: From Shaman to Superstar* (London: Blond, 1985).

Vermorel, Fred and Judy, *Starlust: The Secret Life of Fans* (London: W.H. Allen, 1985).

Braudy, Leo, *The Frenzy of Renown: Fame and its History* (New York: Oxford University Press, 1986; Vintage Books, 1997).

Pilger, John, *Heroes* (London: Jonathan Cape, 1986; new edn Vintage, 2001).

Dyer, Richard, *Heavenly Bodies: Film Stars and Society* (London: Palgrave/Macmillan, 1987).

Roche, George, *A World without Heroes: the Modern Tragedy* (Hillsdale, MI: Hillsdale College Press, 1987).

Hebdige, Dick, *Hiding in the Light: On Images and Things* (London and New York: Routledge, 1988).

Fuhrman, Candice Jacobson, *Publicity Stunt! Great Staged Events that Made the News* (San Francisco, CA: Chronicle Books, 1989).

Sudjic, Deyan, *Cult Heroes: How to be Famous for More than Fifteen Minutes* (London: André Deutsch, 1989).

DeCordova, Richard, *Picture Personalities: The Emergence of the Star System in America* (Urbana, IL: University of Illinois Press, 1990).

Lang, Gladys Engel and Kurt, *Etched in Memory: The Building and Survival of Artistic Reputation* (Chapel Hill, NC: University of Carolina Press, 1990).

Gledhill, Christine (ed.), *Stardom: Industry of Desire* (London and New York: Routledge, 1991).

Magnum Photos Ltd, *Heroes and Anti-Heroes* (New York: Random House, 1991).

Williamson, Roxanne Kuter, *American Architects and the Mechanics of Fame* (Austin, TX: University of Texas Press, 1991).

Bacon-Smith, Camille, *Enterprising Women: Television Fandom and the Creation of Popular Myth* (Philadelphia, PA: University of Pennsylvania Press, 1992).

Fowles, Jib, *Starstruck: Celebrity Performers and the American Public* (Washington, DC: Smithsonian Institution Press, 1992).

Jenkins, Henry, *Textual Poachers: Television Fans and Participatory Culture* (New York and London: Routledge, 1992).

Lewis, Lisa A. (ed.), *The Adoring Audience: Fan Culture and Popular Media* (London and New York: Routledge, 1992).

Paglia, Camille, *Sex, Art, and American Culture: Essays* (New York: Vintage Books/Random House, 1992).

Editors of Time-Life Books, *Death and Celebrity* (Alexandria, VA: Time-Life Books, 1993). True Crime series, chief editor Janet Cave.

James, Clive, *Fame in the Twentieth Century* (New York: Random House, 1993).

Parish, James R., *Hollywood Celebrity Death Book* (Los Angeles, CA: Pioneer Books, 1993).

Stacey, Jackie, *Star-Gazing: Hollywood Cinema and Female Spectatorship* (London and New York: Routledge, 1993).

Gamson, Joshua, *Claims to Fame: Celebrity in Contemporary America* (Berkeley, CA: University of California Press, new edn 1994).

Harrington, C. Lee, and Bielby, Denise D., *Soap Fans: Pursuing Pleasure and Making Meaning in Everyday Life* (Philadelphia, PA: Temple University Press, 1995).

Keyes, Dick, *True Heroism in a World of Celebrity Counterfeits* (Colorado Springs, CO: NavPress Publishing Group, 1995).

Berlin, Joey, and others, *Toxic Fame: Celebrities Speak on Stardom* (Detroit, MI: Visible Ink Press, 1996).

Lahusen, Christian, *The Rhetoric of Moral Protest: Public Campaigns, Celebrity Endorsement and Political Mobilization* (Berlin and New York: Walter de Gruyter, 1996).

Rodman, Gilbert B., *Elvis after Elvis: The Posthumous Career of a Living Legend* (London and New York: Routledge, 1996).

Cass, Devon, and Filimon, John, *Double Take: The Art of the Celebrity Makeover* (New York: Reganbooks, 1997).

Chadwick, Vernon (ed.), *In Search of Elvis: Music, Race, Art, Religion* (Boulder, CO: Westview Press, 1997).

Marshall, P. David, *Celebrity and Power: Fame in Contemporary Culture* (Minneapolis, MN and London: University of Minnesota Press, 1997).

Rein, Irving, Kotler, Philip, and Stoller, Martin, *High Visibility: The Making and Marketing of Professionals into Celebrities* (Lincolnwood, IL: NTC Business Books, 1997).

Wills, Gary, *John Wayne's America: The Politics of Celebrity* (New York: Simon and Schuster, 1997).

Alexander, Bruce, *Celebrity Homes Tour of Los Angeles* (West Hollywood, CA: New Star Media, 1998).

Divola, Barry, *Fanclub: It's a Fan's World, Popstars just Live in it* (St Leonards, NSW: Allen and Unwin, 1998).

Fogelman, Bea, *Copy Cats: World Famous Celebrity Impersonators* (New York: iUniverse.com, 1998).

Fogelman, Bea, *Who's not Who: Celebrity Impersonators and the People Behind the Curtain* (New York: iUniverse.com, 1998).

Gabler, Neil, *Life the Movie: How Entertainment Conquered Reality* (New York: Alfred A. Knopf, 1998).

Harris, Cheryl, and Alexander, Alison (eds), *Theorising Fandom: Fans, Subculture, and Identity* (Cresskill, NJ: Hampton Press, 1998).

Dixon, Wheeler Winston, *Disaster and Memory: Celebrity Culture and the Crisis of Hollywood Cinema* (New York and Chichester: Columbia University Press, 1999).

Leigh-Kile, Donna, *Sex Symbols* (London: Vision Paperbacks, 1999).

Borkowski, Mark, *Improperganda: The Art of the Publicity Stunt* (London: Vision On, 2000).

Cowen, Tyler, *What Price Fame?* (Cambridge, MA and London: Harvard University Press, 2000).

Giles, David, *Illusions of Immortality: A Psychology of Fame and Celebrity* (Basingstoke: Macmillan, 2000).

Moran, Joe, *Star Authors: Literary Celebrity in America* (London and Stirling, VA: Pluto Press, 2000).

Sanders, Mark, and Hack, Jefferson (eds), *Star Culture: Collected Interviews from Dazed and Confused Magazine* (London: Phaidon, 2nd edn 2000).

Scheiner, Georganne, *Signifying Female Adolescence: Film Representations and Fans, 1920–1950* (Westport, CT: Praeger, 2000).

Turner, Graeme, Bonner, Frances, and Marshall, P. David, *Fame Games: The Production of Celebrity in Australia* (Cambridge: Cambridge University Press, 2000).

Wilson, Cintra, *A Massive Swelling: Celebrity Re-Examined as a Grotesque, Crippling Disease and Other Cultural Revelations* (New York: Viking Penguin, 2000).

Barbas, Samantha, *Movie Crazy: Fans, Stars, and the Cult of Celebrity* (New York: Palgrave, 2001).

Carter, Graydon, and Friend, David (eds), *Vanity Fair's Hollywood* (London and New York: Thames and Hudson, 2001).

DeAngelis, Michael, *Gay Fandom and Crossover Stardom: James Dean, Mel Gibson and Keanu Reeves* (Durham, NC: Duke University Press, 2001).

Rojek, Chris, *Celebrity* (London: Reaktion Books, 2001).

Sanders, John, *Celebrity Slayings that Shook the World* (London: Forum Press, 2001).

Showalter, Elaine, *Inventing Herself: Claiming a Feminist Intellectual Heritage* (New York: Scribner, 2001).

Tseelon, Efrat (ed.), *Masquerade and Identities: Essays on Gender, Sexuality and Marginality* (London and New York: Routledge, 2001).

Grand, Katie (ed.), 'The Icon Issue', *Pop*, No. 4 (spring–summer 2002).

Maltby, John, and others, 'Thou shalt worship no other gods – unless they are celebrities ...', *Personality and Individual Differences*, Vol. 32, No. 7 (2002), pp. 1173–84.

Yates, Robert (ed.), 'Celebrity Uncovered', *Life: Observer Magazine* (27 January 2002), pp. 1–62.

# Index

*Compiled by Auriol Griffith-Jones*

Note: Page numbers in bold refer to illustrations